THE WHITE PICKET FENCE

Stories of Individuality as Rebelliousness Collection

Edited by Gina Rae Duran and Edward Vidaurre

In hopes of a future of collective healing with respect for individual thoughts and ideas. We are all a part of something far more beautiful than ourselves. And even though we may not know how, everything we do affects everyone and everything on this planet. We are all connected to all living things, including the trees, the water, the air, the insects, and the animals. All of us. And each living being is already one with the eco-system, we just need to act like we are.

With love,

Gina Rae Duran

Contents

"For the master's tools will never dismantle the master's house. They may allow us to temporarily beat him at his own game, but they will never enable us to bring about genuine change. Racism and homophobia are real conditions of all our lives in this place and time. I urge each one of us here to reach down into that deep place of knowledge inside herself and touch that terror and loathing of any difference that lives here. See whose face it wears. Then the personal as political can begin to illuminate all our choices."

-Audre Lorde

Introduction

Gina Rae Duran

My ideas for this anthology, *The White Picket Fence: Stories of Individuality as Rebelliousness*, first spurred on March 17, 2024, while I interviewed Professor Brandi Wells on my radio show, The Collective. Wells came onto the show to discuss their recent novel, *The Cleaner*, and shared how the main character was queer, and their love interest is nonbinary. Wells made a point to share that the story didn't focus on the characters' sexuality or gender identities. The characters lived their lives without the trauma of homophobia or transphobia. Why would they need to when there were more important things like sinister CEO's? It was a stimulating interview about transformation—analyzing how coming out as nonbinary affected Wells' life while growing up in a rural Georgian town. We discussed how people want to fit in and how some people, like myself, rebel against the feeling of sameness, rejecting conformity and societal norms. It was because of this conversation that I recalled when my little sister wanted to do everything I did, which inevitably led up to an encounter with *The White Picket Fence*.

***

My little sister, Tawni, is five years younger than me. People commonly would ooh and awe, look at me and point to Tawni in her stroller and say, "Oh, now <u>she's</u> beautiful." After she was born, her then bright green eyes lured in the masses. It was then I became green with envy over green eyes—which led to a love of green eyes. Her eyes eventually turned a golden brown and tawny color—quite befitting. And her hair shone the color of a brand-new penny. I loved her fondly.

When I was four, I prayed to God for a little sister. Then shortly after my mom was pregnant. I felt like my prayers had been answered. She was born exactly two weeks before my fifth birthday, so it seemed fair that she was the beautiful one.

When Tawni was two, and I was seven, I cooked her cheese eggs (scrambled eggs with a slice of Kraft cheese), made up bedtime stories and acted them out with Barbies, and read her stories. Tawni loyally followed me wherever I went. She also copied every word out of my mouth—lovingly and pesteringly. My parents called her my shadow. Tawni's lips stretched from ear to ear.

Naturally, the following became a game of cat and mouse. I would run. Tawni would run. I jumped. Tawni jumped. I skipped. Tawni skipped. You get the drift. I couldn't complete a sentence without her trying to finish my sentence. I had to get away. Unfortunately, it was the early 80's and I was considered a suitable babysitter because I had a list of phone numbers and foolishly thought cooking an egg would give me my independence. It just made me an in-home sitter.

One afternoon, I dashed out the front screen door and leapt off the porch and onto the grass. I did not hear the door shut because my "Shadow" was doing an excellent job of keeping up.

Tawni was fast and smart and would later be labeled the smart and beautiful one.

I zigged and zagged, avoiding "The Smart Beautiful One." I couldn't allow her to keep up. She couldn't become me, take me over—clone me—take my place. I needed to think fast. Come up with more clever ways of doing and being, to stay unique and unpredictable. It suddenly hit me; I could jump much farther than her. She was smart, she would know her little legs couldn't jump that far. I ran and leapt up the porch.

And there was *the white picket fence* my mother dreamed of. My father spent an afternoon constructing it and painting it white for her. He made sure to match it with the eves of the mint green house. I can still hear her as they tore out the chain link fence, "Oh, it's going to be so beautiful. It'll be perfect. We'll finally have *the white picket fence*."

I swerved out wide and flew with my braided pigtails flapping
in the wind, off the patio and clearing the planter with *the
white picket fence*. My feet planted firmly on the grass. "Yes!" I
looked back victoriously. I heard Tawni crying. I thought it was
because I finally defeated her, but realized she decided to try and
jump over too. Only, she did not make it. *The white picket fence*
stabbed her right in the chest.

I began to frantically remember where the numbers were placed
on the kitchen counter. I wondered if I should try to remove
the stake from her heart. Would she die, like a vampire? I can't
remember if anyone else was there with us. I just remember the
fear of her death. Then, my parents pulled up in their truck.
They were just down the street. Both of them began questioning
and blaming me. They said I should know better. That Tawni
copies everything that I do. Then Dad said not to touch Tawni.
But it was okay. The stake was not stuck in her chest. They
rushed her to the hospital.

Tawni was fortunate. The stake didn't crack her sternum, and to
my relief, she wasn't a vampire. She was still alive. But it didn't
cure her desire to follow me. So, one day as we crossed through
the laundry room, I whipped around with urgency and grabbed
her by the shoulders:

"Listen, you have to listen to me. It's important." Tawni nodded.
"You have to stop copying me. I'm big, and you're small. We
can't do the same things. We're different. We aren't the same.
We are different people. You have to be your own person. It's
important. Do you understand?" Tawni nodded again. "I don't
know if you understand, but you need to understand that
you have to be your own person. You have to know who you
are. Just like I have to know who I am, and that I am my own
person. We aren't the same. Nobody is. We are all special. You
are special, just as you are. Just like I am special just the way I
am. Okay? I love you. So don't copy me. Be your own person.
Okay?" Tawni nodded.

From then on, I became more determined than ever to be my

own person—to be unique. I didn't care about fitting in. I wore boy's camouflage shoes, let my long hair down straight and messy, sculpted homemade play dough into Claymation, played the cello, and volunteered to teach in my little sister Tawni's preschool and kindergarten classes. I loved her, but that day I learned the importance of not only being myself but of being a responsible and conscientious leader.

The memory of that day made me realize where this desire for uniqueness stemmed from and why I enjoy my individuality. Sometimes, I rebel when people try to force the idea of sameness. I cringe at cliques and other forms of group think. I urgently want others to love themselves as they are, almost like a fear of danger. Then it hit me. *The White Picket Fence* isn't just a physical reality of my story, but a metaphor of the American Dream. It was my mother's dream because it was most Americans' dream. Why? Because we were all sold this unattainable idea that only a very small percentage can actually achieve.

I wondered how so many people of color, women, LGBTQ2S+, special needs, and poor people fit into this ideology. I honestly wondered if white middle class or even rich people felt that they fit into this dream. Does anyone? Why are we all even trying to conform? And if approved of and confirmed conformity does happen, is that person actually happy? Is anyone happy living a dream someone else constructed for them? It sounds like assimilation and acculturation. And if this assimilation is what shaped your life; because this is who you were manipulated into believing would make you happy. Then you were digested into a system not by choice, but forcibly. Then, you are left without an identity.

I mean, who would choose to be digested? Because that is the literal meaning of assimilation in the first place.

In my research, "Sexual Violence and the Assimilation Response of LGBTQ2 Female Identified Latina and Indigenous Americans," for the University of Illinois Urbana-Champaign in 2018, I came up with the term assimilation response, and I listed the assimilation responses and extreme responses. Extreme responses included addiction, self-harm, suicide attempts, and suicide. After working with youth in juvenile hall, I would now add violent and compulsive behaviors.

We are all responsible for what this world is becoming, and we still hold the power to change it. We need to look deep into the darkness of ourselves, and our place of loathing in order to shine light onto our darkness. It is the only way we can free ourselves from our repetitive desire for sameness, as individuals and as a collective. We must allow space for innovation into the already crumbling cogs and dismantle the broken system. We need new tools. We need to break away from our shame and speak our most vulnerable truths. We need more than to tell stories but to actively create new ones together.

Inland

Emily Fernandez

The ocean does not come to me,

but I wake some nights
in a white nightgown,
which I do not even own,
and my house rocks to-and-fro.
I hear the lullaby of the tide
and stumble to the back door
guided by salty wind and silvery moon
onto a deck, which I have not yet built,
and I hold the white banister
waves crashing at my feet.

Ram Dass said he likes to contemplate
the ocean, where it goes –
everywhere, everywhere

but not to me, not most days
and it leaves me with this longing
to be gripped by a swell
pulled under, under, weightless
in the water's cool embrace–
my body deep in the knowing
love is everywhere, *everywhere.*

A certainty I cannot speak
in the inland of my waking hours.

Fleeing the Farm

Mark Hein

<u>Elva (August, 1924)</u>

"This ain't going to work."

I'd been thinking that a couple of days before I said it out loud.

Mighta been a Thursday. But for sure it was back in winter. Byron was on the tractor, harrowing the far field on the hillside, where the snow'd melted, and I was standing by the chicken coop, about to gather eggs, when I said it out loud. Quiet, so as not to scare the hens, who were just cooing and clucking to welcome the sun after the rooster down at the neighbors' had started the day's crowing.

And eight months later here I am—a 26-year-old woman, hidin' before sunrise in this culvert under the road, with the creek runnin' over my bare feet, listening to a team and wagon pass over my head.

"We come this far, girl," I tell myself. "Now just hold on, don't breathe, and we'll be alright."

I'm mostly worried about the dog. I was just about to get out of the creek and start walkin' on the road like I planned when I spotted them a ways off—a two-horse team and a wagonload of tobacco common' right at me. A coon hound riding up next to the driver.

I ducked right under the culvert, curled up as small as I could, and listened hard. I swear I heard that dog jump down and start sniffin' along with his damn nose.

"Why'd he have to bring his dog?" I can feel myself about to shiver. "Calm down," I tell myself. "Breathe once, real slow. Don't get to thinkin' fearful thoughts or it'll smell you sure as shootin'."

I take that one breath, and don't breathe again 'til I can't hear anything but the clop-clop of the hooves, gettin' smaller and smaller. When I don't hear anything at all, I stick my head out behind a spray of switchgrass and peek down the road. They're gone, so I check the way they'd come—nobody—and I crawl out to set on the edge of the road and put on my shoes.

"Now," I say, "we walk into town, as calm as if we own the place."

That winter morning when I spoke out loud the farm had looked so beautiful, with the creek running by and the world filling up with light. It felt like I was cussing in church to say it, but I knew it wasn't going to work. Not in a month of Sundays. It was the drinking. That and the seizures.

What I didn't know about Byron when we'd met was what-all the War had done to him. He's such a handsome man, tall and lean and strong-jawed, with that thatch of hair that falls in his face. And he's a good man, too: Knows how to work the farm his daddy left him, and how to be kind to a person. Folks around here all know him and wish him the best.

But when these "megrims," he calls 'em, come on, he slips away. First, he gets a blinding headache and starts shivering like he's got a fever. But he doesn't -- his forehead turns cold and clammy. Then he has to get off by himself somewhere dark and quiet. He'll spend a whole day or more in the big closet, or up in the barn loft. Can't eat or drink anything. Then it goes to the fits, or the booze.

The fits scared the bejeezus outta me the first few times. He'd start screamin' and racin' around, and after just a minute or two he'd stop and stare like he was seeing a ghost— then, bang! He'd be on the floor, rollin' and moanin' and kickin'. Then bang! Again, and he's out like a light, sleeping like a baby hours, sometimes right through to next morning. Then he'd wake up hungry and thirsty, and fit as a fiddle. When we went in for his arm, that time he sliced it open, I got Doc Harmon aside and asked about the fits.

"They're brain seizures, ain't they?" I asked, remembering my work at Fort McHenry.

"Yep," he said. "Epilepsy. A natural thing. Julius Caesar had 'em. And when they come on, you have to get him on his side and keep him from swallowing his tongue."

So I did that, me wrestling this six-foot man on the floor, trying to get my hand into his mouth… Well.

That actually wasn't the worst of it, though.

It was when the seizures *didn't* come, and he'd start pouring whiskey down his throat to kill the megrims. Then he'd just get crazy, swearing there was some secret I hadn't told him and trying to beat it out of me. Or he'd all of a sudden be back in the War, in France, thinking he was really there in the trenches again with the shouting and the smoke and the shells exploding and dead men and dying men all around him. One time he was sure I was his buddy Hank, and I'd been hurt—fact is, it was him knocked me bloody—and he carried me on his shoulders halfway to the next farm, and made us hunker down in a hollow by the stock pond, in the mud.

I'd seen plenty of soldiers at McHenry havin' these fits, thinkin' they were back in the trenches. But we never did learn anything much to do for 'em, except ride 'em out.

So I knew by that winter I couldn't go on for the rest of my life tending a man who was drunk or crazy half the time. Of all the fellows come back from the War that way, I never heard anybody say any of 'em got fixed. Except maybe the Jesus folks -- they claim they can fix a body by prayin' over 'em til they fall down on the ground and roll around speaking gibberish. Well,

Byron already does that often as not, except for the prayin', and I can't see where it's done him any good. So I made up my mind to leave.

It wasn't so easy. Not in Kentucky, anyway.

That fall, Agnes Marsh had took off after her and Reggie had a row. She was going to stay with their daughter up in Michigan. Well, she didn't get to the county line before the deputies brought her back, suitcase and all. Come to find out under Kentucky laws, a wife is her husband's property, part and parcel—like the house, the land, and everything else. And she can't leave without his permission.

"No more'n his cows can, or his tractor," Agnes told me.

Well, there's ways things should be and ways they shouldn't. And as far as I'm concerned, marrying a man don't make you his slave, no matter what they say in their fancy offices up in Frankfort.

So if anything was gonna change, it was gonna be up to me to change it.

For one thing, I figured, we wouldn't be having no pitched battles like Agnes and Reggie. Whatever I was gonna do, I'd be doing in secret, keeping my own counsel.

And I could see right off if I was to go any distance, I'd need money. So I started puttin' aside a little of the egg money each week. And in town, after church—Byron was a regular one for church, and I didn't mind gettin' off the farm and seeing folks once in a while myself—I made sure we strolled over to the Blue Spot Cafe by the bus station. On the way there and back, I got in a few good looks at the notice board and saw I'd need four dollars to go to St. Louis. So, I set about saving, sometimes ten cents, sometimes less, in an old sock I hid by the henhouse door.

I figured I'd best take off in the summer when the going would be easiest and I could take the least amount of clothes—couldn't see myself getting very far with a suitcase in hand! And it'd have to be the middle of the night, when Byron was sleeping his hardest and I always got up to visit the outhouse and check on the hens.

By March, when the crocuses and pussywillows were just coming up, I had my four dollars. That was a day I smiled, and almost laughed out loud. The rest would be my eating and walking around money. In the spring, I began to think St. Louis wasn't such a good idea. I had family near there—Eva and I had grown up on Uncle Jim's farm north of Salisbury—and Byron knew about that. If he had a mind to, that'd be the first place he'd look. So instead of going up the highway to St. Louis, I settled my mind to go down the other way about the same distance to Memphis. I didn't know a soul there—never been —and I expected the sheriff's deputies would be pretty unlikely to head off that way.

So one night in July, when Byron had just started the hard, hard work of harvesting the tobacco, I got up as usual, pulled on my long summer dress and the sweater I'd knitted in the winter, grabbed the candle and my little purse, and headed out to the chicken coop. I found the sock and put it in my purse, blew out the candle, and I was on my way. I wanted to leave Byron a letter—I figured I owed him that much—but I couldn't take the time.

From the henhouse I went straight down to the creek. I hiked up my dress, took my shoes in one hand and my purse in the other, and walked down the middle of that creek three miles and more to where it passed under the highway. It was cold, uneasy walking, and I lost my balance pretty often, went onto my knees a time or two—but I didn't want any hounds tracking me.

When the wagon's well gone and I have my shoes back on, I walk into Mayfield.

It's still night, so I sit on the bench in front of the bus station and wait for the sun. I'm way too wired up to sleep, and don't feel safe at all yet. Byron and I've only been as far as Mayfield a couple of times, to the feed & grain, and I figure nobody'll recognize me. But the feed & grain is just across the street, so I have to keep an eye out. And wouldn't you know it, I'm checking my watch when I hear a voice.

"Miz McCullom? Is that you?"

I look up and there's Bert, the cashier from the feed & grain. I feel like I'm going to throw up, but I smile and say hello.

"I thought it was you. Good mornin' to you."

"Good mornin' to you, Bert."

"If you don't mind my asking, what brings you to Mayfield today?"

"It's Byron's cousin, over in Murray. She's took ill, and her husband and son are busy working the tobacco, so I'm going over to see if I can't help out a while."

"That's mighty good of you."

"I'm not much use harvesting right now, so Byron allowed as how he could spare me for a week or two."

"Well, it's sure nice seeing you today. I've got to get over and open up shop. You know, we have chairs in front of the feed & grain,and the sun's hitting our side of the street just now. You're welcome to come and watch for your bus there."

"Thanks, Bert. I may do that in a bit. Good seeing you, too."

"Say howdy to Mr. McCullom when you get home."

"I sure will. Thanks again, Bert."

I'm still trembling inside like an aspen leaf when the bus station opens.

It was five hours and change to Memphis, and once we were underway I did start to relax and doze off a bit. In fact, I was full asleep when the driver called "Memphis!" and swung open the door. I hadn't even felt the bus stopping.

Memphis. Home of the blues. It was past noon, and I had an appetite, and the blues made me think of the Blue Spot, so I walked out of the bus depot and onto the main street. Sure enough, over on the corner was a diner with a big neon sign in the window, "Tad's," and a placard, "Breakfast All Day." That suited me fine, so I walked in and took a seat at the counter.

"Free," I thought. "I'm free." I almost said it out loud.

"What'll you have, hon?" A round face with red curls under a cap was smiling at me,while its owner poured a cup of coffee without looking.

"That 'Two Bit Special' looks might good," I said

"Two eggs, two strips of bacon, and two slices of toast. How do you like your eggs?"

"Basted?" I offered, not sure if they said that around here.

"You got it." She turned around. "Hank, I need a two-bit, splashed!"

To look at her, we could have been sisters. She was tall and big-boned, like me, and she kept a fast patter going with a dozen people at once while calling in and serving up the orders, and handling the coffee and tea and water and sides—napkins, silver, sugar, salt, paper, ketchup. It was quite a handful, but she kept it going smooth, chatting folks up, laughing.

I'd taken several mighty welcome sips of coffee and was coming up with a plan when she brought me my plate.

"Two Bit Special," she announced. "You want any hot sauce?"

I wasn't sure what she meant, so I said "No, thanks" and

looked at the name on her blouse.

"Mabel?" I asked.

"That's me."

"I wonder if I can ask you something."

"Fire away," she said, refilling my coffee.

"Can a body get a job here, d'you think?"

"Matter of fact, happens right now you might." She topped a half-dozen little silver cream pitchers sitting on a plate. "We lost a girl Saturday. She got married and moved to her husband's farm." She cocked her head and squinted. "You alright?"

"Yeah," I said, and took another sip to cover up. "Maybe I shouldn't be saying this, but I could use that job. I'm sorta … comin' in the other direction, if you know what I mean."

"Sure do, hon." She put her hand on mine. "Been there myself. You done any waitressing?"

"Back in St. Louis, I worked a coupla years at Mama's on the Hill -- an Italian bakery with a good-size cafe. You probably never heard of it."

"Can't say as I have, but if you can be here at 5:30 in the morning tomorrow, we can give you a try."

"Gee, thanks," I said. 'This means a lot."

"That's alright. Just passin' it on. Now you get after these eggs before they get cold."

Mabel even ended up giving me a place to stay the night, and helped me find a room at a boarding house a few blocks away. She also helped me figure out a new name.

"Elva's too unusual," she said. "Somebody might overhear it and recognize it." We settled on "June."

"And I sure don't want to be 'McCullom' anymore," I told her. "I'll use 'Wilson,' my mother's maiden name. It'll be easy to remember."

We also cut my hair. I cried a little, saying goodbye to the braid I'd worn down my back since I was in school. And we colored it so what was left was almost blonde.

Mabel and I worked well together, getting the place ready to open up each morning. I ended up working alongside of her right through each day 'til it closed. I had nothin' else to do, and needed to build up a little savings. The long days were good. Kept me too tired to go out "lookin' for fun and findin' trouble," as Uncle Jim used to say. And I didn't need many more clothes but what I came in. That made my savings pile up even quicker. I was likin' Memphis.

But I wasn't there a month before Hank took me aside one night after we'd closed.

"June," he said, "bad news. A fella was in here tonight. John Deere salesman down from west Kentucky. Said they're lookin' for a runaway wife. And a reward's out—fifty dollars."

"Fifty dollars!" I said.. "Is that what I'm worth? Shoot!"

"Don't know about that," he said with a laugh. "But it's enough to fire up a bounty hunter.

So, I think I'm gonna need another new waitress. Real soon. You hafta skedaddle."

Hank and Mabel helped me get ready.

"No way you can wear this dress again," she said. "It's got 'farm wife' written all over it. And you'll need a suitcase, with something in it." She gave me a traveling outfit of long, full tan slacks and a white blouse, and I put my long sweater over it. She kept my dress and stuffed more of her clothes into a small carry-on.

That night, "June Wilson" was on the 8:30 bus to Dallas.
I was too wired up to sleep, and just sat there thinking while the
woman next to me snored. I figured that if I could earn a little
something along the way, I could get myself to San Francisco
where Eva and Martin were. I set my sights on that, and relaxed
a little.

Thinkin' back on Memphis, I couldn't get over it. When
a body steps out, not knowing where they'll land, it ain't just
danger they run into. It can be friends, real friends.

All the World's a Firemen's Carnival

Karen Beatty

I saw it coming: the beat-up old Ford grinding slowly toward the curb where I ambled nonchalantly in the direction of the Acme supermarket. The red-faced driver kept me in focus while he surveyed the vacant street and sidewalks.

Thinking about it now, I perfectly fit the profile of a potential abduction victim: skinny and undernourished-looking, ill fitting clothes, a young girl meandering alone on a side street in a small town. Every female child, before she even approaches puberty, knows exactly *what danger lurks*: nasty little boys and dirty old men *out there* waiting for (endless) opportune moments to pounce on your psyche, your spirit, your *body*. My mother warned me all the time. At school they showed you those *stranger danger* films, along with the ones about crawling under the desk when the Communists dropped the A-bomb. As if that, as if anyone, could really save you. And back then, during the mid 1950's, you didn't even have a clue that the enemy was within— within your country, within your home, within yourself.

But growing up with dysfunctional parents in a poor family of seven children, I had early-on concluded that it was up to me to save myself. So I was ready when the sleazy old man stuck his head out the car window and started asking directions, started telling me how pretty I was, how *didn't I need a ride* on this hot day. I was ready, but there at the curb my mind accelerated faster than my limbs could shift into retreat. "No," I stammered, "No, thank you." *Be polite, disengage—don't ignite the electrically charged force field between us. Start backing away, act disinterested, play it cool—at the same time summon every sinew to bolt. No screaming, of course: too embarrassing.* **Don't look up**, *certainly not toward him.* **Don't see** *anything but* **notice** *everything. Just-make-*

it-go-away. At last, he pulls away, but not without a leering, an insinuating, "Are you sure, honey?"

I remembered to breathe, took the measure of my pounding heart, and, at last, my adrenaline-charged mind seemed to be in synch with my benumbed extremities. So now what? *I was certainly not going to tell my parents.* By then curiosity had walloped my more instinctive fear, as well as any residual logic. I actually felt somewhat like a detached observer, rather more indignant than scared. There weren't that many strangers around town, so I figured this itinerant menace must be a set-up man with the annual Firemen's Carnival, which had just pulled into town. Such two-bit carnival operations were commonly leased for fundraising by local volunteer fire companies. Yup, this guy was one of those *bad teeth men* mothers always go on about to their kids.

I headed for the police station…

In our town there was a certain kind of boy who grew up to be *either* a criminal *or* a cop. Such boys were always counted among your friends, and, anyway, you didn't really know until their late teens how it would go for them. Joey Fanelli was one of the older kids who had become a cop and had even once visited my elementary school to warn us about *those strangers*. Since Joey was sort of cute, I thought it would be fun to tell him about the carnival guy. At the police station, Officer Fanelli immediately greeted me, and showed immense interest in my account of being accosted. I was also impressed that Officer Fanelli was taking elaborate notes. Unfortunately, when he showed me the notes and read them aloud, he had greatly embellished my story and his words didn't match my words or experience in the least. I was, furthermore, appalled that the notes were blatantly ungrammatical with multiple misspellings. This was not so much surprising as disillusioning. I thought, *no way this guy is going to save anyone!* Worse yet, he called my parents. I knew they would not (could not) do anything for me or about the carnival man, *but I would never hear the end of it.* Sure enough, decades later, Mom was still asking, "What really happened?"

I don't know what, if anything was ever done about the carnival guy. I think maybe the cops questioned him, but nothing more was made of it. In those days there were no milk cartons with snapshots of missing kids, nor media blitzes projecting images of convicted child predators. That night I went to the Firemen's Carnival, *by myself,* of course. Or maybe I took some of my younger siblings as shields. David, the littlest, would have reveled, wide-eyed, in the wonder of it all; Karla would have thrown up after a ride; and Kathy would have pointed out the dangerous mechanisms on the rickety old equipment. Brothers Bob, Alan and Mickey would also have ventured over to the carnival at some point, alone or with their respective friends. Regardless, I recall that I skulked around the carnival grounds trying to avoid the shame of discovery by the carnival worker *and* the cops, as if *I* were the guilty one, the *exposed* one. After all, I had *told,* and thus, however briefly, unmasked the vulnerability of childhood and the ultimate incapacity of cops or parents to safeguard it.

Addendum

The *carny* man was not my first or even worst encounter with real and potential sex offenders. I'm simply one survivor. Most women can relate numerous stories of threatened and actual abuse, many with dire consequences. Frequently women do not survive either psychically or physically to tell their tales. Call it what you will: sexual politics, a culture of violence, the battle of the sexes, patriarchal imperative. The fact remains that women must grow up anticipating that, at various times in their lives, they will be sexual targets or victims, or alternately, as John Irwin so aptly described in *The World According to Garp,* sexual suspects. (Women derogated as *loose,* seductive, a tease, a tramp, a vamp, a whore, a bitch, etc., etc., ad nauseam.) Of course boys are also at risk, but for females, sexual assault, both verbal and physical, is practically *a given.*

I had pretty much come to terms with this for myself until I had to explain such matters to my young daughter. When she was about eight and had learned a few things about anatomy and reproduction, she once halted abruptly on the street, turned to me and inquired, "Mommy, that thing about putting the penis into the vagina, can a man <u>make</u> you do that even if you don't want to?" Thus ensued our first seriously informed discussion of sexual assault and rape. She was aghast that such things could, and did, happen. I was both depressed and relieved about imparting such tidings. My daughter lost some of her innocence that day, but had appropriately, and sadly forever, *raised her guard* regarding the vulnerability of her gender in the world.

Though I am *there* for my daughter in ways that my mother never was for me, and though she <u>can</u> talk to me, and perhaps others, about her fears and experiences, ultimately I cannot protect my daughter from sexual harassment or assault. Is she smart about such matters? Yes. Is she safe from them? NO. For females, life is, in fact, one big Firemen's Carnival.

A World Made Fresh Each Day

Jeff Rogers

The great hinge point of my life, and one of the hardest things I've ever done, was break it to my dad that I was dropping out of college to move to LA and become a struggling writer.

My dad was my biggest hero: Chet Rogers, PhD, tenured professor and chair of the political science department at Western Michigan University in Kalamazoo. First in his family to go to college, he'd scrapped and scraped out of the poverty and ignorance of his childhood.

It was 1983 and I was 20 years old. I wasn't good at college and hadn't been good at high school. I wanted to read what I wanted to read and write what I wanted to write: stories and poems, not theses and dissertations.

My writer-heroes were the likes of Jack London and Harlan Ellison—rebellious adventurers who learned how to write by pounding a typewriter in impoverished solitude—not from college lectures. Ellison, who dangled this promise about the writing life: "We live alone, each of us, existing in worlds we make fresh each day."

That's what I wanted, more than anything in the world. The urgency boiled in me to *do it*—to launch my quest.

Yet, I knew how much it meant to him that I not fall off from what he'd achieved, how far he'd come. I knew he wanted—and expected—nothing less for me.

He'd been raised by his strict Baptist grandmother in Cincinnati. She gave him a stable home while his mom left and returned through five marriages and divorces. But she forbade him from playing with Catholic girls and Black boys.

Dad's whole adult life had been an act of defiance against the conservative mores of his forties and fifties upbringing—that white picket-fence-archetype of social conformity.

At the University of Cincinnati he became an atheist, and in Kalamazoo after Martin Luther King Jr's assassination he became a civil rights activist, putting body, career, and friendships on the line for what he believed.

In 1970, he divorced my mom to become a swinging seventies bachelor with a bright blue fuzzy couch, subscription to *Playboy*, and a placard on his desk emblazoned in wood-burned letters: If it feels good do it.

He also revered writers. His tastes ran to mysteries and SF, but he treated them with the gravity of great literature. I often saw him hold forth at parties to a circle of rapt admirers on how Conan Doyle invented Moriarty to kill off Sherlock Holmes but was forced by the public to resurrect him, or what Tolkien said about the nature of power in *The Lord of the Rings*.

One late night when I was fifteen and he was drunk after just such a party, about to retire to his bedroom with his girl-friend, he doled out this fatherly advice: "Never let anyone tell you how to live or who to sleep with."

I was my father's son—but not in the ways he had planned. My mother's too, and that was also part of it.

She was the one who read to me every night before bedtime. Sitting on the couch looking out our picture window at the big maple trees in our front yard, leaves lush and green in the spring and summer; or golden and crispy in the fall, dangling from the branches, then wafting down, then piled on the lawn, through the encroaching twilight of the season. Most magical of all: the mysterious creative dark of the winter nights, snowflakes falling softly through the porch lights; or when solid darkness behind the window turned it to a mirror that reflected us back on ourselves: mom with a book in her hands and me leaning close.

The words and stories in hypnotic rhythms and melodies intoned in Mom's voice wrapped me in the silk of imagination—cast a spell from which I've yet to awaken. *The Wizard of Oz*, *Winnie-the-Pooh*, Dr. Seuss, and ultimately *The Hobbit* and *The Lord of the Rings*.

In *Winnie-the-Pooh*, the author addresses the reader before delivering us into the Hundred Acre Wood and so came my first glimmer of the omniscience who hovered behind and above every story—a wizard of sorts, who conjured and placed the words and tones that built the stories that wove the spells. I longed to learn those arts of conjuration—apprentice myself in that wizardry.

At dinner that night in 1983, I saw how my dad struggled to contain himself. A true seventies permissive parent, he never ordered or lectured. At most, he advised. But I'd pushed him up against a wall of everything he'd ever stood for.

"I know you have talent, Jeff," he said, "And I won't tell you what to do. But I've seen a lot of talented and intelligent students over the years make the same choice you're making, only to end up working in a gas station."

Do we choose to be rebels, really? I think we like to believe we do. Or are we made that way? Maybe the great act of individualism comes after we're set apart, pushed outside, when we decide to claim it—like it was our idea all along. Then set off down our individual path of rebellion, kicking up dust as we go.

We moved to Junedale Drive in Kalamazoo in 1966 when I was three years old so my dad could take the professorship at Western.

Junedale was every bit as quaint and classically middle-American as its name: a one-block long dead-end lane of single-story ranch-style houses with two-car garages and flower boxes in front of picture windows, tall old maples and oaks that spread their canopies above wide green lawns that rolled right down to the gravel-studded blacktop street. No sidewalks. And no white picket fences, but more than one split-rail wooden fence, and rows of flowering shrubs or sculpted bushes to separate yards. Wrapping behind the neighborhood on two sides: woods and hills and fields where we ran and hid and climbed.

On Junedale, our family stood out. People were friendly and good neighbors. But every other family went to church on Sunday. We were atheist/agnostic. My parents were the liberals who marched downtown for civil rights, chanting "Fair Housing! Action now!" while most of our neighbors likely constituted the so-called silent majority that elected Nixon by a landslide in 1972. The other men went off to work in business offices or factories while my dad taught American Government and Race in American Politics to university students. My mom, after the divorce, went back to grad school in archeology, while the other women on the block still tended their husbands, houses, and children.

I was the rare only child among sibling-packed families, and the youngest kid in the neighborhood, moving into a complex kid ecosystem of established hierarchies. I was even the youngest of three Jeffs—quickly nicknamed "Little Jeff." Every day of my life I was addressed in the diminutive, made to feel small.

Still, on the day we moved in a pack of neighborhood boys were playing with popsicle sticks in the mud puddle at the foot of our driveway. One boy separated himself from the pack and approached. Like me, three years old, dressed in Bermuda shorts and short-sleeved shirt, sporting a crewcut. He stuck out his hand to shake and said, "I'm Fritz. Let's be friends." We played together nearly every day for the next seven years. So Junedale Drive became home.

In 1970, I became the first kid I knew branded by divorce—first on Junedale Drive, first in Indian Prairie Elementary. Nearly every day someone in the neighborhood or my second-grade class would ask, "Why did your parents get divorced?"

"I don't know," I'd usually answer, head down, sensing I was supposed to feel ashamed but knowing it wasn't my fault.

"My parents would never get divorced," was the nearly universal follow-up. To which I would answer silently, in my mind: "You can't know. I never knew."

It was about that time I started growing my hair long. Funny that I never made the connection until now. Not full hippie length, more early Beatle cut—but long enough to count as my personal flag of rebellion. And since I was only seven or eight, pre-puberty, I frequently heard, "Are you a boy or a girl?" That didn't stop me. It only made me more stubborn.

"Archeologists are weird," Mom said to me, one day around 1972, while I rode shotgun in her powder blue Volkswagen station wagon. "While normal people are working in offices, we love playing in the dirt all day."

In that time and place, after all we'd been through, she didn't have to explain that weird was good and normal was not.

Because normal meant that white-picket-fence complacency and conformity, the folks who made fun of long hair, supported the Vietnam war, thought women should stay home and shut up, who looked down on divorced people; the thoughtless racists and conscious racists; those who still said rock n roll wasn't real music.

Weird exalted the imagination, joy, freedom, racial equality, women's lib, all kinds of music, all kinds of people, the new and novel in the arts. Weird meant the young hippie archeologists my mom studied with, their scruffy beards and long hair, their irreverent jokes.

"Well, I'm the son of an archeologist," I said, eager to claim reflected status, "So I guess I must be weird too."

All I wanted in life was to grow up to be weird: an artist, a writer; to live a rare, even unique life. I lived in horror of somehow ending up normal.

As much as he worried for my future, my dad handed down his old rust-fringed white Chevy Malibu to serve as covered wagon for my journey west.

On September 16, 1983, my high school friend and writing partner John Mattson and I loaded everything that mattered into the trunk and backseat: boxes of books, crates of records, our typewriters, and a suitcase each worth of clothes. John had been accepted to UCLA film school and I'd dropped out. We popped *Talking Heads '77* into the tape deck and headed for Los Angeles.

I loved LA from the moment I got here. I felt like I already knew it, I'd seen it so often on movie and TV screens. But LA can be a hard place for the first couple years until you start to meet the people that make it home. The Malibu was my first car, and I knew nothing about how to maintain it, so I soon burned up the transmission. John and I pushed it around the corner, unscrewed the license plates, and abandoned it by the curb.

Jack London was an oyster pirate in the San Francisco Bay and joined the Alaskan Gold Rush. Harlan Ellison drove a dynamite truck. For all my grand ideas of working adventurous jobs, I had no experience except washing dishes and flipping steaks at Ponderosa Steakhouse in East Lansing, so for my first job in LA I worked at McDonald's. I did get a poem out of it. One morning they closed the main part of the restaurant for a child's private birthday party. The drive-thru remained open so it was just me back there with a big helium tank and a flock of balloons bobbing on the ceiling. I imagined them feeling trapped, conscripted to the whims of some rich celebrity. I imagined setting them free. I didn't. But I wrote a poem in which I did: "Freeing the Balloons," which ends:

Released from the hand of the gentle outlaw

They danced brightly away up to a cloud, crowded,

Bumping there under it for a moment, and then off again

Into a smog-rimmed bright-blue dream

Of knighthood for the freeing of balloons.

Rent was only $500 a month but after a couple months I had to call home and tell my stepbrother to sell my comic book collection and send me the money. If I tell you what I let go cheap back then I might cry. I made more than one desperate call from a gas station phone booth in those first years to dad, mom, friends, begging for a loan to get me through.

All the jobs over the years: mechanic's assistant; night shift in an office building, climbing up and down a ladder to replace florescent light bulbs; various temporary secretarial gigs.

After about two years I got a job at Crown Books in Westwood and that's where I found my first good friends in Los Angeles. By 1986, I managed a small Crown bookstore in mid-Wilshire and one morning when I opened a wild-haired, charismatic woman came in to buy a mystery novel because the play she'd written was opening that week and she needed the escape. She invited me to opening night, I went, and we fell into a brief, torrid love affair that burned out fast. But she gave me my first poetry reading that spring at a café near USC called The Cloisters and ushered me into the LA literary scene.

This morning over breakfast I told my wife Elise I was trying to brainstorm for an essay all the times in my life I'd rebelled.

"You mean every day?" she joked.

I quit that secure and happy bookstore job in the winter of 1986 to drive a taxicab for the stories and characters I'd meet. I sucked at it, but I got my stories—including the day I drove Jay the crack addict around the slums of Beverly Hills while he scored, then tried to beg money to pay me, until a big dude with a gun in his sweats threatened to kill me if I was selling his cousin Jay crack.

I worked for sixteen years at a non-profit, got elected to the board of the union there, organized a group to democratize the union against our despotic president. Ran against her, won, then led the union to its first strike vote in fifty years.

By then, I'd gone through a few love affairs and some years-long spells of loneliness before I met Elise on St. Patrick's Day 1994 and that lightning bolt slammed down that made us crackle together as one, bound in part by our love for the poets Brautigan, Bukowski, and Blake, but so much more than that. We married ten years later, but March 17, 1994, remains our cosmic anniversary—thirty years ago last spring.

I have Elise to thank that I'm now a professional writer. For years, two voices competed over my future. My dad insisted I'd never find a writing job without credentials—that long-lost college degree. Elise called bullshit: I had the talent and writing experience. It was true: every job for decades recognized and utilized my ability to write but never gave me the title or job description of "writer."

So, in 2006 I took a wild chance on a job that took a wild chance on me: Communications Director for a small union. I made three big moves in one: first professional writing job, first professional union job, and first paid gig as a rebel and rabblerouser.

I'm grateful that my mom, already dying of pancreatic cancer, lived to see that happen. "You're coming into your own," she said.

Along the way, I wrote a lot of stories and poems. Wrote blogs, performed choral poetry readings and full-scale theater productions. Found and made community: strong friendships of decades standing, based in love and common purpose.

I also suffered years of crippling insecurity when I didn't submit or perform anywhere—when I feared I'd failed that young self of 1983. But I'd wanted to be a struggling writer and there I was: struggling. A life in the arts can be precarious and I saw a lot of talented people fall off that road into poverty, addiction, death or despair.

In 2014 I broke out of it, submitted and performed all over. I infused my commitment to racial justice into my work. I made friends with other poets, built community, and began to get published in literary journals, online publications, even an essential anthology of LA poets: *The Coiled Serpent: Poets Arising from the Cultural Quakes and Shifts of Los Angeles* (Tia Chucha Press, 2016).

In 2018, my dad flew out for a weekend. He wanted to see me read. I performed downtown and the host made a big fuss over me for Dad's benefit.

On Monday morning, Elise went off to work. My dad sat on the couch while I fed the cats and dogs before we left for the airport.

I set before him a local journal that had published this poem of mine:

Walked Up from Sunset
I sit at the bus stop. "Hey, man!"
Shit, somebody wants something.

Homeless, begging for money.
Maybe lost, needing directions.

I look up. "Here, I walked up from Sunset."
He hands me an unused transfer.

As I worked in the kitchen, I saw him read it. He set it down. Picked it up, read it again, set it back down. Then he rose and stood before the picture window looking down at the street for a long time.

In the car, he told me how much he liked the poem. He

felt anyone could relate to it, even people who don't read poetry.

"Jeff, I'm proud of you," he said. "I really worried about you all those years ago when you dropped out of college. But you found your way. You're respected and valued in your job and as a poet. You're married, you have a house. You've carved your own unique place in the world."

He died in 2020. Neither parent lived to see my first book of poetry, *Right Wrong Night Song*, published in 2022, two days after I turned 60. But I know they'd both be proud and delighted. "About time," they'd probably say.

A Day in the Life

Thomas Adrian Davila

A disability is defined in the dictionary as a physical, mental, cognitive or developmental condition. A disability also impairs, interferes with or limits a person's ability to engage in certain tasks, actions or participate in typical daily activities or interactions.

My name is Thomas Davila. I am a 37-year-old Chaffey College student and I was born with the severest form of Spina Bifida. According to the Centers for Disease Control and Prevention, Spina Bifida is a condition that affects the spine and is usually apparent at birth; it is a type of neural tube defect.

For nearly two decades I have been going to school to obtain my associates degree in "something." I just did not know what that something was until recently. I started my college career at Mt. San Antonio College (Mt. SAC) and that was a waste of time, because I never went to my classes. Instead, I opted to socialize and develop a cigarette habit. After dealing with some health issues, I decided to enroll at Chaffey College in Chino. I had been a student at Chaffey since 2005.

I went to the Chino campus because it is closer to my house in Chino Hills and it is a lot smaller than Mt. SAC or even Chaffey's Rancho campus. I have been to the Rancho campus, and like I said, it is too big. At the same time even though I prefer the Chino campus, I felt claustrophobic being there because there are always a bunch of people in the way of wherever I want to go, and I have to wait for them to move just so I can go faster. Sometimes, I think they walk slow on purpose.

I liked my classes during the day because I feel that I accomplish more at that time. I guess everyone must feel the same way because my classes are always full. When I am in class, everyone is obviously taller than me even when they are sitting down which makes it harder to see because I am not always in the front row. Instructors that put me in the back row say that it is a safety hazard to seat me in the front row.

I had to take a semester off from school when the covid-19 pandemic began because I had to have surgery in February 2020 to remove kidney stones. That was my 20th surgery in my life. The process leading up to the surgery is not fun. I will just say that having kidney stones was not painful for me.

It has been more than 4 years since the pandemic began and I am no longer a student at Chaffey College. I graduated with an Associate of Arts degree in Journalism. That's right. After being at a community college for so long, I finally found my niche. The shutdown caused by covid-19 allowed me to follow my dreams. I had the honor of writing for The Breeze while I was at Chaffey College.

Before graduating from Chaffey College, I was accepted into 5 universities: Arizona State University, Azusa Pacific University, Cal State Los Angeles, Cal State Long Beach and Cal State Northridge. I elected to go to Cal State LA because it is closer to my family. I also had the privilege of writing for the University Times while pursuing a Bachelor of Arts degree in Journalism and I will be graduating in Spring 2025.

I just want to say that you may be going through something right now, but whatever it is that has got you down now will not keep you down for long. So, get back up and start something new today. If you are saying to yourself that you are too old: you are not. It has taken me almost twenty years to get to where I am in my educational career, and you would think that after going to school for so long I would be burned out by now. I am not. The way I see it I am just getting started.

Never Gave Up on Me

Gracie Azua

I could have been a good girl, or I could have held her fingertips in my hands—made her like putty in my palms. For 4 months and 20 days, gay marriage was legal in the state of California before Proposition 8 killed the hopes of thousands across the country. For my insulated world, this was a gift from God. Jesus's response to the dozens of prayers lifted in His name during daily prayers to keep our families pure. Keep girls like me under the covering of the Bible's commandments. My heart was different. Queerness streaked in red in my hidden diary. I justified my ache for the femme form as tender friendship. My obsession with boys most times was just daddy issues manifesting—not true love.

Internalized homophobia cultivating from the biblical seeds sown by the altar. I bowed cross-legged on Friday Youth nights talking to Jesus about my sins. The featherweight mistake which fueled my mother's anger. The fib I snuck into a conversation about my addict father with my friends. The boy in English I obsessed over out of desperation for masculine love. The girl in Spanish my smile couldn't get over. The crown of thorns laying on Jesus's head punctured my skin—His love a spotlight to my sins.

I dreamt of women in the moonlight instead of the sunshine. Queerness lived oppressed in brick walls as I did. My curls crackled with strong hold hair gel, and my cheeks covered in adolescent whiteheads unironically belting to When We Were Young by Adele. I spent my Friday nights on the football field for marching band or my church's Youth Night. My first youth pastor, bald-headed and an ex-con, always spoke about the importance of God's love.

"God is love," he would scream. His voice shaking the glass doors.

However, God's love never extended to my dreams about kissing girls. "It's Adam and Eve, not Adam and Steve," He would make us collectively say during youth nights. Forced all the girls who got "too close" to walk apart. My hands grew clammy when the older girls in the group swung their arms into mine to race to the front of the altar to get the first seats. There was always one girl though–a senior in high school while I was just a freshman. Her caramel hair twisted into finely woven braids, she consistently knew every bible verse and every song by heart. Her name sprung out of my mouth like a frolicking bunny in a wildflower field. She tied every heart together towards God with one look of her teasing eyes. And my heart danced with her around. I was too nervous to sleep in the same bed as her during a youth conference trip, so I made my bed on the floor next to the air vent. She was comfortably asleep dreaming of Hillsong and For King and Country melodies. I kicked the metal vent all night, afraid her hair would frolic onto my pillow, and I would be made.

Queerness lingered in the back of my mind into my adulthood. Made my body so devoted I believed my mission was to be a pastor's wife. Fit myself into the mold of a perfect helpmate who could juggle the woes of an impoverished pastor's family while carrying the burdens of all in the congregation. So I sang. I courted God through every note. I taught Noah's ark and the Ten Commandments to hyperactive children with iPad addictions every month. Stood on the stage of outreaches to tell my testimony to dozens of lost souls. This act of righteousness could make up for the consciousness I would slip into a night of passion. Save my soul from my twitter search history or fanfiction.net saved stories. Merida x Rapunzel fanfiction and clips of fem porn always led to my fingers crawling between my thighs.

Led me to being a youth leader with the same youth group I went to. A few times a year, the youth leader, now a woman in her 20s, would break the boys and girls into gender-specific gatherings to bond with an older man or woman. These adults were meant to be seen as the prime example of what living a Godly life could look like to youths headed down the wrong path. The youth pastor and I would rope the girls to the back rooms stuffed with eye-stinging children's toys and jars of stale animal cookies. The youth leader loved to connect—she was a school counselor for low-income students. She would widen her bright Oreo eyes and rope their attention to her. She would reveal her own sin she gave up to God.

"Girls," she said proudly, "I gave up liking girls. I prayed to God for healing from this, and although it is hard, He is my provider. He has never given up on me. I am waiting for the one He has for me."

As the other female youth leader, I was meant to move on from this sin, but my eyes couldn't help but melt under her brown skin. My mind recounted our home bible studies–where she would tell stories with the ear-catching flips in her voice. She was sweeter than wine to me. Every Friday, she would pick me up in her parent's van, introducing me to the beauty of Christian Rap music, and I couldn't help but love to take photos with her at Andy Mineo's concert. I couldn't help but document the way her laugh turned me into tv static. She was Ruth, steadfast to God and her family. I was Lot's wife, who disobeyed God and turned around to the destruction of Sodom and Gomorrah. I turned to salt. I was not worth being named.

My sin was simpler—listening to worldly music like Adele and Cardi B. It was an easier sin to ask God for forgiveness—something I could divulge to the girls in the group and actively live up to my promise. My queerness was never an option.

Queerness lived in me longer than my endurance for the word of God. Isolated in a 500 square-foot studio behind the police station, COVID-19 gave me context of how life just...

stopped. Prayer didn't save me from my anxiety disorder and depression. Years of therapy did. My genuine desire to help the community could be done outside of a religious context. A passion birthed from being closed off flourished into my first book, helping others with their grief too.

I accepted my bisexuality fully in the middle of a Hooters over a garden salad drenched with ranch and late-night special BBQ wings. I sat across from my cousin and our friend, who was also staring at the waitress in her tight uniform. I am so sorry! Their notice went to my gaze. When the questions popped up, I vented about every girl crush, my fanfiction addiction, my twitter search for femme porn, and my guilt for calling myself Bi when I possibly wasn't. But I was. And my husband, cousin, and friend knew it.

I gave up twirling like a dolled-up monkey for a circus I wasn't fond of anymore. I blocked my ex-pastors on social media. They didn't need a connection to my life anymore. I unliked all the songs tied to religion on Spotify, so they weren't on my "Liked Songs" playlist anymore. I never wanted to shuffle the playlist and hear "My God Is An Awesome God" after listening to Olivia Rodrigo. My childhood Bibles stayed for the nostalgia of my doodles and childish handwriting but were tucked away in storage. Stored in the boxes next to my mother's things. I waved the Mexico Pride Flag at my first Pride Festival. My feet ached, walking along all the corridors watching others be proud of being themselves too. I wasn't scared of retaliation anymore.

My bisexuality was here to stay. The church wanted to have my soul in their heaven. I wanted to have my soul on this earth in the sunlight.

My queerness never gave up on me.

What Can I Offer You?

Angela Townsend

I want to give you *cake*. I just don't want to give you cake.

Please don't misunderstand me. It is important that you have dessert by any definition. It makes my shoulders slump when you dismiss the wheel of cheesecakes at the restaurant. When you lay your hand on your belly with anything other than awe, I fight the urge to give you a five-minute education in your magnificence.

It gives me peace that Entenmann's exists. I never admire my stepfather more than when his smile returns to kindergarten, and he butters his Butter Cake. I will give impassioned invocations against margarine and meal plans. The world is as thin as November, and I am a flag-bearer for the plushy, fleshy revolution.

You are not a degenerate for eating the entire sleeve of Fig Newtons. Your deadbolt still works, no matter how loudly shame claims that your ricotta gave it the key. You are entitled to string cheese and soul music. You are sinew and tendon and the apple of your ancestors' hungry eyes. You are a child of sheltering Sweetness.

I just don't want to give you cake.

Blame the child I am on the child I was. An endocrinologist stood outside my epicure like the cherubim guarding Eden. His flashing sword would keep me safe, if I agreed to know nothing of grape juice or eclairs. I had Type 1 diabetes. I had surrendered my ticket to the ferry that crosses frostings. The date-nut bread was off the calendar. The Oreos were empty of meaning. The world was full of peril.

Contamination cackled. I deputized Diet Cokes to convince my belly it was full. I read about "free foods" and proclaimed cucumbers and sugar-free Jell-O my favorites. I had panic attacks when my parents filled the fridge for guests. I slathered my fear with guilt like buttercream. When the pie passed me by at Thanksgiving, I drank black coffee with three Sweet n' Lows and smiled so big that my face hurt for hours.

Times and pies have changed since the 90s, and today's diabetics command cake and dignity. I have excommunicated myself from the church of celery. I have declared anathema against shame's sugarless Sparta.

I have even crawled back into the kitchen. I stack cookbooks like booster seats until I am tall enough to have a place at the table. I have recurring dreams that I am the Sugar-Plum Fairy, all pink and winged. I don't get out of bed until I've asked God to help me to stuff people fat with worth. I unscrew the lid from my sprinkle jar and pour gluttonously all day. I binge myself breathless telling the cashier and the coworkers and the kinfolk that they are the sauce itself. I find the nougat in the nincom-poops and sell them on their own sweetness.

I love to give you *cake*. I just don't want to give you cake.

When my delivery truck is empty and the loaves have reached their destinations, I want my clean room, my crumbless count-ers, my carbless cocoon. I can believe it's not butter. My faith comforts me. I have a fractured relationship with food, but I've bent my bones into a peace sign. I do not want to feed and host. I cannot part with the hope that I am still hospitable.

I can picture you with blue frosting on your cheek. I applaud the melty mirth-cheese on your sleeve. I give thanks for your margarita toasting every green and lively thing. I drive past Applebee's and Olive Garden and am relieved that the lights are on.

I see the light in you, and I hope my sight satisfies. I hide hot-pink Peeps in your cubicle, and I hope you hear a song. I find purpose in feeding you. I just can't feed you.

Can you forgive my need to bumble between cucumbers? Do you believe you'll always have a place at my table?

Will I lick the frosting from my finger before the Great Feast begins?

Don't wait for me. Do accept my offering. Please.

A Purse Full of Paint

Karen Cline-Tardiff

I carry around paint in my purse. Not the actual cans of paint, but the little square pieces of paper with color on the front and a name on the back. Names like *Lights at Sea*, *Lavender Blaze*, and *Goose Island Orange*. I go for the tropical colors, the island sunsets and little Caribbean houses bright against white sands. That's what I carry around in the bottom of my purse.

What the little paint cards don't say is *Someday, Maybe*, and *In Your Dreams*. That's the crux of it, isn't it? Finding a place that's finally home. A place where I can paint the walls, the furniture. I could paint clouds on the ceiling and throw sand all over the floor. Create my own paradise.

I've been told I need to settle down. Build a life. Raise a family. I've tried. I had the two-story house, I had a son, I painted his room like a jungle full of happy giraffes and hippos, monkeys painted hanging from a palm tree. I dumped all my paint chips out and started dreaming room by room. I even tried painting my husband in the bedroom, but the paint wouldn't stick and the marriage wouldn't last. The jungle room is probably some-one's grey dining room now.

Sometimes, most times, dreams just don't come true. I've been trying to find that home my whole life. The small town I was raised in was too small and too backwards for all my dreams. I left on the first road out of town graduation night. My feet and four wheels have taken me all over the United States. I'm still traveling. Still moving. Still looking.

I thought I found home again. A dream home with a deck view of the bay. Turquoise blue with lime green trim. *Breath* on the ceilings and *Tiptoe* on the living room walls. It was only half a dream in the end. The promised kitchen never materialized, the bedrooms never finished, no sheetrock for paint. Another lesson in loss. It took 14 years and only everything I thought was home to realize it wasn't. At the end of it all, it was just me.

They say blood is thicker than water, but I've spilled enough and shared enough to know blood isn't thicker than the ropes they try to bind you with. I just keep moving. Moving on? Moving away? Moving up? Just forward motion. With a purse full of paint.

Splintered Heart Photograph

Raquel Reyes-Lopez

It is April 2008, three days before my father's birthday, and even in this photograph we are women at the center focus. The men divide behind our backs. My father hides his face behind clothes hung on the clothesline. My brother walks away from all of us with a Modelo in his hand. My mother and I are left spirit split, together we regenerate our hearts, and blister between our current disconnect. We have lost our home in the housing collapse and we will be evicted in three months. My mother and I face the burden of healing from damage we did not create. If it isn't pain caused by a collapsing economy, it's the pain we live by being in this house, and it reminds us how little we control.

From my mother's pain, I learned that your partner will strike your face when illness controls you. I saw her become just another schizophrenic to people, instead of her name. From her, I learned that you could birth a son into this world, and he will still look away from you, embody violence, and lock you into disdain. Even if you gave him more love than your daughter, it wouldn't matter. The men in our lives taught us that being a woman wasn't enough. There was always room for them to hurt us. We were never protected. We were always hated for never giving more of our obedience and forgiveness. How could we ever be enough? We questioned the men when they failed us. When our grocery money would be taken for alcohol or gambling, mother and I didn't stay silent, we held them accountable.

I was still a child. I was only ten. I took my Kodak disposable camera and tried to capture a photo of my mother, who sat centered on the white hood of our white 2002 Nissan Sentra. I couldn't get her to smile, no matter how many times I pleaded, "Mama, por favor sonríe." My mother's life was always on the verge of collision, constantly caught in the wrong moments. I was always a forced spectator, trying to pull the beauty out of her pain. It was the purity of being a child that made me want to teach my mother to love herself, because loving herself was the most rebellious act she could practice in front of the bitter men in our family. I lost my childhood in the effort to teach her. My mother was always at the center of my focus, yet I never understood that she was never comfortable being seen. She didn't want her dreams, vulnerability, or beauty to be looked at closely. She reserved those intimate parts of herself in the privacy of a mirror when she did her make up.

Nobody took photos of the women. I wanted to change that. I broke my piggy bank and bought a disposable camera at Walmart. I would photograph her regardless. I clicked the button on the camera. I realized my mother would never be able to smile through this poverty. Sometimes there wasn't enough money to keep the gas on, food on the table, or to buy me pads. How heartbroken she would be when she would hand me socks to layer over my underwear when I was on my period. Now she was coming to terms that she would never be a homeowner again after this. I was content in knowing she would not force a smile—not even for me. I then understood this moment deserved to exist for what it was. We will be remembered. The pain caused by these men will scar us, but this photo would be our defiance. We will be visible. This pain will go in the album of what we would survive. That shot was the last one in the roll. I held on tight to the camera. I was determined to save up my allowance to get this photo printed. Whatever it took, I did not need the men in our house to give me permission. I would make sure to frame and hang this photograph in our house.

Two weeks passed. I finally had enough allowance money. I asked my dad to take me to Rite Aid. He didn't ask why, he just nodded. I wanted to surprise my mom. I handed my disposable camera to the employee. "We can have them ready by tomorrow twelve in the afternoon at the earliest." I nodded and walked back to my dad. "So, we're coming tomorrow again then?" he asked me. "Yes, papa," I told him quietly as we walked back to the car. That night, I almost couldn't fall asleep. The anticipation wanted to keep me awake. I didn't let it. I would rest well so I could carry the weight of that photograph.

When morning arrived, my father and I made our way to Rite Aid. We didn't speak a word—a silence I had come to expect, but it still hurt. When I paid the cashier and received the developed photographs, my heart raced. My dad stood behind me as I looked through them. Little did he know I was only interested in one. My eyes widened when I found the shot I took. I felt so proud before I said anything. My father huffed, "All that trouble for that photograph? Your mom doesn't even look that great in that photo." His remark knocked the smile off my face. "Hey kid, do you want an ice cream?" he asked. I fumed. Why would I want an ice cream from him? He couldn't even acknowledge or see all the pain he's caused my mother. "No thanks. Can you give me the money you would have paid for my ice cream? Please?" He shrugged and said sure, and walked over to get himself an ice cream. I sprinted towards the picture frames. I picked one that was mahogany the color of her bible, with a wooden frame that would be the right size, and once I paid for it, I put the photograph in it. My father came back with one ice cream in hand. I rolled my eyes and turned away.

When we got back, I rushed into the house yelling, "Mama, mamá! Tengo un regalo para ti." My mom walked out of the kitchen. She looked up and saw me, her face relaxed, she still had her yellow gloves on, because she was in the middle of washing dishes. I ran up to hug her and then I shoved the picture frame into her hand. "¿Qué es esto, mija?" she asked, "Míralo para que veas mamá!" I said, ecstatic. She turned the picture frame, and she was quiet. She then finally managed to say, "Soy yo." I nodded. "Sí, mamá, eres tú." I really wanted to say, "Yes, it's you, you are your own person, despite everything." My mom began to cry, and she turned away from me. She then crouched down and looked at me. Her face was highlighted with joy. It had been such a long time since I saw my mom fully present and happy. She kissed my cheeks and told me, "Gracias mi corazón. Eres tan linda." I wiped the tears from her eyes and I told her, "No mamá, tú eres linda. Quiero que tu seas tu propio corazón. No yo." I really wanted that for her—for her to feel beautiful, for her to be the heart she needed to be, a heart that was kind to herself, and a heart that would give up waiting for others to treat her right.

My mom then put the picture frame in my hands, "Uno de estos días te voy a pedir esta foto patras." I understood in that moment that I would keep my mom's history safe. Little by little, I'd tell her story, knowing I was a part of it. I would survive my brother and father, even if she couldn't. I would leave this house, even if it meant leaving my mother behind. I promised myself that as I hugged the picture frame. I hung the picture in the living room on top of the fireplace. I understood that even if we did not live a picture-perfect family life, I still loved my mother, because despite all the challenges she faced she was still resilient, and beautiful to me. I didn't care that this framed photograph would only sit over the fireplace for three more months. I knew from the ashes of what's ending, my mother and I would rise above whatever was next for us. This photograph would remind the men in our homes that we are alive despite it all we will live.

Pleasure: Sacred Paint Chips and Memory Fragments

Thea Pueschel

> "Trust in him at all times, O people."
>
> —Psalms 62:8

I notice a scent in The Grand LA that massages my nostrils as soon as I walk in, and it asks me to remember something. It is my first time there, so the memory calling forth is from another time. My Complement and I walked hand in hand through the Jean-Michel Basquiat: King Pleasure exhibition. We paused in each gallery and gazed into the multifariousness of his work. The blues, blacks, reds, yellows, and whites of his manipulated media share a strong perspective. Political and avant-garde, a mixture of house paint, spray paint, acrylics, and oils.

The representation of the broken systems of society in his work took me on a meta journey within, to my own devalued placement in the hierarchy of my family system.

***

"Keep your fingers away," my father says. The blow torch lights and the paint under the heat buckles. My father takes his putty knife and scrapes large strips of paint off the wood. Some smolder and melt like a marshmallow; other areas snap back with a pop and a crack and catch flame while stubbornly adhering to the wood then go out.

"Can I go back to the truck and sleep for a minute?" I rub 7:00 A.M. out of my 12-year-old eyes. I hate mornings. Working for him means standing around and doing nothing for long swaths of time.

He scrapes along the windowsill. He shakes his head, and his tongue sits in the corner of his mouth. "I don't pay you to take naps."

"Can I, do it?" I ask.

"Maybe when you are older, it's dangerous."

***

There's a pleasure in cracking paint, a pull that calls to fingers, like my childhood memory of the paint on the metal handles on the merry-go-round lifting. The draw of the red paint satisfyingly pulled away from the metal bar with a stretchy, oily quality. When the paint stretches and lengthens, it may snap but it might not. The thinning in the middle is the determiner. Or the allure of an old French window that has a strip of white paint lifting its ruptured head (among other pieces that shrink and crack from weather). I must fight the urge to pinch my thumb and pointer finger on either side of the lifted piece, as it asks to be a full paint snake, removed in a long strip. But the window is not mine, and I am too old to vandalize the property of others.

***

I have a box of paint chips secured in a drawer in a closet in the guestroom of my home. The box is blue, the paint chips are white and swirled in art nouveau form of organic nebulous shapes. They were pulled and scraped from a metal bistro table—I have yet to refurbish—that I bought on a whim from Craigslist.com for $60 a decade ago.

***

In one exhibition gallery, a dark work jumpsuit covered in spatters and splats laid across an armed chair. The purloined traffic signs, the projection Jean-Michel painting, and the remnants of his loft and life are scattered in an intentional lived in way. The air remains the same, and it holds an echo.

47

My olfactory epithelium sensors decode the sensation. It's the scent of drying paint. Most galleries carry the aroma of cleaning solvents or dusty vents. But this one houses the essence of paint, both visual and aromatized. Unsure if it is present because of the newly constructed exhibit or piped in to allow us to commune with his spirit.

This redolence blends with the texture of my life experience. My father would come home in his painter whites splattered with the rainbow. I would pick at the large drops on his shirts and attempt to pull them off the cotton. To this day, when I smell paint thinners, turpentine, or wet paint, I feel the itch of nostalgia and I am coated in a sense of home. Paint is in my DNA. My grandfather was a painter, and my great-grandfather too.

***

One piece that caught our attention hung on the wall of the gallery, tattered, and suffering from being constructed of standard textiles (not archival), its fabric pulling away from the wood, the paint cracking. My Complement looked at me and said, "It will not last much longer. It's degrading."

"That's the beauty of art. It is ephemeral. It is not intended to last," I respond as my eyes continued to dance over the textured surface of the textile. "There are pieces that have survived hundreds or thousands of years, but those are the outliers. Think of how many pieces have ever existed and now they don't. This piece might be nothing in twenty years."

"You're such an artist." My Complement laughs. I shrug.

He's right, I am an artist. Though the Larry Gagosians of the world will not knock on my door and offer me a show in their posh gallery, it isn't what I need. It's the paint and surface that calls. When paint rings, I connect to the vibration in my fingers, to press the nozzle, to sashay a brush through acrylic/latex, to add texture, to kiss the canvas or the board, to find myself in the meditation of creation.

***

Paint telepathically communicates with me while wet, as I brush long strokes, and it also speaks when dry, in rooms with recessed lighting and great works. The texture and shapes of the table scrapings called to be stored for later use. My Complement couldn't hear them. He thinks I am quirky in my gatherings of materials to adhere to mixed media pieces. I know the chips want my muse to allow their shapes to readjust to a foreign surface not intended for their presence. Though the pieces are not sentient, there is a connection that I cannot place other than to personify them.

"Love and firmness are needed to produce the desired result."—

The Watchtower, April 15, 2015 (page 31)

The paint on the table had buckled and required removal. Shapes broke free to design a new life. Like I had when I separated myself from the faith of my family and embraced the world. My sin was inconsequential and not worthy of expulsion, but my indignance and lack of penance labeled me unrepentant.

I tried to fulfill my childhood dreams of blow torching the paint until it sighed, bubbled, and then busted; scraping my putty knife or scraper under and over the surface of the paint until it had to let go and crumpled. However, my attempt only made the metal hot, and I burned my hand. I grabbed and secured the chips after I scraped the surface with a putty knife and wire brush.

***

"You know, they didn't do this right, this right here. No, this is a case of a bad paint job, no primer. You can't paint metal without primer. What were they thinking?" He shook his head and smashed his lips but none of us were listening, the

49

impromptu lectures of poor workmanship plagued my sisters and I every trip to Disneyland or Knott's, or anytime there was a wall or pole to be felt, my father would take his nail and flick a piece of paint off any surface with a slight paint bubble.

***

The air is crisp in the Basquiat show. The exhibition gives us a sampling of his life. It pulls from his childhood, his adventures, and his creation. He is not flat here; Jean-Michel is multi-dimensional. He was a man with a family, he is still loved and remembered by his sisters to this day.

He was more to his family, and I am less to mine. King Pleasure drove in the point that I am a fracture, a piece of a whole that no longer exists. I am unsure where I live in my sisters' memories or hearts. Posthumously, there will be no archives, keepsakes or relics preserved by them in a matter of tribute.

***

"See this right here?" My father asks us. His hand sliding up and down the surface of the interior wall of a hotel room. "This wasn't sanded. It's a shame." He moves his hand side to side. The lack of professionalism in the painting trade hits him hard. "It's a shame that someone didn't want to take the time to do it right. Real shame."

My father hides his humiliation, fear, and anxiety through keeping a single focus on paint finishes and the inappropriate use of materials. If he were to stop touching the walls, he may disappear and start connecting with his emotions and fears.

***

I traded in my blue-collar history for that of a white color one and did what none in my family had done. I went to college and deepened my love for art. Now, I paint with words in technical report form, updating individual service plans for services to be rendered for those who seek support navigating the world of independent living. I sculpt bodies through asanas and gloss the subconscious through meditation and hypnosis journeys with vivid language. The brush calls, but I rarely answer it.

***

In another gallery, family footage and documented veneration of the lost artist danced between monitors. Basquiat's sisters share memories, friends and colleagues testify to his spirit. The conversation moves beyond Andy Warhol. He and his soup cans are an afterthought. The video clips and slices together Basquiat's life as a genius, beyond the disinformation that he was a tragic drug addict that depended on the connection of others to enter the art world. He was his own connection. He is not Icarus in the eye of memory, rather a prolific force that didn't get enough time in the sun. A runway model, a painter, club kid, a brother and more.

***

Hyperbolic and tragic with or without the art is what I am. I too am prolific, but my family will never know. Jean-Michel's sisters saw him as something more than a coffee table picture book of creativity and caution. I am a biblical caution-ary tale and have broken the spiritual bond of my family—shunned—lost, not forgotten. My elder sister has not spoken to me since my excommunication, and the little one found Jehovah again a decade ago. I have broken the spiritual covenant and thus they are showing loyalty to god and loving me through the discipline of shunning. My disfellowshipment was supposed to bring me to my senses. Instead, it sent me further into self-expression.

The Truth is a broken structure that I cannot blend with others. Perhaps that is why objects lure me to place them somewhere they do not belong.

***

Where my father sees flaws in painted surfaces, I see stories and opportunities. A smooth wall does not make a good story. The buckled paint, the skins underneath, speak to dreams or thoughts of the before times. I crave the story.

***

Jean-Michel was the son of an accountant, and he knew the secret of mesmerizing others with unassuming materials and complex thoughts. He employed degraded materials and turned them into something new. He did what was wrong on purpose. Form, structure, and rule were suggestions intended to be broken.

***

I paint too, I lack film or video to prove it. A gallery housed a solo exhibition once. I've had three pieces featured in a museum and work in random neighborhood shows. I vacillate between being unknown and invisible. My art and my father are the only things that remind me I used to be part of a bigger structure. Impermanence keeps my feet to this earth. My father's calls and texts are the only pieces that give me a glimpse of the gestalt.

***

The box of chips reminds me I am called my father's son, the third of four daughters and one day those paint chips will cling to a canvas with other media transforming them into something new. Eventually, the ephemeral nature of the piece will degrade. Perhaps it will be on a wall in an exhibit and an unknown emerging artist will comment on their love for the temporary nature of things and I will become part of the evanescent canon.

My Father Does Not Wear a White Shirt and Tie to Work

Anna Y. Loebe, Ed. D.

September 1960: First grade, first day of school. I am led to my desk where my name card spells out "ANNA" not "ANA," my given name. I do not speak English and fear opening my mouth during round robin reading of the *Dick and Jane* primer. The teacher hands me a sealed envelope to take home. I am anxious about its contents-I haven't done anything wrong. My father is asked to meet with the teacher. She directs him to speak only English to me. That was the day our communication changed at home. Speak in Spanish to my mother; speak in English to my father. It took several more years to do away with this imposed, inefficient arrangement. I returned to speaking in Spanish to both of them.

1961: I never told my parents the principal slapped my arm as she demanded that I stop speaking Spanish on the playground. My seven-year-old self recalls a mute response: "How dare you tell me what to speak during my recess time! I'll obey you in the classroom only!"

The language holds us together.

En mi hogar, el español nos une.

Lengua de cuna. Lengua del corazón.

El español me asegura de mis raíces.

Raíces españolas, raíces indígenas.

Mestiza.

The language pulls us apart.
"This is how you'll write your name in English."
"Speak to her in English at home."
I'm so afraid to speak-to mispronounce.
I'm so afraid to speak.
¡Pues, ya verán, que a mí no me quitan el español!

Mestiza.

5/10/14

My father drills me in the pronunciation of the word *resurrection* as I learn the prayers in preparation for First Communion.

I work hard to acquire my second language. Soon, I become my mother's translator. I excel in English language arts. All the while, though, as I make my way through the *Dick and Jane* reading series, I compare the drawings of Dick and Jane's parents with mine. My mother does not wear heels and an apron at home. My father does not wear a white shirt and tie to work. He does not carry a briefcase. He carries a black metal lunch box. And sometime early on, I learned that you never ever pack a burrito in your school lunch bag. Only Rainbo white bread will do.

July 4, 2024. The social milieu is abuzz with what to do with the upcoming presidential election. People who live in houses (or minds) with white picket fences are busy trying to recreate "Leave It to Beaver" days."

Bilingual education programs snuffed out in 2000 returned in some areas as dual language programs. A state school superintendent reigns again looking for ways to knock out dual-language programs. English-language learners languish as they sit in English-only classes getting further and further behind in other subject areas. It seems not to occur to lawmakers and social economists that these students may well become the people they criticize as the poor, uneducated fray of society who subsist on welfare.

School boards across the nation censor books addressing gender issues and those that dare to bring to light parts of history that some would rather hide. Teachers are under threat should they utter the words "critical race theory" in their classrooms. Louisianna lawmakers mandate that the Ten Commandments be posted in their public-school classrooms.

School funding continues to mirror the economic status of the school neighborhood. Charter schools and tuition vouchers serve to segregate schools.

Students who do not live in a suburban house with a white picket fence may survive grades K-12 through sheer will. Some begin to drop out mentally and emotionally in third grade. Some may have the good fortune to have guides lead them out of preordained systems to keep them in their place.

The strike on my arm for speaking Spanish on the playground started me on a road to quiet rebellion. I shall speak, read, and write in my first language. In 1970, my American Government teacher woke me up to the raging issues of the Civil Rights Movement. I began insisting on the correct pronunciation of my Spanish name "Ana." I refused to enroll in typing and shorthand high school classes to keep me out of clerical work until I could "settle down and marry." In 1972 during high school graduation ceremonies, I was presented with the achievement award for four continuous years of Spanish language studies.

¡Pues, ya verán, que a mí no me quitan el español!

Mestiza.

I proved the neighbor lady wrong three times- she who would tell my mother I would never finish college. I graduated from college and completed a Master's degree. Today, my doctoral dissertation is housed in the Library of Congress. . . all without living in a house with a white picket fence!

Glory

Isaiah Kye Diaz-Mays

There's glory in resilience. Throughout my life I practiced all of the things I wanted to say to him in the mirror. Emotions I needed to get off my chest. A large portion of those feelings involve anger, bitterness and judgment. Words like coward and asshole are some of the kinder labels I'd used to describe him. I thought the long drive over from New Jersey would grant me ample time to draft the perfect speech. No matter how many times you visualize something in your mind, things hardly ever play out exactly how you imagined.

It's been 25 years since I've seen him. Back in 1998, I was an energetic three-year-old who was warm and bubbly with everyone, according to my mom. This makes sense since all of my pictures from the 1900's feature a wide bright smile. Or a gummy one. Even the few photos that I have with him are seemingly happy as can be. I don't remember those days, nor much of anything about him at all. Theoretically, I'll be shaking his hand for the first time tonight.

I park my Wrangler by the corner in front of a bodega at the intersection of 189th and Boston Road. The Bronx has a gritty reputation, but in the calm moments of fog and silence it can be quite charming at night. A ghastly cloud departed just moments ago, leaving behind a path of crisp rain droplets along the sidewalk. My inky leather shoes kick up water from a few subtle puddles as I anxiously strut toward the palatial front doors of the funeral home.

I walk in with my sweaty palms tucked deep into the pockets of my long Black trench coat. The place is enormous, and packed with bodies from front to back. The smell of freshly vacuumed carpet would've dominated had it not been for the multitude of perfumes being worn. Scents of citrus, flowers and musk all battle for the demand of your nostrils.

Most people chat amongst each other while others sit solemnly and listen to the gospel music being amplified through the speakers. The first person I see is my uncle Jason who's standing tall at 6 '4 about 30 meters down the hall next to a man I don't recognize. Him and I make eye contact, then he makes a waving gesture with his hand encouraging me to go greet him. As I step forward, all eyes set on me. My legs begin to feel like noodles out of nervousness. Regardless, I place one foot in front of the other, doing my best to hide my true emotions.

I don't recognize any of the faces staring at me. Some of them lend a heartfelt smile, to which I return the sentiment. Others gaze with curiosity, wondering who this 6'2 stranger is. Uncle Jason holds out his arms and we tightly hug. He wears that cologne that OG's from back in the day typically wear. The kind that smells like smoked bourbon and tuscan leather. It's been almost a year since I've seen him.

"Nephew! What's goin' on? How you livin'?" He asks.

"I'm cool Unc. Blessed. How you doin, how you holdin' up?" I ask him, with his sister in mind. "Sorry for your loss by the way. I wish I got the chance to meet her."

"Nephew, it's all good. Just know that she happy you here. Believe that. She woulda loved to meet you. She'd always mention ya. Thank you for comin'," he says with reassurance.

"Of course, Unc. You already know," I say solemnly.

"You know your father's here, right?" He nods his head toward the lounge area where a larger group of people stand and chat. "Right over there. You want me to bring you over?" He asks with concern.

I thought about that script I'd been rehearsing in my mind during my drive here. I thought about the multitude of harsh words I promised myself I'd use the moment he greets me, in my finest attempt to make him feel the pain I felt for most of my life. Make him regret his greatest mistake of abandoning me.

"Nah Unc. I got this."

I trek forward, each step symbolizing the leaps I've made without him. As he stands against the wall, I recognize him immediately. I knew we look alike due to pictures, but I didn't expect to be his clone when it came to all of our features. A much better looking clone, of course. The crowd of people that was standing around him moments ago, now form a lane for me to pass through. My frantic heart is about to leap from my chest and burst through my Black turtleneck sweater. We made eye contact, and for the first time in my life, I feel sorry for him. I can see the pain in his eyes. I recognize it from the nights when I was younger and cried myself to sleep wondering why. I immediately spot the embarrassment and regret. I can hear the crowd that surrounds us whispering "Oh my God, that's his son. That's his son."

"Wow. Wow. Is that my son?" He asks. His bottom lip trembles.

Those sentiments of revenge I felt for so long died instantly, evaporating into the bleak atmosphere of the funeral home. I realized his expression of surprise meant that I won. Me being the man that I am, leading the life I've led, walking in here graciously with my head high unashamed, told him everything he needed to know. My existence is the victory I've been searching for my entire life, which means that I conquered this war a long ago.

I extend my hand out to him, firm and powerful.

"I'm Isaiah. Nice to meet you."

He extends his, and we shake. His eyes turn watery, forming a lake of sorrow around dim pupils. A tear falls down his left cheek. He makes no attempt to wipe it away.

There's glory in resilience.

Why I Don't Wear Skirts: UncertainWinds

Gina Rae Duran

…sometimes change is in a gale…

Jacob's sinewy arms flex as he lifts and slices the air with a katana. The light reflects off his glasses as he discusses his lesson plan for me. He has taught me how to sword fight and refreshed me on grappling. The thing about Jacob is that—he's not my dad. I know Jacob won't hurt me. He takes me to his backyard to teach me how to protect myself. It's a huge lot with a big dirt area dedicated to archery. I've gone to shoot bows and arrows there, so has my son, Rain. Sometimes, Jacob gives him lessons in martial arts, sword fighting, respect, patience, the responsibilities that come with the skills in fighting.

"Now you see…Gina…I think you need to change the way you look at a dress." He becomes very methodical in his lesson for me. Jacob studies a lot of religious philosophies aside from martial arts and strategies of war. The thing about Jacob is that he loves me. I know that he has my best interest and he lets me go to him. When I call or text, he is always receptive and ready to chill. Today he wants me to know that my dress is not a symbol of my victimization, it is a symbol of my strength.

"I want you to think of your dress as a suit…as something that transforms you into the person you have always been—a warrior." He looks at me "It is the thing you put on when you are going into battle. Because you are a warrior, Gina. You just don't know it yet. But I'm here to tell you that that's who you are. You are strong and probably one of the strongest women I know. You love Wonder Woman, and you need to know that you are Wonder Woman. Plus, you look like her."

I blush at his speech but feel empowered. He explains that he is going to teach me how to fight as if I were wearing a dress so I will feel confident when I put on my dress. He wants me to feel like a warrior— and I do.

I feel more inspired to go to school and face the other newspaper editors, at the Breeze. I am definitely not going to let them convince me to quit. Even though I am emotionally run down, and exhausted by gossip. Beto is sitting at the photo editor's computer (my spot) in the long line of computers in the newsroom, he is a lot nicer now that I basically told him my life story. However, it could be that nobody else is around. I tell him how I won a contest for one of my nonfiction pieces and I'm supposed to read it on campus, at the Wignall Museum of Contemporary Arts. I'm not sure if I should edit it and since he basically knows my life story, he won't be surprised to read a story about my ex swerving and speeding in his Toyota truck when we were dating in high school, or the fact that I got pregnant two months before my nineteenth birthday.

"Do you want to read it?" I ask. "Maybe, you'll have some edit suggestions?" I try to nonchalantly hand him the pages.

"Sure." He takes the page. As soon as he begins to read, I see his eyes grow sad and the furrow of his brow deepening. It's really good. I have no idea what to edit. I'm a journalist. I'm sure it's good. Ask Aella, maybe she'll help you. She edits Ashley's work."

"I don't know. She's always busy. I'll edit it later. I have my shitty demo job to go to."

"What's a demo job?"

"Ugh…You know those ladies who serve food samples to people in the isles at Costco?"

"Yeah."

"That's me."

"Well, it's a job."

"Yeah. A job where I get sexually harassed by gropey men that snatch food from each other and small children. But yeah, it's a job. I just need a new job."

He tries to act like he cares but it's too much for him. I can't help that my life is shit right now. But I haven't worked in several years, it's like having no work experience. Sometimes the job is degrading when men do things like come up behind me to reach over my shoulder to get food or place their hand in the small dip of my back. Plus, it's weird that the majority of the people serving demoes are Chicano/Latino. I don't want to be another Mexican servant. I need to transfer, I don't know why I haven't left Chaffey yet. I go into the school bathroom to change into my black slacks and button up T-shirt. There's graffitied arguments about God written in different markers, obviously by several different people. I laugh—and sometimes gasp when I see that door. I purposely go into that stall to see what frustrated women are arguing about on campus—it's generally about oppression. Then a random comment saying something like "Cats are cool" next to a generic doodle of a cat head. Sometimes I photograph the comments and post them on Instagram. The walls have entertained me enough to pull me back out of my head, and I'm prepared to head off for my four hours of belittling comments by greedy lips. *Later my son will refer to sampling food as the job that made me hate life.*

Today the wind is blowing leaves into the huge Costco entrance, and I wish I was hidden deeper into the store than the candy isles. My thin purple hoodie, that my boss thinks is blue, keeps me warm. For the sake of not freezing my ass off, I pretend it's blue. My body numbs, not from the chill but from misery, as I beckon customers to take a cookie sample. I look down to place the last of the snacks into the white paper demo cups onto the red fast food serving tray and see a dainty Caucasian woman's hand with well-manicured nails, and a silver thumb ring reach out for a sample. My heart is nearly pounding its way into my throat as I gasp— "Aella." She smiles and says she's been watching me and waiting for the right time to say hi. Then she floats off as she and her skirt wave goodbye. I stare to watch the flick of her gold spun curls sway towards the refrigerator section. Then remember to exhale. I've heard she likes to visit students at work. I feel a little less numb. She knows I've been struggling. I'm happy for the support. Dreams of becoming something more than a food sample lady take over. If I could ever impress that woman enough to take interest in at least this woman...well at least make her proud of me. But first I have to make some emotional improvements.

By the time I'm home from work I realize I have spent at least two hours out of my body, and I crash on my bed relieved that Selene is still at work. I hate that I only got this job because she referred me. I despise; the hairnet, the silver carts, the smell of the food wafting in the air, the people—and everything. An ache for healing, vulnerability, and more adventures linger in my fingertips. The struggle to pull myself out of depression leads me to create a mental list:

1. Call my acupuncturist and write about my search for healing for my next nonfiction assignment.

2. Call my therapist for an appointment.

3. Text Dawn for a massage at her place.

***

Gusts of crisp golden brown leaves rush along the cold November earth. The glass door to Patty Johnson's Acupuncture presses up against the migrating air. Patty lights up when she sees me, her long red hair is tied up in a bun and today she's wearing one of her long flower skirts and white lab coat over a purple T-shirt. It makes me smile to spend time here, a place of healing, safety, and meditation. I see her small framed, grey-haired husband Bob sitting hunched over in the waiting area, watching television. He always has a big toothy smile ready to greet everyone that walks through the door. I quickly sit down to fill in my SOAP chart with little x's to mark all the areas I'm hurting—my ovaries and my heart have the big X's. I don't know when shit will finally get better, I just want some rest. Patty gives me my usual room two doors down on the right side of the office, she makes sure that the room is cool because I can't handle the heater, and this room doesn't capture as much heat as the others. She takes time to find out what's happening in my life before she leaves me to undress. Today Patty offers me a job working as a massage therapist and tells me I can learn color therapy with her if I have time. I tell her I would love to work with her but both massage schools I went to closed down. I haven't figured out what school has my old transcripts to get the new state licensing. It's nice to know I have support and if I could get my license, I would rather work with her than serve demos. Maybe then I could finally move away from Selene and not have to deal with her immediate need to date. My memory flashes back to the first week I asked her for a divorce. Selene found her next girlfriend online that week, they quickly hooked up in a hotel in Ontario. When Selene came back two days later, she smugly told me "I moved on already. Get over it. You should move on too."

As I lay naked under the sheets, I wonder how I could ever trust again. Or maybe I have learned to trust, just not to give anyone available my heart. Why fall in love with a straight woman? Whether Aella is straight or not, I still needed to mend my pieces. My stories about my childhood, adolescence, my marriages, and my angry daughter are spilling over from my mind and hampering the way air enters my body. *Inhale... Exhale.* Patty places the thin needles all over me. She usually goes for the "less is more" method, but today I remind myself of a character in a movie aching to find silence covered in needles and left to cry out the angst. Although, my scene isn't so dramatic. I'm not going to leap up from my padded table and sob as I make a mad dash for the exit with nothing but my sheet. Instead, my tears silently stream down my cheeks and the needle in my third eye draws me into silence. The glow of the lamp cascades across the ceiling. I close my eyes and listen to the calming sound of ocean waves that Patty plays— knowing I like the sounds of water. I begin to meditate and see the swirls of red, blue, purple, and indigo in the depths between my eyelids and my forehead. I feel like today Patty is letting me stay a while longer than usual, so I can gain rest. I give myself permission to drift off inside myself, but not as an escape from life—today I get to escape my thoughts. When I wake-up I decide that I am going to say yes to my next opportunity to take risks. I hear Patty's gentle taps on the door, and I invite her back in to take out the needles.

Once I'm dressed, I look down at my phone: it's Dawn asking me what time I'm going to want my massage this weekend. She's excited because I swore, I would never visit her at her place. I smile, preparing for my next adventure— to a nudist resort.

***

The bright sun is accentuating the gold in the dry grass along the winding roads of the Colton hills. I pull over to let the black rag-top of my little white Fiat down. This car is not the best for steep roads but it's cute and it hasn't failed me yet, despite people's banter about my choice in cars. Plus, I get an average of 42 miles to the gallon. (Laugh at that people.) As I pull up to the Olive Dell Nudist Resort, I call my friend Dawn to let her know I've arrived. I let the people at the greeting area know who I am, and my friend pulls up in her white pickup truck. She's excited to finally have me over and tells me to follow her to her place. It's been about 7 years since I've seen Dawn.

Looking back: the last time we saw each other we did a massage trade because my ultrasound at the gynecologist found a growth conclusive to cancer in my bladder, so Dawn gave me energy work. A week after the massage and a week before I went in to see my urologist for an exam, I became very ill in the middle of picking my son up from a jazz band performance. My body was weak and shaking. Sweat poured out of my body soaking my

65

clothes and the driver's seat. I immediately pulled over wrenched in demobilizing pain. The next week I went to the doctors, and I no longer had a growth. My guess is that it burst when I was driving. The cancer scare was over. But Dawn has always been a nurturing person in my life. She and I met at a health spa when I lived in Riverside—about a month after my nervous break-down— "51/50." She was my support when my ex took every-thing, because he wanted me "to know what it is like to have nothing and no one"—and my mom beat me with my suitcase and punched me repeatedly. She let me sleep on her couch when I was homeless. I would help clean her place and tutor her son, Cash, in reading and writing the weeks I stayed over. Now here I am searching for healing, once again. I know that I don't have to, but I will repay her kindness.

I see a lot of trailers, motorhomes, and mobile homes as I drive through the dirt path. It kind of reminds me of camping, until I suddenly see about five naked men literally hanging out on the corner. "Oh yeah, I'm at a nudist resort" I say out loud to myself "I should have expected that." I chuckle to myself.

Dawn's mobile home is a little higher up the hill and somewhat separated from the rest of the homes. She has a beautiful view of the hills, and she points out the trail she takes hikes on regularly. We head off to the back porch and I show her the Tawny Port I bought for dinner. She says the plan is to make a shrimp scampi and I'm drooling at the idea but as we sit and chat with our glass of wine before my massage, she casually throws out her suggestion "Well, unless you want me to order a vegetarian pizza and then we can go down to the pool?" She smiles with her steel blue eyes and until I see the gap between her two front teeth.

I take a sip of my wine and place my glass on the table and casually answer without doubt "Okay." I know that the pool is not clothing optional.

"Wait...What? Are you serious?"

I laugh.

"Let's do this then."

"Okay."

"Wait what about your massage? Do you still want your massage?"

"Oh yeah, let's do that first." I laugh again.

Dawn never thought this day would come so she quickly sets everything up and orders a pizza. She heads me over to a big room with her old massage table and explains that she hasn't massaged in a long time, but she knows that I need it because of everything that has happened. She asks if it's okay to do energy work. I answer "Please, do energy work. I need it."

Her once little and now very tall and lanky son, Cash, walks into the room with a sound bowl. "What about this, Mom?"

I look over from the massage table "Oh my gosh. You've grown" I exclaim "Sure, play it."

Cash grins with his bright and gentle blue eyes. He starts to hand it to Tami.

Dawn looks at Cash and asks "Why don't you do the sound bowl? You've been practicing. Would you like that, Gina?"

"Yeah, that sounds great."

After Cash plays the sound bowl for a few minutes, Dawn asks him to leave as she starts her energy work. We talk about my divorce as she massages me and I cry because I feel like I will never find someone that loves me deeply, the way a lover should. I need to spend time on myself, and I don't think I can be in a relationship until I understand why I keep picking unhealthy relationships. I mean it must be me...I've failed. And now I'm in love with a straight woman, who will never love me back the way I love her. Dawn reassures me that it's not me, but I still believe that there must be something. I tell her that I want to fall in love with my best friend and not settle for anything less.

My massage is over, and Dawn serves me a glass of wine. "Here liquid courage, for the pool."

I reach out my hand to grasp the stem, then sit it down without a sip. "Oh, then I don't need that. I want to be fully present for this. Otherwise, it won't count."

***

Dawn takes me into the pool area and leads me to the undressing room. I'm a little nervous and can't believe I'm about to take my clothes off in front of my friend. "Now listen…" Dawn starts to direct me "There are people in the pool. I can either introduce you and you cannot say this is your first time, but you will have to be comfortable and play it off…or I can say this is your first time and they will be really nice and ask you questions and try to make you feel comfortable…"

"Oh my God. No." My eyes start to bulge out "Please don't say anything, that sounds worse."

"Then you are going to have to pretend and remember not to be shy and don't stare."

"Oh, don't worry, I won't stare. I can't believe I'm getting naked in front of my friend."

Dawn chuckles.

"I'm shy. It's okay." I laugh "Oh my God. I can't believe I'm doing this…I know, I'm a warrior. Wait, even better… it's a performance. I'm on stage. I'm an actress. I'm acting. It's a performance…It's a performance…It's a performance."

"You're funny. You'll be okay. I'll be here the whole time and if you feel uncomfortable, I'll make up an excuse and we'll leave." She opens the door to the changing room, and we walk out. I'm

68

so nervous I get a little Catholic and do the sign of the cross, like I would have in my childhood.

I look straight out and perform as if I am a nudist, and I feel comfortable in my body. I tell myself I am proud of my nudity and the hair on my body. My breast. I am beautiful and confident. I'm a warrior. I remember my yoga breath. Inhale... Exhale. I try not to think about my stretch marks from carrying my babies. Then I realize that these people don't care, and they are used to seeing bodies like mine. I see Dawn glide down into the pool from the shallow end. She is strong and confident. She has stretch marks. She has curves and is full-figured with large breasts. She enters the pool like she owns the place, with comfort and sass. She says hi to two older gentlemen and a woman with ease. So, I continue to carry myself as if I belong here, acting like I'm a nudist. Only I hop in from the edge into the deep end of the pool, to fully immerse myself. As if I'm comfortable with diving nude. I rise up from the deep and I am more aware of how my breasts float in the water than I have ever been before. I laugh at myself and swim over to Dawn.

I'm naked and I'm okay. Inhale...Exhale. I'm safe. For the first time I feel safe about my nudity, and nobody is trying to touch me. Nobody wants sex. We are all in this pool without clothes on because it is natural to be nude, and nobody is staring or making perverted comments. I'm safe. I'm naked. I'm a warrior. It's a performance. I feel a gentle breeze kiss my cheeks and I smile.

Dawn is conversing with everyone in the pool and begins to introduce me. I remember that this is a performance. Then walk over to them and shake each of their hands as if I've done this before and I know everything is going to be okay.

I Was a DEI Hire

Daniel Acosta, Jr.

Preface

I quickly learned how discrimination worked in a society that was mainly white and how some whites actually thought that they were entitled to the better things in life because of the color of their skin. In grade school, the white bullies told us that they were "free, white, and 21" and us brown kids were not and did not belong in America. I learned that when a Chicano said something nice to another Chicano, the response was invariably: "that's mighty white of you". It was our inside joke to counteract the discrimination we saw in our daily lives and supposedly not fortunate enough to be born white.

I did not know that Texas would later become the envy of the other states in the country. It created the myth that anyone with ambition and determination could make it and have a good life here. The image of the rugged Marlboro man on his horse comes to mind, which reinforced this belief that Texas was the place to succeed in America, even though this cowboy was meant to sell cigarettes. Of course, one saw a white man on a horse; if you were Mexican, Black, Asian or an Indigenous American you did not fit into this world of whiteness in Texas and America.

I grew up in El Paso in the 1950s and 1960s desperately wanting to make it in America's predominantly white society. I graduated near the top of my high school graduating class, was first in my pharmacy class at the University of Texas in 1968, was drafted and spent two years in the army, and completed my doctorate in pharmacology at the University of Kansas in 1974.

While I was studying at KU, I met a young Kansas woman, who was five years younger than me. Patti's father was Irish; my grandparents and mother were immigrants from Mexico. I was essentially a first-generation Mexican American from El Paso who married a white Kansas woman after a brief courtship in 1973. She completed her degree in German a semester before I finished up my PhD work in pharmacology and toxicology at the end of the spring semester.

I turned down a postdoctoral fellowship at the prestigious Karolinska Institute in Stockholm to accept an assistant professor position at my alma mater. Patti declined an interview with the CIA. We completed our packing and loading of the U-Haul truck in August, 1974 to begin our trek from Lawrence to Austin. Would we regret our decision to start a new life in Texas?

When I was hired, I was never told that it was a diversity, equity and inclusion (DEI) or affirmative action (AA) position. Neither DEI programs nor AA policies existed when I was accepted into pharmacy school, nor did they play a role in my admission into graduate school. I later learned about the impact of these diversity programs in recruiting more people of color at the University of Texas.

In effect, I was one of the first DEI faculty hires at the University of Texas, unsure what that meant personally for my career. But my training in an elite graduate program at the University of Kansas gave me the skills to succeed as a professor. I did not expect much help nor any special treatment to reach my academic and research goals. I never thought I was unqualified or unworthy to be a professor at the University of Texas.

The University of Texas has had a long history of segregation. Because of the new AA policies established by the federal government in the 70s, UT was forced to hire more faculty of color. I was the second Mexican American PhD professor hired at the College of Pharmacy since its founding in 1893. After a few weeks into the semester, my immediate supervisor called me into her office and bluntly informed me I was lucky to be a DEI hire. She told me that there were more qualified white candidates vying for my position, which I seriously doubted. It was clear that she'd make things difficult for me if I did not toe the line. I was told to keep quiet and be satisfied that I got the job.

That was when I became aware of the stigma that some Americans place on minorities because they believe people of color are given special considerations over whites for admission into college and for obtaining good jobs in corporations and universities. I thought I was hired because of my academic and research honors. I graduated first in my pharmacy class at UT, received a nationally competitive graduate fellowship from the National Science Foundation to study at the University of Kansas, and was offered a postdoctoral fellowship to continue my research training at the elite Karolinska Institute in Sweden. I was now stigmatized as a DEI hire who was given unfair advantages over whites for the successes I earned during my career.

A New Beginning in Austin

Austin in the 70s and 80s was still a laid-back college town, whose motto was "Keep Austin Weird". State and city government workers, professors, students, white-color professionals, blue-collar workers, cowboys, musicians, slackers, and hippies co-existed together and gave Austin a special ambience and mellowness. But I knew from my experiences as a Chicano student at UT in the mid to late 60s that race was still an uneasy topic of discussion among city residents and university officials.

When Patti and I started to look for a place to live in Austin, we knew that we had to find a home in the new suburbs where affordable housing was more available. Not realizing it at the time, we were one of the first families of color to buy a home in a new west suburb. Historically, many Black and Mexican families lived in east Austin, with I-35 the dividing line between west and east Austin.

About nine months after starting our new life in Austin, our first daughter, Anna, was born, and our next daughter, Elise, was born about 18 months later. Our third daughter, Dani, was seven years younger than Anna. Patti's family lived in the Kansas City area, 700 miles away from Austin, and my parents were in El Paso, about 600 miles away.

With two daughters under two and without much assistance from relatives, Patti was on her own; I was not much help. I was so glad that Patti was not alone; she quickly made friends with another faculty wife. Another assistant professor from Indiana was recruited into the department at the same time that I was. He and his wife became good friends with Patti and me. It helped that the two wives were very compatible and loved to talk on the phone when their husbands were working long hours at the College, and especially when they both had their firstborns a few months apart.

For a while, Patti took on a couple of part-time jobs with the IRS and as an assistant to a UT professor of Romance literature to help with living expenses. In the end, Patti and I decided that with small children to raise it was best that she remained at home to care for them and to not continue working. We squeaked by each month with a few dollars left in our checking account. We never had credit cards while we were students, but we quickly learned that a Visa or Master card was sometimes needed to help buy larger items for the home, or even simple items like diapers, which filled the trunk of our car when they were on sale.

We were one of the first homeowners in the new suburb of Lakewood. As the suburb grew there was an influx of white families; very few minority families bought their homes there. I suspect that some of my neighbors did not know that I was a Mexican American, and the kids in the neighborhood thought Anna, Elise, and Dani were white like them. If you were to meet them for the first time and not know that their family name is

Acosta, you'd also guess that they are white; they have more of the skin tone features of Patti because of her Irish and European blood. In their early years, Patti and I did not necessarily stress my Mexican heritage, but as they grew older, we had to talk to our children about race and ethnicity, especially because they were living in a city and state with a racist history.

It came to a head when Anna was playing at a friend's house; she heard the little girl's father talking about all those dirty Mexicans coming across the border into Texas from Mexico. When I came home from work, Patti was upset when she told me that Anna asked why her friend's father thought Mexicans were dirty. We had a conversation with Anna and Elise about their mixed heritage-Mexican and Irish-and that they should be proud of their cultural makeup. We had a similar conversation with Dani when she was older.

By the time Anna and Elise were entering the sixth grade, the Austin school district was facing the problem of racially segregated schools that were predominantly white or mainly Black and/or Hispanic. The school district's solution was to bus some of the white students to schools where many students of color attended. In our Lakewood neighborhood, several of the parents started a petition to protest this busing. When one of those mothers knocked on our door to ask us to sign the petition, Patti and I declined. The mother got angry, and I saw the hatred in her eyes for people of color.

Anna had an excellent Black teacher who wanted her students to learn more about each other's heritage. Anna proudly told the class that she was a Mexican American, but her teacher thought that could not be true, because Anna was not brown like some of the other Hispanics in the class. Her teacher advised Anna to talk to her parents. Anna was perplexed about what her teacher said about her heritage.

Patti had a painful conversation with the principal about the matter. The principal was posed to reprimand the teacher and wanted Patti and me to write a letter of complaint to place in her personnel file. But I asked to speak first to the teacher to hear her side of the story. I learned more about her life as a Black growing up in a poor section of Chicago, and she heard my story about growing up as a poor Mexican boy in El Paso. She did not know that during the 1800s and early 1900s there was extensive discrimination and racism against Mexicans by whites in Texas. She did not know about Anna's Mexican-Irish background and just assumed Anna was white. We informed the principal that Patti and I were satisfied about the teacher's explanation and wanted Anna to remain in her class.

The Education of Danny Acosta

I think I proved my supervisors wrong about my being an unqualified DEI hire. I received tenure and promotion to full professor in a shorter period of time than many of my white colleagues. I later took a position as a dean of pharmacy at another university in 1996 after I was told that I was not suited to be an administrator at Texas. In the final years of my career, I was one of few senior Hispanic administrators at the FDA during the Obama and Trump administrations.

DEI hires in academia, industry, and government are often denigrated as unqualified for the positions to which they were initially appointed. The Supreme Court, because of its recent ruling that color and gender can no longer be used as factors in college admissions, has opened the doors for the weaponization of DEI across all sectors of American life: employment, education, health care and medicine, and of course, politics.

It is now quite common to question how people of color and women have succeeded in the business, education, medical, legal, and government worlds. Some Americans contend that these individuals received special advantages and treatments in employment hiring, promotions and raises, and admission to certain colleges, mainly because they think that DEI has unfairly treated white men in these areas. This is nonsense because most top CEOs, university and government administrators, legal and medical leaders, and elected officials are white men.

Politicians and others feel entitled to attack "DEI hires" as unqualified in their specific jobs and professions solely because of their gender and/or color and not even consider that these individuals are often more qualified in the areas of education, qualifications, training or experience than many of their white male colleagues. These so-called DEI hires are unfairly stigmatized for the success that they rightly earned through their own qualifications, persistence and hard work during their careers.

The acronym, DEI, is used as code by some white Americans to demean women and people of color and to hide in a subtle manner one's racist and sexist viewpoints. It is not surprising that America continues to harbor people who feel threatened by the changing demographics across the country. In several states the population of its citizenry is majority-minority; that is to say, people of color make up a majority of the state's population. Texas is one of those states.

The societal value of diversity in the workplace and classroom has never been adequately explained to the American public and to employers and employees. The hiring of more women and people of color in jobs mostly held by white men slowly advanced diversity in many blue color jobs and white color professions.

But these incremental changes may stop because the Supreme Court has stepped in and ruled that America must turn a blind eye to matters of race and gender in college admissions and hiring practices, even when discrimination is so evident in the classroom and workplace.

Final Thoughts

Patti and I were looking recently at some photos her sister
Jackie had taken of our rehearsal dinner before our wedding in
Overland Park, forty miles away from Lawrence. I had never
seen the photos; the album had stayed with her mother and
sister in Kansas for over 50 years. Patti had often seen the album
when she visited her family without me while I was teaching or
attending toxicology conferences.

There were a couple of photos (she was unaware of them being
taken) that captured her youth and innocence, but also the
disbelief and bewildered look of a girl (young woman) who
seemed to be wondering why she was getting married. Several
of the photos showed me gesturing with my hands and laughing
at the dinner. Patti seemed to have a half smile and at one time
tried to grab my hand which I had placed from behind on her
shoulder. I was wearing a black t-shirt and slacks, which accen-
tuated my maturity, and she had on a dress that was buttoned
to her neck, which definitely gave her a little girl look. She told
me, after laughing at my observations, that this was fashionable
attire for young women in the early 1970s.

When I saw those photos, I immediately apologized to her
that I should have been more caring and understanding of this
important change in her life. We had known each other for only
eight months. There was one high school friend of Patti's at the
rehearsal dinner, and the rest of the young people were mostly
my friends. She appeared to be alone.

***

Our lives evolved such that Patti became my equal partner in
the establishment of my professional career. Because of her close
interactions with my graduate students, we endowed a graduate
fellowship in pharmacology and toxicology at the University of

Texas in both of our names. In addition, I became very active in my discipline's professional organization, the Society of Toxicology, which is the largest organization in the world for academic, government, industrial, and consulting toxicologists. Patti was there with me.

I was elected president of SOT by my peers as its first Hispanic president in 2000-2001. At my side was Patti, who helped the SOT executive staff develop ideas and ways to raise income at its annual meetings through the sale of clothing items and other memorabilia. We have continued to have a strong relationship with SOT. Because of our interactions with graduate students who are interested in careers in toxicology, we decided to establish an endowment for students of diversity to learn more about toxicology and to support their travel to the SOT annual meetings.

When I interviewed for the dean of pharmacy position at the University of Cincinnati Medical Center in the mid-1990s, Patti met many of the faculty at the college during those interview days. After I had been offered the position and we had settled in Cincinnati, a couple of the faculty told me outright that the major reason that they voted for me to be the dean was because of Patti. They saw that she was an independent thinker and did not always agree with things I said at the interview. Throughout my tenure at the University of Cincinnati Patti significantly helped me with my professional and social responsibilities, especially with the sensitive task of talking to alumni and friends of the college to donate money to the college.

Fifty years later, what is it now like to live in Austin during our retirement years? As a first-generation Mexican American from El Paso, I wanted to be accepted as an equal to my white professional and scientific colleagues in Texas and elsewhere in America. In other words, I accepted the premise that all immigrants and their children must strive for assimilation and acceptance into American society. Patti and I still have hope that America will guarantee to all Americans and our three daughters their inalienable rights of life, liberty, and pursuit of happiness.

One Hand Clapping

Donald Vogel

How is a kayak trip a metaphor for a socially awkward person making his way in a life marred by sloth and envy? The trite answer is it's a journey. My hope is both excursions are worth hearing anyway. The kayak trip is one I embarked on recently during which two people, one an older woman and the other the group leader, were lost. There were 15 of us on a paddle to Bannerman Castle, the ruins of a Robber Baron estate on an island in the Hudson River. We started at 10 a.m. on a mid-October day, diagonally across from West Point, cannons booming for a football game. It was to be near 70-degres, and though a drought was ruining the colors of that spectacular autumn weather, bursts of yellow, orange, and reds still greeted us during the approximately 12-mile trip. Only, there was one more surprise burst to come, which shouldn't have been a surprise as this was a serious paddle club.

Diametrically opposed to other groups I have kayaked with on drunken shallow water excursions, this was the touring set. Each member, including myself, had no less than 14 ft craft, meant for serious water, to cut through wind and wave, and a list of requisite safety equipment, including wetsuits with the water in in the 50s that day. The adage is to dress for immersion not the air, but it was the air that became our problem. We began the day with about 5 knot winds to our backs, but the leaders warned everyone before putting in that it often changes. By our first break, we could see white caps, and the trip leader gave us a choice, to explore a creek or head across the river right to Bannerman castle and then home, knowing we would be against the wind and tide. In a decision that seemed like the old joke of searching for lost keys in better light, not where you lost them, we chose the creek because it was sheltered. The winds only increased during that time.

This was obvious as soon as we left the creek to confront the challenging river cross, in two-foot chop. We kept to the plan to still visit Bannerman Castle. Skills and age divided the larger group into subsets, leading to us outpacing two compatriots. Like the military, this club paddled with a 'leave no one behind' credo and structured all excursions to prevent such an occurrence: one co-leader in the front, two on the sides, and the trip leader in the back, all with radios to report direction, hazards, and laggards. If you've ever paddled in rough water you are most stable while moving and, where possible, cutting directly through the waves without looking back. Mother nature wasn't that cooperative as the swells came at angles. By the time we reached the Castle, sheltered but fatigued, we noticed the leader and an older woman not with us and not in sight of the horizon.

The majority of the group waited 45 minutes without a visual of the two, though the co-leaders were in clear and calm communication with the leader escorting the woman. It became a little like *Lord of the Flies*, as our small community broke down. Some paddled to the western shore to ready for the trip back, some stayed by Bannerman. One woman, not a leader but who had her own radio, kept interfering with the necessary communication among the others, screeching for updates, creating a cacophony on the air waves. She kept threatening to leave or call for a rescue, even while the leader confirmed that he and the struggling woman were okay. The panicked woman decided to leave and began paddling on her own into shifting winds and swells to venture solo approximately 5 miles. A co-leader and myself thought it prudent to, first seek permission to follow for her safety and to remove her obstruction of the other rescue.

The trip back would have been better had we stayed on the other side of the river with the cover of the cliffs, but to cross and then back again, would have been doubly treacherous. So, we slogged, the co-leader in the front, and me taking up the rear to ensure the woman did not fall behind. This formation is safer if you cannot paddle three across. You dare not turn your head to look back without the danger of getting swamped. Slow, calm, and steady was the rule, even when it seemed we were paddling in place. Though the wind muffled communication, one couldn't miss the woman squawking her incessant justifications for leaving. Eventually another member of the group caught up to us and passed as the co-leader fell back to calm the woman. Perhaps out of frustration with her and a burgeoning of my self-preservation instinct, I left them behind me as I focused on following the other paddler. He and I made it back in enough time to clean our boats and load them on our cars before other members of the group straggled back, including the co-leader and boisterous woman. The leader and woman who fell behind earlier were both weary but fine. The leader and another paddler had to rig a towline to get her back.

Not one of my shining moments, I'll admit, especially knowing what being left behind feels like in my own life. This is one of my many issues as a socially awkward person, including raising a child who is in the autistic spectrum. Like my son, I grew up reticent, with limited friends, and spent a lot of time by myself, eschewing sports and social activities, though I have never been diagnosed on the spectrum. What worries me is if my son mirrors me in my envy of the neuro normal and the sloth that has me say 'fuck it all.' My son just graduated college and is working his first job as a music teacher in a private elementary school, a temp job for another teacher on leave. He is fine, except that he has not made any acquaintances with colleagues, and spends most of his time at home, weekends included, playing his trombone. Unlike what I did that day on the Hudson, I will never leave my son behind to fend for himself in life. Along the way in raising him, I have grown weary of regrets and self-recriminations on how I could have guided him to be more sociable. Maybe that is what I should leave behind.

Kayaking as a solo or a group activity says something about me. I've always taken to the nonteam sports, biking and swimming as well. I was uncomfortable with athlete culture's

one-dimensional view of tough manhood, because I didn't fit
the mold, although I was a good athlete when I applied myself.
The basic types of kayaking, recreational and touring, which I've
done for 12 years, suit both sides of my personality, and I have
a boat for each. Recreational yaks are in the 8-12-foot range and
meant mostly for calm lakes or rivers. Anything larger, 14 foot
or more are the open water, day tripper variety meant to glide
with less effort. Funny, the Hudson trip was both, starting one
way and ending the other. Luckily, I am experienced enough to
know that this was a trip for the larger boat. When I go in my
rec boat, I'm usually with people who, after a mile or so, are
ready to crack the first beer. My touring colleagues are the oppo-
site, all business and safety. With all of the trips I took this past
summer, group or solo, do you know what the best one was?
Me, floating on a lazy river, a 90-degree day, listening to Chuck
Prophet sing "It's a Summer Time Thing", feet up, while sucking
a cold brew and vaping. I was the envy of anyone passing that
day.

In general, I have found that life can be like it was early
on the morning of that Hudson River paddle: little wind,
favorable current, water like glass. That to me equates with the
ignorance of youth, untainted by experience that teaches you
to prepare for the unexpected wind to come. Thinking back,
my youth was not worthy of a memoir in an age in which the
word 'compelling' in that genre is equated with 'shock value'. I
grew up uneventfully working class and all that it implies with
a divorce and the broken individuals that it produces. The man
today has on one shoulder the devil of pride saying, 'hey be
proud, you're first generation college educated' and on the other
the demon that says 'yes, but look at the gulf it has produced
between you and some of your no-load siblings.' Before getting
any deeper, what I do know at age 60, that the answers to life's
questions lie is in the muddled middle between the wind of
philosophy and waves of experience.

Of course, the kayak trip provides a convenient meta-
phor, with the middle of a turbulent river in a speck of a boat is

the most dangerous place to be and the only way to get through it is to keep paddling without looking behind. The goal is to get back to where you were before, because the shores are lined with rocks and treefall. I'm eschewing it as a model of the path to self-discovery, as I returned grateful for being safe, but with others eschewing me because I broke the cardinal rule to not leave anyone behind. No, I'm weary of knowing thyself, and trying for a metaphor of self-acceptance. If exhaustion does not swamp anyone dumb enough to think they can stay fighting in the middle their entire life, loneliness will as anyone closest to you will get exhausted from constantly trying to rescue you from yourself.

Not that some form of self-knowledge on my part is not required, such as recognizing my sins of envy and sloth and the damage that both have wrought. I wonder if it is the combination that infects anyone we call a 'slacker.' It is something I see, but find hard to accept, and in discussing it I feel like it puts me in the place of the woman on the river I got weary of and left behind. On envy, it is as I mentioned before, being socially awkward growing up, wanting to be among the privileged, in looks, money, and networks. In high school, you would have found me among whomever occupies the social classes of the goths and stoners today that tend to produce brainiacs, artists or, regrettably, the maladjusted. This is the sin I never want to admit and one that I stashed behind the false idol of being an astute social critic of those groups I most wanted to be among. The self-preservation view to have was they were always shallow and self-absorbed, whereas I found my own self-satisfaction in being deep or enlightened. In reality, I most desired their emotional felicity, perhaps just their joy.

Music and books seem to be the coin of the realm among the socially inept, perpetuating customers and creators of each. My son and I fit both of those molds, but each of us speaks in languages the other may not understand. Jazz is my thing, my son's peripherally, and I find free jazz to be the language I prefer, though my tastes are eclectic. My devices and shelves house a Ph.D. thesis of either musicology or psychology. The thesis statement would be about the search rather than the destination. The same could be said of books. Reading this essay should give some evidence of the creator in me. Where I can't reach my son's level is in the depth of music, expression and interpretation, he has reached. The kid has studied music from single notes up to composition, across instruments, but funneled it all through his trombone. A good critic, of which I am not, could write about emotion and intellection, maybe even intent, in the noise of his practice I hear several hours a day. Might there be some common ground when it is organized cacophony that draws me to free jazz. My vocabulary here is limited.

Sloth itself is like being on a river without a paddle, unable to help anyone or myself, barely staying afloat. I wrote an essay about this, that was meant to be comical, but thankfully, was never published. Its premise is that of a guide giving a tour of a house of sloth with dust and disproportion visible due to regrettable attempts to fix things, and what it says about the owner. Missing is what sloth has wrought in relationships, because that isn't something I want to figure out (another example of sloth?). As that is like the rough part of the river, the muddled middle, I'll contemplate if I could have done more to ensure my son doesn't wind up like me: self-aware without self-acceptance. Bro-culture was the route my wife and I were most familiar with, and it involved sports. However, that stopped when my son, always uncaring about a game or inter-acting with the rest of the team, pulled down his pants in the outfield of a t-ball game. His answer to my later admonition, "I had an itch."

His issues were more glaring with scouts, with its empha-sis on team building activities, the pinnacle of patriarchy which still dominates our society. I was a co-den leader with a surfer dude father. Most of my time was spent working to get my son to interact with the other boys in activities than it was helping with the overall activities themselves. I envied the felicity with which the surfer dude led the others. The kids loved him.

Scouts, like t-ball, didn't last, but my wife and I were adamant that my son had to choose something to stay connected, and he relented on band. For a brief time, he flourished in drama, and one of my greatest memories is of him dancing joyfully with the chimney sweeps in his high school junior year production of *Mary Poppins*. Alas, that interest faded as he preferred the pit with the band. That has led him to where he is now, an artist in search of a teaching job. I spent his school age years failing to connect with others in our town, envying them and their lives of shared community, jocks, beauty queens, and socialites perpetuating their kind. I guess we were fated to do the same.

This is being borne out as we head into the next phase of our life. Right now, our generation's sons and daughters are transitioning from college to the working world and eventually, to their own families. I am not sure that is the trajectory for me with my son as the only progenitor. We see signs of our fate in the extended family: a brother in law in his late fifties living alone in the family home; a nephew turning 40 who lives solitary in his own home. This is just on my wife's side. You might be surprised that envy is still my sin here, because my family, represented by my youngest brother, is the example of those people who shouldn't spawn, but did anyway. The result is a niece, though she is the best thing about this no-load shit brother, who was mostly raised by my mother and smarter than her patriarch. She is currently living in her own home with her boyfriend. This is quite the opposite of her cousin, my son, who has never dated and is pathologically shy around women. Time and again I feel like the woman in the lagging kayak, watching the other version of me paddle ahead and out of sight.

Not that my son will never settle down and have a family, I just wonder how he would do it and how well. This is a kid who, because of his issues, is mostly non-conversational, garnering certain types of glances at group functions from people who don't know him. He gets annoyed when my wife has to ask a thousand questions just to get anything out of him. At most any gathering, he sits looking at his phone, or staring into space. You've heard the old saying that 'even when a fool is quiet, people will think he's wise', well for my son it seems to go 'even when a kind soul is quiet, people will think he's unfriendly.' Look, in the wake of so many lone wolf scenarios making the daily front page, I am grateful for who he is, though I sometimes worry if the sideways glances at him could launch a bad trajectory. At the very least, I see the possibility of a future with my wife and I silent among friends sharing pictures of grandkids.

I have to wonder if not caring what people think is a step toward self-acceptance or the rally cry of the slothful. Yet again, competing forces, like wind and water. I may never find an answer, but so what, I hit the lotto every time I get a belly laugh out of this kid. I have spent more time thinking about ways to get him to laugh, than about teaching him how to live life. The world educates you whether you ask for that or not. One gift of being the awkward outsider is seeing the absurdity of life and how that can also be funny. Thank you, Robin Williams, rest in peace. Add comedian to those who are spawned by our awkward crowd. Our best moments are when my son and I are on long drives and I'll say whatever comes to mind to see what clicks, and then riff from there. I'll leave it God to forgive me if there is a lowest common denominator at times, but I can get the kid going and responsive. Conversation it is not, but I am reassured by the fact that his finding the humor is an awareness of the reality that makes it absurd.

I am writing this at the beginning of the Holiday Season, and our just completed Thanksgiving dinner, out at a restaurant, was either the first, or one of the few times my wife, son, and I, ever ate it outside a home. It is an indication of how life whittles down the social networks you do have. Our parents, who used to host these Holidays, are gone, and most of our siblings have moved away. Some cousins are what remain of the extended families, whom we see at various times. This too, is like that day on the Hudson in which the larger group gets separated by circumstance, age, or skill. I'm torn between my envy of friends who have large families and ongoing traditions, and the part of me that has always liked less noise and crowds, and thus appreciates this stage of life. I am noticing how the commercial part of Christmas favors the former, and is unkind to those who are alone. One of our recent Holiday family traditions that will continue, is going to see a jazz or classical Holiday concert. When I hear those old carols, it is more about nostalgia than making memories. In line with the clichés we all adopt as coping mechanisms, I appreciate each moment more now.

I am naively hopeful that the pandemic provided direct insight into the life of the socially awkward, and for that crowd, my son and I, a break from the Fear of Missing Out (FOMO). It helped me to mostly get over mine because how can you envy anything that is not happening. Schadenfreude also helped, as I remember at the beginning of the lockdown biking past homes that had set up food pantries for the less fortunate to come and take what they needed. I am most grateful I never had to do that, pray that it never happens, and also have a bit more perspective on life. My type of otherness is nothing compared to theirs, and a point at which I should consider dropping back to help those left behind. Still, I write this after yet another lone wolf shooting that killed five people in a Walmart. The shooter's suicide note alluded to being bullied and ridiculed for being socially awkward. Too many of these individuals fit that profile. I don't empathize with that person, nor do I have any answers on preventing the next one. I can only speak for myself and ask forgiveness for sloth and envy and pray against self-fulfilling prophecies.

One person I have mostly forgotten about in my convenient paddling metaphor, is the trip co-leader who stayed behind with the struggling woman kayaker, as I forged ahead of them. Sometimes a life coping mechanism is allowing a paddler to come alongside and offer wisdom, while another is finding it in yourself to focus on what's ahead, as I did to keep pace with the kayaker who had surpassed us. If neither is your thing, know that in my sometimes-solitary world of books and music, I have found wisdom, grace, and empathy in the fellowship of unintentional communal moments one finds across years or distance, reminding me I am not alone. Reality is quite often not so altruistic, as I certainly wasn't that windy day on the river. Sometimes instinct takes over, whether that's our tendency toward selfishness or survival. Looking back is helpful, and other times it might take your life. Readers should listen to me, because there is a great tutorial video out there of me on another kayaking trip, that got 45,000 hits in an hour.

Me and my recreational buddies were on the Upper Carman's River on Long Island. We were heading back from paddling upstream against the current and the wind. It was midsummer and I had the requisite safety equipment. We three were headed downriver in a swift current, navigating lots of treefall and jagged rocks, exhausted from the first half of the trip. Fortunately, my buddy behind me caught my deft maneuvering on a Go Pro for posterity. We reached a curve in the river where the flow increased significantly. I was in the middle of the line of boats, and watched the man in front negotiate the treacherous bend. My turn. In the video you will see me, geared up enough to give kayak adventurers a boner, nonchalantly approach, as I was pushed sideways by the current into a tree limb hanging over the swirling stream. In that moment I figured, 'simple enough' and reached up to push way with my right hand.

Removing my hand from the paddle necessary to control the boat was the first stupid mistake in a confluence of dumbass one might study if you were to make this a lesson on what not to do. Remember, I said before that my recreational buddies were the ones to crack the first beer after the first mile. We did six miles that day. Anyway, the effect of me pushing with my right hand, instead of using the paddle to brace or navigate, created a force counter to the flow underneath, essentially capsizing me. You might think my expert survival skills from years of paddling kicked in and I made a seamless wet entry into my boat that would be the envy of the kayak community. Nope, I just stood. Outside of this being the first time I ever capsized in over a decade of paddling, the most embarrassing thing about the incident was that the river we were on averaged about two feet in depth. The video closes with me pumping furiously, and my buddies fore and aft taking bets on how many pumps it would take to dewater. The lesson here is simple, it just might be as stupid to make a kayak trip a metaphor for life.

Freedom was a Red Silk Thong at the Sam Ellis Department Store

Karla Cordero

When I was twelve, I wanted a thong. No, I needed a thong. A need that manifested into a monstrous obsession, a wish to any star that would grant me my very own strip of cloth. I wasn't picky. Give me a thong in cotton or silk, animal print, the color choice was never a deal breaker. I wanted the kind of underwear that my butt cheeks would swallow up for the fashionable purpose of ghosting any pantyline into extinction.

The year was 1999, MTV was still dubbed as the channel for playing a wide variety of music videos, before it was fully consumed by the treacherous uprising of trashy reality TV. Cisco released his one hit wonder, the iconic "Thong" song. Back then my young brain didn't recognize the visuals or lyricism written toward the objectification of women in the video. I was mesmerized by the women that danced like goddesses, shaking their glistening bodies in thong bikinis in public without a mother's scolding voice or God looking down full of judgment.

In the evening when my mother worked late hours at the mercado, I watched Pamela Anderson from our wooden television screen as she ran across the beach in Baywatch. She would sport her cheeky red swimsuit, saving lives with her bleach blond hair and bronzed tan. Other nights I witnessed John Travolta's character Danny Zuko glide across a high school gymnasium with Cha-Cha to Blue Moon playing in the background, as three high school boys dropped their pants exposing the whitest cheeks I had ever seen.

After school, rollerblading through the neighborhood meant passing by Jose with his open garage door while he attempted to play electric guitar like Santana. It was hard not to notice the poster of Carmen Electra wrapped in dental floss. Her image hung across the garage wall for neighbors to take notice. Then there was JLO, the one Latina making moves in the music industry, who shook her behind and the world went crazy. Sir Mix-A-Lot shouted "Baby Got Back" from the radio, confessing his animalistic urges for thick women. Music gave me more butt content than I could handle.

If music and media weren't enough, the family drive out of our hot little border town to escape for cooler weather, entailed a drive through the scenic route. We passed by large mountain ranges and valleys as we made our way toward San Diego. We were all crammed into a van and as kids we knew we were halfway to our destination when we drove by a large collection of boulder-like mountains. My cousins jokingly named the largest of boulders, Butt Mountain, as their way of expressing their own humor and attraction for women's body parts.

These were the images that flooded my middle school mind, teaching me what was deemed beautiful by mainstream society. I was in no hurry for a boyfriend but wanted more to feel like myself, pretty and comfortable in my own skin. I attended a private school, Our Lady of Guadalupe Academy located in Calexico, a city found at the bottom end of California. The girls who crossed the border every day from Mexico to attain an American education, were dropped off by their plastic surgery mothers who were obsessed by the two B's: Boobs and Butts. The girls at school that developed way faster than the rest of us, made it their life's mission to make sure we knew our chest and behinds were as flat as washboards.

During lunch, halfway deep into a bag of Hot Cheetos garnished in nacho cheese, I overheard Tania Garcia talk to the group of big boobed girls about Erika Sanchez. They mocked how she bent down to take a drink from the water fountain. They pointed and stared at her pantyline. The first time I had ever taken notice of such phenomena. In the colder season, our school allowed us girls to wear khaki pants instead of our plaid shirts. Tania had an eye for guessing the kind of panties girls would wear when they would reach down to tie their shoes or sit on the bleachers. Tania would say, those are parachute panties or granny panties. Sometimes Tania would spot a girl at school without a pantyline like some scientist spotting a rare animal in the wild.

"Look at her. She's definitely wearing a thong," Tania pointed with the kind of excitement you get when you win a large stuffed bear at the fair.

A thong equated to no pantyline. I was on a quest to own one and eliminate any trace of underwear peeking through my khakis. I desired to be pointed at by Tania's perfectly manicured nails, stared at by the big boobed girls, as they complimented my flawless no panty line ass. But it wasn't the kind of item to add to a birthday wish list or Santa Letter. There was no way I would ask my mother for the funds or ride to the store for a thong. This was no, "We're out of milk and eggs. Let's go to the store," situation. This was defying my mother in ways that would surely fracture her heart by my request. As I approached my teen years, my curiosity meant the risk of hearing my mother's voice spit fire back with disgust and denial.

My mother migrated from Mexico when she was five and was raised witnessing her own mother be submissive to an abusive husband. Turning to religion and devoting her life to serving the big man upstairs was how my mother stayed strong despite the hardness of the world. My mother was blessed with the gift of raising four daughters, surviving thyroid cancer, all while maintaining her family's needs and the business at the mercado. Reputation and hard work as a woman of color was a wealth my mother valued. When it came to showing skin, my mother was a conservative. I never saw my mother's legs past her knee or her cleavage.

Wearing a dress on Easter Sunday or a pair of denim shorts on days when the temperature would hit triple digits were but a few exceptions that allowed my skin to be exposed more than normal to avoid heat stroke. Bathing suits during the summer months was the closest thing to ever seeing my body outside of a bathroom. My mother still encouraged me to wear a T-shirt with my bathing suit to avoid sunburning my shoulders or perhaps a way to dodge the inappropriate gaze of an older man at the public pool. I was convinced every woman showing mid-belly or upper thigh never had a mother, or at least not like mine.

Right before the start of the school year, I lost to my sister's quick hand at "rock, paper, scissors," and in return was the sacrificial tribune to accompany my mother to the local department store, Sam Ellis. Sam Ellis was our version of Nordstrom Rack full of big named clothing brands marked down to affordable prices. The deals were excellent for buying saddle shoes for school and fresh white socks in bulk. As my mother and I walked past the women's nightwear the image hit me in slow motion. It was the forbidden fruit of all underwear. A bin full of thongs stared back at me in polka dots, white lace, floral prints and classy black. The loudest thong of them all stood out in a vibrant red silk. Red like all good things: apples, Hot Cheetos, Valentine hearts, licorice. If freedom looked like anything that day, it was this red silk thong, cut and sewn to a perfect size small, made for me. I wiped off the swampy moisture from my palms along the side of my jeans. I avoided making direct contact toward the pile of underwear but my eyes disobeyed. The temples of my forehead beaded in sweat then disappeared as I thought about my khaki pants without the pantyline. I grabbed the red silk thong like the winning lottery ticket to middle school coolness. My mother finished her conversation with the check-out lady and as she turned to me, I said it.

"Mom, can you buy me a thong?"

My mother's eyes dropped wide open and all I could see were two giant oceans full of scorpions swimming in volcanic lava.

"Why, so can you have sex? No, put those back," she said walking away toward the store's exit.

My mother's response was megaphone loud for all to hear. The lady at the checkout counter stared deep into my soul as if I needed an exorcism.

Sex? I thought to myself. I knew sex required kissing, but how did a thong play a role in such activity? I was clueless never having received the talk about the Birds and the Bees from either parent. I learned about body parts and birthing babies in Sister Lilia's Health Education course, but there was never any dialogue or textbook visual of a thong. I was confused more than ever with zero opportunity to plead my case for eliminating my pantyline.

That day, on our return home, I looked down the hallway to confirm that the coast was clear. I locked the door to my room and pulled my jeans down. I stared at my butt in the mirror. My twelve-year-old bubble butt, an inheritance from my mother's side of the family. And then I thought about my ancestors, before TV and dial-up internet. How they must've sat on their behinds grinding corn into maza, talking about their children, exchanging stories of the gods and hoping for a plentiful harvest so their families would live through another deadly winter. These were women surviving with butts full of wisdom and story. Surely these women didn't have 100% cotton underwear by Fruit of the Loom.

With determination to still acquire my own thong despite my mother's embarrassing response, I grabbed my underwear and hiked them up into my butt crack. I gave myself a wedgie to replicate the look of a thong. I pulled my pants up and took a few steps before the cotton material turned into sandpaper. There was no way I would last five minutes walking around in my homemade thong.

Up on my bookshelf, sat an abandoned Barbie from my younger years, naked and collecting dust. Barbie without underwear, smiling back at me, as if to say, "You don't need them." I removed my underwear, freed myself of my wedgie, and walked around my home with a secret that was all mine. Commando. It was liberating to move without the constraints of cloth wrapped around my thighs, no itchy tag escaping from the back, waving at every passerby. I cartwheeled into the living room, ballerina twirled past my mother in the kitchen, and skipped outside to welcome my father home, as he pulled up into the driveway. I felt invincible.

Google once told me that the phrase "going commando" dates back to the Vietnam War. Soldiers would remove their underwear to avoid chafing and even bacterial infections. I too was at war, gone commando, shamed by my overprotective mother with good intentions. I tried seeking validation from Tania Garcia and the big boobed girls at school, but it was no longer about a thong, it was no longer about validation–it was about the power of choice. To choose to live a life where acceptance came from within. Liberation is an internalized act that takes place in the body without needing anyone's approval. Being a twelve-year-old gone commando meant that even though I lost the battle with my mother, the war to free my butt cheeks and the rest of me was just the beginning.

Concentric

Maximillion Martini

The sun hasn't even started its bullshit though the birds have. The streets are lined with soldiers dead on their feet. The smell of rot and ruin lingers everywhere, piling up every Wednesday night and then disappearing Thursday morning. I'm the one that disappears it. I'm the one that rolls by your house like the rising sun, emptying trash cans and eliminating their filth. It's a job well done and I'm proud to do it.

Once your side is done, all that's left is the other side. It's a simple problem. And yet the solution is anything but. A trash truck is unwieldy, even if it's just a pickup with some modifications, like mine is. And, believe it or not, yours isn't the only road in town. This place isn't big, but it has managed to cram in a lot of damn roads into not a lot of space. If I have any hopes of getting everyone's trash not just efficiently but *well*, that is, *elegantly* - and elegance is absolutely the mark, despite what most people think of trash and those of us that collect it - then this is a situation well worth thinking about.

Consider this. Let's say I make a left at the end of your road just to keep things moving forward. Now I have a real decision to make: should I take this new road to where it ends and make another left to keep that process up, doing a big loop, counter clockwise? Or should I make the next left immediately, and follow *that* to the end, but this time make a double right instead of another left, and keep *that* up, zigzagging back and forth through the neighborhood?

It's not an easy decision.

Regardless of what Wilkins says.

There are two sides of this waste management debate and they both have their merits. I'm not calling anybody stupid. On its face, I say I can understand that zigzagging gets the job done. On its *face*. That's simply because with a good zigzag through town, you don't miss anything and you don't waste any time. Everybody's happy.

But that's not good enough, not for me. The problem is that zigzagging is an *ugly* way of going about the job. It has no *grace*. It's not *natural*. Back and forth and back and forth - it makes me feel like an oil drill or a hamster wheel. There's nothing beautiful about back and forth - there's nothing fun about zigzagging. And yet, some people - I'm not naming names - say it's the best way to collect trash. They say it's the only way. But here's the deal: the zigzag is only preferred *because* it's preferred. It's how the world's lawnmowers move. It's how your grandma's vacuum moves. People like what they like. They know what they know. And they can get defensive. Scared even. People don't like change. You know how they are. People like to do things by the book. But that's the problem. Because the book in this case is actually just called *Waste Management* and it was written and edited and published and reissued and loved just to death by a bunch of city people. I guarantee that they've never even seen a town like this.

And it gets worse! Because these cities, where the city dwellers dwell, where the power pools, they were all built with the zigzag in mind. So as the authors of *Waste Management* sat around in their sky lofts and rooftop pizza parlors and high fashion DGs - I don't have any idea what's going on over there - they looked around and thought, "Ah yes, the zigzag is God's gift to waste management and we shall not question it." Of course they did! The zigzag does work in their pristine, boxed out, zigzaggy cities. But that's only because the cities were *designed* to be zigzagged! Meaning we have a zigzag bias baked right into the pie! It goes all the way back to Rome and the ancient traditions. Irrigation canals or whatever. If the Romans even had pie, I don't know.

Let me just say it: this is not Rome. This town's a damn mess! It's not on a grid, nothing is straight, and there is rarely enough space for more than one vehicle on the road at a time. In other words, things are not so easily zigzagged. Hell, most of the streets in this town were not planned at all. John Wilkins is the Town Planner here and he doesn't know jack shit about waste management. What he does know jack shit about is telling me how to do my job. He says I *have* to zigzag. According to him, it's the only way. He says it's a "best practice" and "just common sense" and "get your shit together." But he's wrong! And I've told him as much to his face. I said just last week, "You don't see what I see! You can't even comprehend the *problem*." He doesn't collect trash - he *only* manages it. And he's been that way his entire life. His dad, John, Sr., was the first Town Planner here. Senior took that opportunity to name half the town after himself. Can you imagine the head on a guy like that! Then his damn son made it a family business. This is the guy that's up here now trying to tell me how to collect trash.

I don't want to cast aspersions on Wilkins or any of his zigzagging. I just try to say it like it is. This town *is* a mess. And we cannot rely on the powers that be to clean it up. The future will not fix itself. Have you seen John's kid? His face does not inspire optimism. This damn child - he's John, III, now - he couldn't be more than ten years old - I found him in the junkyard one day after I did my route. He was kneeling down between the residential waste and the junk cars, just interested as all get out in whatever it was he had in his hands. It could have been anything. People are incredible with what they throw away. He was trying to steal from me. I know he was. So I snuck up quiet-like and I yelled hey or something and I spooked him and yes I know it's just a kid but he wasn't so afraid of me that he couldn't look me straight in the eye. And he had the same smug face and the same mess of too much blonde hair as his daddy. I know that stupid hair all too well.

As we made eye contact, time seemed to stop. I forgot what year it was. The sun reflected a thousand times off the stack of wrecked cars I keep in the middle of the yard. It was so quiet I could practically hear the snails sliming around. Then - boom! - I was back forty years ago. And Johnny III was back there with me, too. Together, we saw the boy's daddy. There he was, a specter from the 80s in the middle of my junkyard wearing a green zoot suit, his blonde hair all over the place. I was there, too, wearing my dead uncle's huge suit and a fedora. I remember purchasing that hat from Goodwill with my own money specifically for prom, so I could honor my uncle, who had only recently overdosed. So, me and Johnny III watched as my ghost - looking damn good, if I may say so - said, "I sure am glad my street isn't named Wilkins Boulevard or some shit." The real me had to laugh at that. It was a pointless thing to say, deliberate shade thrown at the richest and most popular kid in school, but it was brave in its pointlessness. And true! Unfortunately for me, though, that's when the violence commenced. Because the ghost of John II shouted some things and threw some punches and ultimately tossed the ghost of me headfirst into a trash can just off the dance floor. He thought he was better than every-body just because he was in this suit that his mama had bought for him brand new and because the damn road to the school was named after his pa. "I own this town," is what he said. He literally said that as I was swimming in trash and my feet were flopping around over my head!

The Wilkinses think their superiority is spelled out all over town and proved by every street or fucking dog park with their name on it but that only proves their arrogance is congenital. Because John, Sr. - this is the head of the line - he just happened to be in the right place at the right time. The inter-state came to this town and everything was blowing up. More importantly, John, Sr. *knew* the right people at the right time. This old man was *connected*. And he was connected not because he was so great or beloved but because he sold moonshine all over the county when it was very difficult for people to get drunk anyway else! That's it! That's the whole damn story! That's how he got his start! It's bullshit! Three generations!

Long story short, I am quite sure this kid stole something from me and was not afraid to do it because he knew his daddy wasn't afraid of me either. It's not a secret that John is technically my boss. So, yes, I threw some shit! And, yes, I said some things maybe I shouldn't have said to a child. But I was mad! It's my trash!

Thankfully, not everything is up to the John Wilkinses of this world. I have done the *research* and I have figured it out.

What I do is called concentric circles. It goes like this:

I start at a corner of the town and I go straight, picking up trash on one side of the road until it ends or extends beyond my purview. If it ends, nine times out of ten it actually Ts, so you can turn one way *out* of town or the other way *into* town. Instead of zigzagging back in, then, I stay on the outside. Enough of this and pretty soon I've circled the whole town so that I'm back to back to where I started. Obviously, then, I don't want to do the same stretch *again*. Instead, I turn at the very last intersection before the starting place and start a new loop, one in from the last, like the next layer of an onion. I can do that over and over until I hit the center of town, the middle of the onion. At that point, we're halfway done. I simply turn my ass around and head back out, making the same circle but in the opposite direction, looping towards the outside.

It's that simple. And it's that major.

For three generations now, the Wilkenses have been sitting on a mountain of zigzag money and telling me I have to get in their zigzag line. They sit in their ivory tower and drive their unwrecked cars and write damn emails full of their lazy, zigzagging directions. But they're not in charge of everything! Trash people like us can beat the Wilkinses of this world. We can do it! I am doing it! I am literally running circles around these bastards. But it's more than just a matter of bottom lines and best practices and efficiency. I don't care about that shit: I'm striving for a higher standard. It's something Wilkins can't even understand. My circles are beautiful. They're graceful. They swirl within themselves like curling ocean waves making and remaking the beach. They pout like puffed up pillows in the sky that block the sun and bring life-giving rain. It brings to mind the moon which pushes the pulls, cycling the air and the water and the blood in each of us, the earth on which we stand. Trash is not separate from the earth - it is the earth. We should not be trying to square things that aren't square. We should be making circles.

As we speak, thousands and thousands of rainbow-hewed snails are sliding in and around and on top of my dump. They make their shells layer by layer, oozing some nacreous thing from themselves and swirling it in slow motion. They ooze and circle within circles until they've built a defensive coating that is also a home. It's functional and effective, yes, but it's also more than that: it is beautiful and it is graceful and it is natural.

Why do we have to pretend to be any different?

Wonder Twins Reactivated: A Search for Connection

Juanita E.Mantz

The Wonder Twins' are Zan and Jayna, alien siblings from the planet Exxor with shapeshifting ability, but they can only activate them when they touch hands.

My twin sister Jackie and I fight. We fight hard. We fight ugly. We fight unfair. There are no belts to hit below when we argue. We aim for the heart, for the head and for the soul. We crush one another.

My day job is as a lawyer in mental health court. Jackie works as an English teacher with troubled kids at a continuation school. Our lives have often mirrored each other. We graduated the same year with English Literature degrees after waitressing our way through university. We both went on to graduate school.

Despite our academic achievements, we have not been successful in our relationship. Our fights always end ugly, recreating the chaos of our shared childhood. It has even gotten physical at times and I recall fighting with Jackie in the street at a writing conference in our thirties. Typically, we explode at each other and say awful things and then after the battle is over, it is almost like it never happened. It is a vicious circle.

Jackie called me after one of our fights recently and told me that she realized through therapy that the chaos our parents exposed us to made us both co-dependent and gave us a fear of abandonment. This, in her opinion, was the cause of the cyclical fighting and forgiveness aspect of our relationship. It was like a lightbulb went off in my head.

Writing this, I wonder how Jackie would feel about this essay. A better question is whether she would even want me to tell it. The answer is likely a resounding "NO!"

Like many hard things in our lives, especially from our childhood, this essay may remain buried and maybe one day, I will light this essay on fire.

***

Our relationship of learned warfare vacillates from anger to forgiveness. It was passed down. It is our shared inheritance. We were raised in a house where fighting hard was normal. Growing up, mom and dad fought ugly and often. "John, you're a fucking asshole" was a phrase I knew by age five, or even sooner. Maybe Jackie and I heard it in the womb. I imagine us grimacing in utero our ears perking up and our mouths turning down.

Words were not my parents' only weapons. Plates were

routinely thrown and holes punched in walls, by both of them at times, but mostly it was my mom throwing and my dad ducking. If my dad was drinking, it was even worse because then my dad would engage with her, after holding it all in for far too long. He would often try to deescalate my mom to no avail with his standard, "Judy, calm down, I'm home now aren't I?" After they fought, Mom and Dad would make up and go get us Pizza Hut or McDonald's. Fast food was our treat for enduring it all, I suppose.

Mom and Dad did get along at times, especially when they would go out country dancing. Mom would dress up in her jean suit with fringe looking like a Mexican Loretta Lynn and my dad, who was a white cowboy from Montana, would put on his Stenson and his shit kickers and they would go to the Crazy Horse bar to line dance and listen to dad's favorites by Johnny Cash and Willie Nelson. The good times never lasted longer than a few days.

***

One time, when he was drinking, my dad threw a sewing machine at my mom, and it hit her on the side of her face. My sister Jackie and I watched from the patio outside looking through their bedroom window. My little sister Annie shivered alongside us. I've written the story as a scene, but it is fragmented, broken like the sewing machine into pieces.

A decade ago, I asked my mom if she remembered the incident and she said she did. She said that it was the one time my dad really ever hurt her physically. She was surprised I remembered it. My mom admitted that she had been pummeling my dad with her fists and that she forgave him. It didn't make sense to me back then and I wondered why my parents would both choose to stay in such a destructive relationship. But looking at it in my fifties, and after being married for a decade and a half, I almost understand it. It's fucking complicated. Marriage sure as hell isn't easy. It's not like in my mom's Harlequin romance novels I devoured as a kid. Truth is, my mom loved my dad to distraction and they stayed together until the day my dad died at 69 from pancreatic cancer.

After his death, my mom was transformed into a different person, calmer and more loving. My dad was the trigger for any rage my mom had and now that he has gone, it has dissipated. We're very close now. She lives down the street from me and I take her grocery shopping and to all of her doctor appointments and with us on vacation.

And sometimes, just sometimes because I am working on it, I am more like my mother then I want to admit. I yell. I scream at my husband when I am frustrated with my exhausting job as a deputy public defender and my life not being all that I imagined it would be. Then I apologize to my husband. I justify that I never use my hands as weapons or throw things. But still, it is not pretty.

***

Now, in our fifties, Jackie and I no longer physically fight, but a few months ago, we tried to do a family Christmas which is always risky. Growing up, Christmas always resulted in fights, and usually ended with me and my sisters sitting at the park down the street, or us girls sitting on our roof together, waiting for mom and dad's argument to calm down.

So, on this Christmas, Jackie was hosting at her sixties style house in Palm Springs. Jackie is a thrift store antiquing queen, and her house is decorated as if Frank Sinatra lives there in colors of blue and orange. Jackie was anxious as hell because she had a rough week at work and her husband was stuck in a meeting instead of helping her prep. I got to her house late and she was annoyed because I was supposed to be making deviled eggs. Jackie was more than somewhat rude and wouldn't show me where the parsley and mixing bowls were.

"They're up there Jenny, just look," Jackie said petulantly. I responded, "Well you're the one who can't peel the eggs correctly."

All of a sudden there's an explosive twin fight.

"Why do you always gotta be a bossy bitch?" she screamed.

"Why do you always gotta be an asshole rude jerk?" I yelled back.

We ranted and raved at each other and shouted out more insults. I threatened to leave. My mom took a walk. My husband put his head in his hands. Eggs are such a petty thing to start an argument.

Looking back, I should have understood it was a lot to host. Cooking is not the Mantz girls' forte. I thought, how many good days have we ruined in this way? We made up, of course like we always do, but the fight cast a shadow. If my dad was there, he would have said slowly in his Montana drawl with a sad look in his blue eyes, "Girls, don't fight."

It pains me to think of all of the experiences Jackie and I have missed because we can't get along. We were so close as kids. United. It was always us against the world since we were in utero. Mom says we had our own language as babies. We dressed exactly alike for most of our childhood, until we were old enough to be embarrassed by it. We were best friends all though our childhood. We called each other wonder twins. We would reenact our favorite Justice League twin characters who wore purple spandex outfits and touch fists and chant "Wonder Twin power activate!" We would wear our under roos and tie towels as capes around our necks and fly off the sofa.

Now as adults, Jackie says I don't support her or like her. She says that I judge her, and I do. I'm an asshole. I put on my lawyer voice to distance myself from people. I know this. Authority is my armor. Sometimes, Jackie will call me in a loving voice and say kindly, "Hi sis, what you doing?" and I will be short and abrupt just to hurt her feelings because I am having a bad day. The niceness doesn't feel normal to me. I would rather have sarcasm and dark banter, but is that normal? Why can't my twin sister be sweet to me without me being cruel? How can I be so cold to her yet kind to strangers and loving and supportive with my friends and my writing community? How can I have empathy for my clients, most of whom have been accused of horrific things, and not love my twin sister unconditionally?

I have to heal this. I have to find that connection and hold her hand and heart close to mine. Does this sound sentimental? Well, I've been anti-sentimental for far too long. I need to take off that protection. That's part of my goal in writing this down, it's to try and understand how my trauma has shaped my relationship with my twin sister who should be my best friend.

Nowadays, Jackie judges me back. She says I need to quit drinking and smoking and she is right. She's trying to save me. Most days, I feel like I'm all alone adrift in the sea looking for the shoreline, escaping into oceans of beer until I am numb and cannot feel the dregs of loneliness in my gut anymore. I have washed them all away. But have I?

Wonder twin power activates, form of a melting heart ice sculpture. Tears of icy water falling down. "I'm melting!" Isn't that what the witch from The Wizard of Oz said as she lay dying? Help me Justice League God, are you listening? It's me, Juanita.

***

What I am avoiding telling you is the reason for it all.

When we were kids, my mom would hit Jackie. Why you ask? Two reasons.

First, my mom was jealous of Jackie's relationship with my dad. Mom was jealous of cocktail waitresses, of my dad's ex-wives, of my dad's two daughters from his first ex-wife but

108

most of all, my mom was jealous of Jackie who was my dad's favorite. The second reason my mom hit Jackie is that no matter what, Jackie would rarely cry. I've described it in a story as her lonely tree stance. She could take a lot. I would always tell her, "Jackie, just cry when she hits you like I do!"

It's hard to say these things, but I know they are true the way I know a just verdict. It's in my bones. I've lived it. I sometimes joke that I was raised by wolves, but that's just hyperbole. I was raised by two fractured and grief-stricken broken people who both lost young children to horrific accidents before they met and who were doing the best they could.

When we were little, my mom would lose her shit and go off on us, usually because my dad was out at a bar getting plastered instead of coming home after his job moving furniture for the Mayflower Moving Company. Our little sister Annie would run and hide. I would scream and cry if the hits came, and Jackie would stand still or fight. Jackie was brave. I'll give her that. Jackie would go toe to toe with my mom as a kid. Jackie is so brave she once got into a fistfight with a chola for me as my proxy. She saved me an ass kicking that day, but I never was able to save her.

Maybe it is not about each of our histories, but about our shared history. We have different perspectives, of course, but we lived together in the womb. I find it interesting that Jackie and I both write about our childhood. We are both clearly living in the past.

***

When we were kids, my mom would hit Jackie over and over and I would watch. This happened often, at least once a week. The not knowing was the worst part. Not knowing if my mom would explode. We never knew whether it was going to be a good or bad day. I would intervene at times and beg my mom to stop hitting Jackie. I remember one time, my mom totally lost it on Jackie. Jackie had broken my mom's doll who

109

lived in a glass dome, a present my dad had gotten her. Mom came home and saw my dad was not home from work and then she saw the broken glass. I remember my mom shaking Jackie over and over and slapping her repeatedly so hard I thought Jackie's head would fall off. I remember screaming "Stop MOM, STOP!" My mom snapped out of it and left the room. We were both crying and Jackie rarely cried so I knew she was terrified.

I don't want to remember these things. It's not fair and maybe if I remember how bad it really was, I will not be able to love my mom the way I love her now. My mom and I have healed our relationship, yet Jackie and I have not. Is that ironic? Maybe it is just so fucking sad.

***

I remember when Jackie urged me to try and graduate high school with her senior year. "Just get it together Jenny," she said. "Stop fucking around and graduate." I didn't listen and dropped out five credits short. I remember watching Jackie graduate from my vantage point hiding under the bleachers with a cigarette in my hand, tears running down my face, ruining my Siouxsie Sioux eyeliner. I was so sad but also proud of Jackie for graduating high school, at least one of us had made it through and yet, my happiness for Jackie was all mixed up with sadness at my own self sabotage.

***

Let me think of a happy story. Jackie and I are riding our bikes. It's a sunny Saturday in Ontario, California in the 1980s. We have matching yellow beach cruiser bikes with bells. We are wearing our florescent Wham UK style sweatshirts. Jackie's sweatshirt is yellow and mine is green. Mom said we could ride until sunset because she had to take our little sister Annie to the dentist. We took off mid-morning and we rode and rode from Ontario to the Montclair Plaza, a trip of at least ten miles. We arrived out of breath and parked our bikes and chained them up.

"I'm starving. What we gonna eat Jenny?" Jackie said with a grin. Food was always a priority for us.

"Corn dogs definitely. I think I have enough quarters for two. But we have to drink water." I said with a big grin.

Jackie winked at me and I felt a plan hatching when she said. "I want a lemonade and some pizza, where there's a will, there's a way."

I nodded and right then, we both said the exact thing at the same time, "Operation begging for quarters." We could always read each other's minds. The "con" was that we would go up to old people and say in our best twin falsettos, "We lost our wallet and need a ride home. Can we have a quarter to call our mom?"

That day, as a twin dream team, we raised a record breaking five dollars. The mall was packed and that helped. We stuffed our faces with pizza, popcorn, corn dogs, lemonade, and candy. We rode home ringing our bells, high on junk food, with huge smiles on our faces. When we got home, we told Annie who whined, "It's not fair."

Another story that sticks in my mind is not a happy one. We were four or five years old and at my mom's godfather's house in Norco who had a huge dog. I watched Jackie pet the dog on the porch. Annie was inside with my mom. Then, all of a sudden, the dog lunged and ripped into Jackie's face right below her eye. Jackie sat there in shock as blood streamed down her face like in a movie, and I yelled, "Mom, *my* face is on fire! Help! Help us

Jackie just stood there, a quarter of her face gone as I screamed over and over, "It hurts so bad, it hurts." I felt Jackie's pain that day. I know I did. I remember feeling it. It hurt so bad I felt like I was dying. My mom rushed Jackie to the hospital and stood by her side for days comforting her along with my dad. The doctors saved Jackie's face with plastic surgery.

Looking at Jackie now, you can't even tell she was ever bit by a dog in the face unless you look close. You have to squint in and get in really, really close to see the faint lines below Jackie's eye and above her lip. The scars are barely visible, but I know.

Look closer is what I will tell myself next time I see her. Look really close and really see her. You must. She's part of you. You are one. Don't ever forget it.

Cholos vs. Deathrockers

Facundo Rompehuevos

When we visited my brother at juvenile hall my hair was spiked up with Aquanet hairspray (the purple extra super hold can) and I was wearing fishnet sleeves on my arms, a tight black shirt with a spiderweb design, a bondage leather belt with big chrome metal loops and tight black jeans with a bunch of deathrock band patches.

My family tolerated that I was a deathrocker (for those who don't know, it's kinda in between a punk and a goth but none of that velvety-vampire aesthetic shit). They had given up on trying to get me to change because I kept dressing this way even after graduating high school and going to (and then quickly dropping out of) community college.

But they still cringed when we would go out in public or to family events. They felt the eyes of strangers and family members alike staring at their eldest son with looks of disgust, immediately questioning their son's sexual orientation—almost certain he took it up the ass (I didn't).

My mom didn't like to call it juvenile hall. It was the Challenger Memorial Youth Center, so to her credit technically it wasn't. Although it was administered by the same government agency, the infamous California Youth Authority, or how it was more commonly known, the "YA."

My brother was affiliated with the local gang—which shall remain nameless—in one of the bad parts of the San Fernando Valley—which, too, shall remain nameless. He had been busted for some serious shit—which also doesn't need elaboration. He was facing some serious charges. After hopping around from various youth detention programs and "camps," he finally landed at the Challenger Memorial Youth Center.

It would take us about an hour to get to the camp from our apartment. Sometimes we would stop by In-N-Out on the way. Drive-thru, of course, in order to avoid the masses' judgmental eyes on me and by extension my accountable family. The guards and staff—or "camp counselors," I guess, in following with my mom's wholesome delusion—would let us bring him food. To their credit, they treated us—even me—with respect. They never made fun of me to my face. They were polite and professional enough to wait until we left. Then they'd harass my brother about his weird and gay-ass-looking brother. But he defended me, and by extension himself. He didn't take shit from anyone. Family is family, no matter how weird.

On the ride home I'd already be thinking about how I could get fucked up that day. Either drunk—alcohol was easier to get even if I was underage because we had a small network of liquor stores in the Valley that sold to us on the downlow). Or high—drug dealers never card, of course. Or both. Preferably both.

When we would get back home, I'd go straight to the room and scrounge for change. I only needed a couple of bucks for a 40 or tall can.

The room seemed bigger now. I no longer had to share it with my brother.

We had a small two-bedroom apartment. My parents stayed in one room, and we stayed in the other. The traditional poor Mexican-and-Central-American family arrangement in the poor Mexican-and-Central-American *barrio*.

But here's the thing: there was nothing "traditional" about me.

I didn't look like the rest of the kids my age on my block.

Them—*los cholillos*—with their shaved heads, rocking flawless pairs of Nike Cortez, Ben Davis, Dickies, FB County and 501s, everything ironed, starched and creased. Listening to gangster rap, oldies and sometimes *corridos*. Drinking and smoking (but not like us, nothing like how we got down).

Us—the rocker foos—with our crazy-ass long, spiked and dyed hair, painted nails, pierced lips, septum, tongues, eyebrows, rocking boots or dirty and worn-out Chuck Taylors, ripped up jeans and hoodies, covered in band patches sewn on with white dental floss. Listening to all sub-genres of punk and metal and everything in between. Drinking and smoking, too, but not like the *cholos*.

We smoked meth and crack, snorted Special K and coke (when we could afford it), shot up or smoked heroin, dropped acid, ate mushrooms, popped pills as if they were Tic-Tacs.

Whereas the gangsters were arrested or died from *la vida loca*, we were the truly *loco* ones. We declared it. We were admitted into psych wards. Many of us died from drug overdoses.

***

It was February. It was me and another punk whose identity is forever lost to the permanent amnesia of my alcoholism and drug abuse. We were coming back from getting drunk in an alley up the street. In order to be respectful to my family, I rarely got drunk or high at home. I was a freak and veritably insane, but c'mon, I had decency.

As we turned down my street, we ran into two of the local *cholos*. I don't remember their names so we're just gonna go with Lil Humpty and Big Dumpty.

"Sup foos," Lil Humpty said. "Where's the party at?"

"Sup," I said. "It just finished!"

"Aww, *pues*," he said.

"*Invítanos* next time, holmes." Big Humpty said.

"*Órale*," I said.

But we weren't buddy-buddy. By no means. It was détente. If they didn't mess with us, we wouldn't mess with them.

After we walked away, I saw a Christmas tree abandoned on the curb. Although it was mostly dried-up and brown, you could still see some green at the bottom. I dug out my lighter from my front pocket and walked over to it.

Because it was so brittle and dry, it lit up pretty quickly. I could see my friend slowly mouth the words "oh" and "shit."

"Hey!" Big Dumpty said. "What the fuck you doing, *ese!*"

The *cholos* ran up on us.

Alcohol is a funny thing.

I didn't consider myself brave. If anything, I was cowardly. But you get some booze in me, I'm unstoppable. Not sure if you can call that fearlessness or recklessness. In many ways it was self-destruction. And if you were to take that apart and delve deeper into the psychology behind my recklessness, it gets darker.

One time I was so drunk I ran through traffic on a busy street with my eyes closed.

But I didn't feel brave. I felt determined to kill myself. It wouldn't be my last attempt.

So, no, although the outcome was the same, it turns out I wasn't brave. I just didn't give a fuck.

***

Lil Humpty and Big Dumpty were brothers. Although they were affiliated, their family had just recently moved from another street in the neighborhood.

Gangs have a pretty basic set up. A gang can be exclusively based on a street, like Valerio Street or Blythe Street. Or it could be based in an entire city or neighborhood like Van Nuys, Pacoima or San Fernando. But with the latter, the neighborhood or city gang is often made up of smaller street-based cliques. Like Delano Street, which is within Van Nuys.

But while the cliques belonged to the larger gang, there was a certain level of division—a sort of street-pride territorial rivalry.

So, to me, because they weren't originally from my street, they were more outsiders than me. Even though I look like I didn't belong. Even though I wasn't a *cholo*. Even though I wasn't Chicano enough.

So whothefuck they think they are, I thought to myself. *Whatthefuck does it look like I'm doing*, I thought to myself.

"Whatthefuck does it look like I'm doing?" I said.

Lil Humpty and Big Dumpty looked at each other with confusion, each one waiting for the other to give direction—*you wanna handle it or should I or should we both stomp on him or what?*

But I didn't wait for either of them to respond.

"I said, 'Whatthefuck does it look like I'm doing?'"

I was defiant now, pissed. The malt liquor was like molasses slowly coursing through my veins, clogging up whatever part of the brain was responsible for reason and logic and the fear of consequences.

"Where you guys from, huh?" I asked. "I'm *from* here. I grew up on this street. I've been in this hood all my life, all my fuckin' life. You foos are new. Where the fuck are you foos from!"

I don't know exactly why they didn't kill me or at least beat the shit out of me and my friend. But they didn't. They stayed silent. They stepped back and allowed me to continue.

Before the fire got too big, I grabbed the Christmas tree by the base and dragged it into the middle of the street.

It was late, so there wasn't any traffic, especially not on a small street like ours. It was dark because half of the streetlights didn't work.

I walked back toward my friend on the sidewalk. The *cholos* had walked back to their apartment building's stoop. We left the Christmas tree ablaze in the middle of the street.

My friend and I walked back home in silence. I was hoping my parents were asleep so I could sneak him into my room. But my dad hated when my guy friends would sleep over. We were too old for sleepovers, so he assumed we were gay—but we weren't, or at least I wasn't. If my friend was Black, it would be worse. Insult to injury. *Not only is my son a fag but his boyfriend es un pinche Negro.* I was more scared of my dad than I was of the *cholos*.

***

There were many rocker foos that weren't white, but we were still seen as white. Or wanting to be white. Not *authentically* Black, brown or whatever else enough.

It's true that the majority of the music we were listening to was played by mostly white musicians—from Bauhaus and The Smiths to Amebix and TSOL—and that the majority in attendance at a show were often white (except the backyard shows—it was the opposite in fact—shout out to Pacas and East Los!).

Today you see mobs of non-white rocker foos all over the city, but it wasn't like that back in the 90s and early 2000s. It was more antagonistic. We'd get into fights with the *cholos* who acted like the vanguard of Chicano culture—sometimes we would win, but most times we would lose. They always outnumbered us.

We were smaller, more alone.

But it wasn't until I stopped being a deathrocker that I realized I had some of it wrong.

Not all of the musicians in the bands were white. Of course, we always knew about brown punk bands like Los Crudos and Union 13. But there were also bands like The Adolescents (the late bassist Steve Soto was of Mexican descent), Catholic Discipline (friggin Chicano Elvis himself Roberto Lopez, better known as El Vez, was their keyboardist) and The Bags (frontwoman Alice Armendariz, better known as Alice Bag). These were my people! With Spanish last names! Fellow Rocker foo comrades!

And what of my favorite band, Christian Death, the originators of deathrock?

Their late singer Rozz Williams? White. Rick Agnew? White. George Belanger. White. John Albert. White. James McGearty. All white.

But not Eva Ortiz, better known as Eva O, who did backing vocals for Christian Death's debut masterpiece "Only Theatre of Pain" and then went on to become a full member.

¡*Pinche* Ortiz!

I've seen this woman perform. Watched music videos, recorded shows. I've listened to most of her discography. But *pinche* Ortiz is always covered up in thick corpse-like makeup.

It may seem shallow but after finding out she's Hispanic (she grew up Catholic so I'm going to deduce she's Chicana) I love her and her music more.

Because maybe we shared similar upbringings.

Maybe she got picked on, too.

Maybe the *cholas* jumped her and stole her lip liner.

Maybe she didn't fit in with her classmates, her family, her neighborhood—with their culture, with her *own* culture.

But so, what? Look at all the good that struggle and conflict have produced. In art, literature, music.

I don't think I would've been a writer if it wasn't for being picked on, for not fitting in—not with the white kids, not with the Chicanos—for all the trials and tribulation of growing up poor and working class, the drugs, the alcohol, the textbook trauma.

So, the next time a *cholillo* hits you up and asks, "Hey foo, you a rocker, huh?" just tell him, with your chest out, with your hair spiked or shaved or long, with your makeup on point, "*¡A wi wi, mi vato!*"

La Pierna del Diablo
(The Devil's Leg)

Tomás Montoya

When I found out that Lucien Freud was related to Sigmund Freud I threw my bagel in the air and let it fall to the ground. My love birds stopped singing at the snap of my Jewish bread hitting the floor. What kind of cultural nepotism was this? My anxiety rose inside my chest, a watery tar on slow boil. I hear Paloma Picasso sells overpriced jewelry. I can just imagine a gnarly Italian debutant on a sunny terrace, holding up a P.P. original and between her a.m. dirty martini sips, saying "You know *this* is a Picasso..." And they laugh and laugh because it's true. I wipe off my bagel and call my mom. She knows about these things. She was married to a famous man. Not Picasso or Freud famous, but famous enough to have had many a family breakfast interrupted from San Francisco to Albuquerque. A giddy former student claiming my father's admonishments had changed their life. Hapless state workers who would ask him if he could recite the final words of the speech he gave, at the anti Pete Wilson rally in 1994. He'd always nod politely until they left him alone and then he'd turn to us and shrug. "Putting people on pedestals is a social construct!" my mother yelled through the phone. That was her answer any time I came to her with this dilemma of establishing myself as an artist. She had said it to us so much I no longer believed in heroes. According to her no one was above anyone else, and if they were it was only because a bunch of other people put them there (undeservedly). My dad's fame might have truly been a social construct, but like other mutually agreed upon constructs like money, class and race... it could cut deep into the fragile psyche of a young kid trying to follow in his old man's footsteps.

Amidst my search for place and purpose within my father's socially imposed shadow, I wrote a short essay entitled, *If my dad was a plumber would you still like me?* The feeble premise I proposed was; if my dad was as good at plumbing as he was at being a teacher, artist, activist, poet and musician, would society see *me* as someone special, based on who my father was? Would people assume I was amazing at unclogging hot water pipes too? The piece was understandably an expose of cringeworthy self-loathing, but something about the act of writing it and asking the question aloud, gave me the courage to seek out my other siblings and see how they established themselves in spite of our father's fame.

In a bungalow overlooking Echo Park, my older brother (from a different mom) and I, sat on either side of a substantial mound of blow. He was born the same year of the Cuban Revolution. His mom was a Mexican/Lebanese, darling daughter of an influential farmer in 1950's Fresno. I saw a picture of her once. Imagine Rita Hayworth and a young Liz Taylor had a kid. He's a playwright. His answer began:

"At least dad was there when you were little! When we were kids, he was out fighting the dam revolution and forgot all about us! And then when he did come home, he'd just sleep or drink and then head right back out for The Cause! Why are you complaining anyway? He was already old and retired when you were born. You got everything I ever wanted!"

The two nefarious characters who'd driven in from T.J. to provide the booger sugar for our little heart to heart, sat behind my sensitive brother, nodding in unison. They'd obviously heard this rendition before. We cried and hugged and waited for the sunrise. My brother was right. My dad had confessed some of these things to me. He'd also told me that with his GI money and his first teaching stipend, they were able to move out of the housing projects in east Oakland and get a small three-bedroom house. He made all five kids sleep in one room because the third room was going to be his painting studio. As we drove home and the sun was rising over West Hollywood, it didn't feel right telling my brother that my dad and I were planning a month-long trip to Spain later that Summer.

Nicolas Kim Coppola AKA Nicolas Cage is Francis Ford Coppola's nephew. If Nicolas Cage deemed it necessary to change his name for Hollywood to take him seriously, then best believe, the struggle of which I speak is real.

Back in Sacramento I sought the counsel of my older sister (from a different dad). She is an administrative assistant for a prominent architectural firm. My sister's biological father was a lawyer and frequent bodyguard for El-Hajj Malik-El Shabazz. Soon after my sister was born, the political violence of New York in the early seventies was not something my mother wanted my sister exposed to. They moved to San Francisco where my mother and father met at a poetry reading. My sister was ten when I was born. Her answer to my inquiry was concise and honest: "That's your dad, not mine homie…" At least we had a great lunch after that. We were at my favorite Panera.

Not finding any solace in my siblings' words I decided to shake off the urge to be an artist by committing myself to full-time proletarian labor. I was hired at a door factory. I worked twelve hour shifts and slept all weekend. In spite of the long workdays, I found myself arriving at the warehouse early, and sketching the sun as it peered over the empty fields behind the pallet stacks. I did demolition work for a while because no poet ever did that, right? On my breaks I'd sit alone with my cigarette and coffee and write sonnets about the tragedy of tearing out the flooring of a house where a mother had gone mad and killed her only daughter. Around this time I also quit drugs and drinking to combat the swashbuckling Bukowski-esque persona my dad had so carefully crafted throughout his formidable years of terrorizing Beatniks along Telegraph avenue in the early 60's. Sobriety was boring. I decided to go to the source.

Upon entering my father's house I could hear Eydie Gorme careening from the backyard. Her soft whine was always soothing to me. He was in his garden. It wasn't actually a garden. It was a large Olmec head statue with a chunk of the nose missing, and a cactus. The head and the succulent rested in a six-by-six square of soft earth, under the shade of a Mulberry tree. He cared for that space as though it were an old loyal dog. (In real life he hated dogs). I opened the back door and entered the yard. His back was to me. He had one of my kids' toy rakes in his hand and was moving the dirt around the cactus, careful not to scratch the plant. I felt guilty. With each step I took, I inched closer to shattering this old man's peaceful Thursday afternoon.

Is Jaden Smith even talented? Can talent be extrapolated from kin to kin? I remember taking a writing class in my early twenties. It was my first attempt at coming out as an artist like my dad. The teacher was an older Mexican-American fellow who looked like he could be my uncle. He had a thick mustache and a long tight braid. Throughout the semester he shared a few stories from his formidable years in South Central L.A.. I happened to be writing very similar stories about growing up in gang laden Sacramento in the early 90's. He knew who my dad was but made sure to mention to us that Ishmael Reed was *his* mentor. One night during a class critique, an older blonde woman told the instructor that the way his characters talked didn't seem truly authentic. It sounded too "literary" to her. After the surprise subsided, he turned to me and said,

"Maybe we should ask Mr. Montoya here to help make my voices sound more authentic…"

My dad chuckled at this story. "Fuck'em!" he said, before taking a sip of his coffee. The tiny rake was leaning against his chair. I couldn't tell if he meant the instructor or the student, or both. My dad was old school. It was best not to ask him questions directly, it made him uneasy. It was best to present him with a sort of anecdotal conundrum, a tale of sorts, in need of solving. He'd consider it and then give his answer with an equally obscure parable. It was all terribly stressful, but necessary if you wanted an honest answer out of him. If you came at him too directly, he'd get flustered and worried and then ask where my mom was. And you didn't want my mom around at times like these. My mother and nuance are mortal foes.

One afternoon after a long day at the door shop, I headed downtown to gala the arts council was hosting to celebrate my dad's Poet Laureate appointment. When I arrived, the place was packed. I wasn't just underdressed, I was covered in a thin veil of soot and sweat. The event was free and open to the public, but when I got there, a man in a tuxedo ushered me into a low lit corner near a staircase. My dad was at the podium saying how grateful he was that John Trudell had agreed to come to Sacramento and read some poems for the upcoming event. My dad paused before beginning his next sentence and squinted in my direction, just as I stepped into my spot under the stairwell, "I see my son just walked in… glad you made it mijo!" A hundred people in suits and gowns turned to the back of the room. More than half of them tried looking past me because surely it couldn't be this dusty kid with neck tats. He went on with his speech. The man with the tuxedo rushed over to me with a forlorn smile and asked if I wanted a seat near the stage.

Reminding my dad about this story would have been too forthcoming. He would have dodged the implied query about getting special treatment because of who he was, and made a joke about how maybe neck tattoos weren't the best choice. I tried to muster up the guts to ask him how to transcend or at least circumvent his reputation and establish myself as an artist. Being the kid of someone "famous" wasn't so bad, I guess. It was like a bearable purgatory… A lukewarm shower when everyone else had cold baths. I slowly accepted that when you were the kid of someone famous, it was superfluous to create a full, independent identity. There was already a little mold all set up for you.

After a long, peaceful silence my dad stood up and grabbed his little rake. "There's some dynamite chile verde on the stove if you're hungry mijo.." He went inside and left me, Eydie Gorme in the backyard.

I chickened out that day in my dad's garden. I never brought it up again. I'd spent my short life as an aspiring artist suspended in that liminal *to be or not to be* cliché, and I'd let it defeat me. My ambivalence became my reality. I stopped making art altogether. I had some kids. I got a job that honored casual Fridays. I went to matinees on my Tuesdays off and opened up an IRA account. I fell in and out of love without a poem or painting to help make the heartache bearable. I read novels as a passive witness and not a scavenger of style and technique. I trained myself to see things for what they were. I realized the moon was just a rock in the sky and not a pale muse I worshiped in secret. I learned to see the river as a body of water and not a life-giving tentacle of a loving universe. I taught myself to see a plucked flower as just an object on a table and not a bloody allegory of aborted potential.

Mama Married a Mormon

Audrey Harris Fernández

In college, I thought I fell in love with a Mormon. He was a year older, with brown eyes so big I thought I might fall into them and divine the secrets of the universe. He was from Utah, where my father was born, and had served a mission to an impossibly foreign country. I found out later that he was the son of a big player in Salt Lake business circles, and it fit his slow self-assured smile. A mutual friend suspected him of being a know-it-all, but I fell readily under his spell.

The daughter of a Mormon father and non-Mormon mother, I grew up in San Francisco. My dad instructed me in religious matters from a young age by reading me stories from the Old Testament about strong women, like Ruth and Esther. He'd spend long afternoons helping me polish short essays on lessons from the Bible, and I would read them in special meetings to the whole congregation. These experiences were a fertile training ground for a future career as a literature professor; however, I began to suspect that my dad was a bit unorthodox. In my Young Women classes, I chafed at being taught how to someday tend to my husband and children and I left at the age of sixteen. I knew I was right to leave the Church, but my defection left me with a deep sense of spiritual and cultural emptiness.

How strange but fitting it felt, to leave a religion only to fall for one of its practitioners. He and I were both studying abroad at an ancient English university. Our differences were clear—I spent weekends dancing to Kylie Minogue with my roommate in cramped pubs and drank strong cups of black tea in the Junior Common Room every day at four, while he refrained from alcohol and caffeine. Nevertheless, we slipped into an easy companionship amidst the soaring spires, cobblestone streets and the courtyard library of our co-ed boarding house, spending so much time together at one point that people began to nudge each other when we passed.

"Sister Harris," he'd call me teasingly when we were alone together in the kitchen. "Brother B-," I'd reply, my face burning at the traditional greetings and the feelings they stirred. In one of these conversations, I remember we discussed the red rock marvels of Moab, in Southern Utah where my family was from, and that I felt chills when he called it "God's country."

Part of his allure was the call of Utah. I knew it from extended family reunions filled with campfire songs, second cousins wearing name tags, and silly skits. Utah was my grandparents' apartment near Temple Square, the dishes of homemade pickles and chocolate pie. One winter, when our plane touched down in Salt Lake, I cheered along with the rest of the passengers, dressed in Sunday best, as they applauded the captain for landing us safely. My family was from Pine Valley, a tiny mountain village where my many times great grandfather is said to have lived with four wives in four houses, one on each corner of the same street. The dubious honor of taking many wives was designated to the powerful. I always wonder what happened to the others, the males who weren't deemed worthy to marry. I imagine them as the gay uncles, artists, fire walkers, moonshiners, cross dressers, and cowboys. I think they're the ones I would have gotten along with best.

One night I persuaded my roommate to help me cook dinner for my crush and one of his friends. I made a run to Tesco and baked a succulent chicken, with clear gravy and mashed potatoes. After dinner, probably sensing my ploy, he folded his napkin and grinned slyly at me. "Audie, will you marry me?" he jested, using my childhood nickname. My heart beat wildly, even as my inner feminist shook her fist. On another occasion, during a train trip through the Scottish Highlands, we sang "You take the high road and I'll take the low road" in unison between fits of laughter.

I didn't know many Mormons in my regular life growing up, except at church where they tended to come and go, the kids of medical and dental students, or army brats. Though many did settle in California, sent out by Brigham Young, San Francisco isn't exactly a hub for Mormons. With my crush, so many things felt familiar. That afternoon in Scotland, I remember falling asleep on his shoulder to the gentle rocking of the train. The gesture was meant as a not-so-subtle sign, but the sense of comfort it brought surprised me. Never had I felt such a strong and sturdy spiritual presence beside me, except my dad's.

In Mormonism, grace illuminates the simplest human gestures, and the search for love is the search for God. On a group movie outing, I remember the song "When you Say Nothing at All" played during the opening credits, possibly the version sung by Keith Whitley and Alison Krause. Sentimental as it is, I loved it then and still do. I thought I heard him hum along to the opening bars. Even then, the irony wasn't lost on me: I'd travelled all the way to Europe just to meet someone who pulled me back to the place I was from.

His feelings for me, however, were far less clear, expressed in feints and retreats. Watching other couples chatting at candlelit cafés, I began to wonder why he never asked me out and became prickly and withdrawn. We grew apart. Then one night as I stood in the kitchen, I thought I heard him complaining about my cold treatment of him on the phone in the courtyard below. I decided to reveal my feelings, thinking he cared. His answer: silence.

I did my best to forget him. Then back at our home university he came to my row house, hung out on my bedroom floor, joked with my roommates. They hinted that he liked me, but I took his silence abroad for a definitive answer. A week or so later, a mutual friend had a birthday party; my crush sat next to me in the dimly lit foyer, but I left early on the arm of a member of the track team, wanting to show him what he had lost.

It took my friend, one of my oldest, years to forgive me for leaving her party after it had barely started. The runner took me directly home, ran his hands over my body. I rejected sex, and never heard from him again. Suddenly the friendship approach seemed a million times better. Wanting only to be back in the sunshine of his attention, I visited my crush's dorm room a few days later. He wasn't there, but I found a scrap of notebook paper on his bed filled with a list of people I knew. My own name was crossed out.

I think now we were destined to enact this mutual rejection ritual. In part because we weren't right for each other, but also because I had already chosen to leave the Church, for irrevocable reasons, and he had to marry a Mormon. I know the part of me that loved him is the part that wished I could have stayed.

The feeling of being on the outside was familiar from past family gatherings. Even with my mother's skirt still swirling around my head, I could already feel the invisible line in the room that divided our cousins, full Mormons, and my sisters and I. Recently, one of those cousins mentioned a children's book my grandpa used to read to him before bed so often he memorized it. He never read it to me. My mother hints at deeper snubs: the wedding my grandfather never attended (my grandma went on her own, on the arms of her other children); the pressure to be a housewife (my mom was a working lawyer and helped support the family so we could live in the city); the implication she might be a hippie when she hadn't borne a child by twenty-eight.

I landed a job in New York shortly after college. My crush went his own way, married a Mormon woman, had a handful of children, and moved to Utah. My path to settling down took much longer and feels hard won. To quote Gloria Steinem, first I had to become the man I wanted to marry. Today I live in Long Beach with my free-thinking husband, who never left his feelings for me in doubt. I teach literature at local universities and explore different worldviews. I keep some of the traditions I was raised with, transform others, and discard the rest to cultivate something pure and wild, something I can believe in and pass on to our daughter.

One Sunday of my senior year, I dressed up and visited our campus church in a naked last bid to see my crush. After the meeting, he spoke little to me but introduced me to his father in the lobby. I left as soon as I could, craving fresh air and solitude. As I headed out of the parking lot, his dad pulled up next to me in a Porsche and offered me a ride. He had his son's self- assured smile, but in the face of his persistence I shook my head proudly and walked myself home.

Arabic for Dummies

Alex Poppe

Hanging onto the Land Cruiser's roof rack with my left hand, I let go with my right, twisting to take photos of the stampede of children chasing us. Riding the back bumper evoked the exhilarated invincibility of youth. *This is why I came here,* I thought. *This is wh*—the truck hit a deep rut in the dirt road, and I went flying.

It was 2012. The year prior, I had moved to Kurdistan, Iraq, motivated by desperation and curiosity in equal measure. I was forty-five years old.

***

Summer 2011

I woke to the wail of New York City sirens, assailing the streets. Outside my bedroom window, clouds drifted zoologically over squat, repurposed factory buildings in the early morning light. Rolling over on my air mattress, I was greeted by a steady, hissing whisper. The mattress had deflated almost to the laminate hardwood floor. The toilet flushed, the bathroom door clacked open, and the ZZ Top-bearded man from whom I sublet the bedroom padded down the hallway, probably scratching his belly.

At that time, I was the director of marketing and operations for an internet startup which provided concierge-like services for apartment buildings lacking a doorman. It was a position formidable in title only. The founder and sole other employee would interrupt strategy sessions to ponder Kim Kardashian's breast size while wolf whistling at pictures of her tits online. My position was so poorly paid that I had to wait tables two nights a week at an unglamorous Upper West Side Italian restaurant. My fellow servers and busboys gossiped that

I was an undercover agent for US Immigration and Customs Enforcement (ICE) because they didn't understand why someone like me—white, legal, and educated—was working at this under the radar restaurant at my perimenopausal age. Meanwhile, the owner's wife watched me like a hawk.

"Why haven't you bought your own place yet?' my Israeli almost-boyfriend admonished, skirting the fact that he had dealt a lot of drugs to scrape together the seed money to start his handyman business. To be fair, the equivalent of an apartment down payment was probably hanging in my closet. I suffered from a different type of Cinderella Syndrome; the belief that wearing the right dress would change my life. Many of the vintage and designer frocks I owned still bore their tags. Neither they nor I got out much.

"So, you never married or had any children?" messaged a former colleague from my business analyst days at Mobil Oil. Her daughter had just shown her how to use Facebook. My ex-colleague now lived outside of Princeton, where she'd earned her master's degree. Her daughter had decided to become an actor, which made my colleague think of me because the last time I had seen her, I was doing implausible murder mystery dinner theater in Philadelphia's Old City. How could I explain the permanent restlessness of my soul? That I hadn't married because I couldn't guarantee that my life path would run parallel to a partner's. That I thought having children was thankless. From conception, there is a tiny person kicking you as it grows, and you can't kick back.

A few days later a "How did your life turn out?" message came from a college friend I hadn't seen since 1989, when I had a terrifying perm. This friend had been named a "Women to Watch" by *Advertising Age* in the early aughts. Now, she was the regional creative director for Coca-Cola, Asia Pacific, had a daughter, and lived in a spacious high-rise in Hong Kong, where she was part of a competitive crew team. After trawling her Facebook feed, I lay on my leaking air mattress and stared at the ceiling, feeling my age settle around me. Two floors below, there had been a recent drug bust, and the super or the police or the tenant, depending on who told you the story, had removed the front door so the police wouldn't break it down the next time someone got caught dealing. A tear slid from my eye to my ear.

I had been the top grad of my university's undergraduate business school. Where had I derailed?

I tiptoed back along a mental trail of breadcrumbs to my Mobil Oil days in the early 1990s, to sharking corporate happy hours, running on a corporate track team, bumping my head on the corporate glass ceiling. Everything I heard, I had heard before, and I couldn't listen any longer. I chucked my corporate existence, along with my family's expectations, to embrace an actor's life despite never having been on a stage. Twenty-three and green, I auditioned for my first play.

From the humility of hindsight, I doubt I wanted to be an actor as much as I wanted to live a variegated, visceral artist's existence, where all the colors ran. In reality, I was more the unfulfilled housewife played by Rosanna Arquette in *Desperately Seeking Susan* than the bohemian sprite played by Madonna. Acting was a reprieve from my sheltered Catholic upbringing, an exploration of possibility where I could let desire and instinct creep. Every set was an opportunity to create family, and every performance was a playdate with an audience.

In 2003, I became friends with the writer/director Larysa Kondracki while acting in a short film of hers. She asked me to read her new screenplay which would become her debut feature, *The Whistleblower*, starring Rachel Weisz and Vanessa Redgrave. The main character is real life Kathryn Bolkovac, a UN peace-keeper in post-war Bosnia. She outed UN officials for their role in facilitating and then covering up sex trafficking. Reading her script reignited my childhood desire to become a spy. I devoured Larysa's source material and continued down a literary rabbit hole reading books by *New York Times* journalists and interna-tional aid workers.

Emergency Sex and Other Desperate Measures: A True Story from Hell on Earth by Kenneth Cain, Heidi Postlewait, and Andrew Thomson changed the direction of my life. In the book, Andrew, Ken, and Heidi detail their work for the UN on the frontlines of Cambodia, Somalia, Haiti, Rwanda, Bosnia, and Liberia. The authors' deployments were everything I craved: escape from the doldrums of ordinary living into adrenaline-fueled moments of feeling intensely alive. They did important work, partied like they meant it, and formed brothers-in-arms type friendships. In contrast, pursuing the chance to play someone else's life seemed frivolous and indulgent, especially when I realized I wasn't living my own. I was auditioning, occasionally performing, shopping for magic-making dresses, and waiting tables at an upscale tapas bar. I wasn't challenging my personal limitations by having new experiences.

Those vintage and designer dresses cajoled from the closet as I alternated evening play rehearsals/performances with evening wait shifts. I'd close the tapas bar at two in the morning, cab to my illegal sublet in gentrifying Williamsburg, wake up at six to ride the subway back into Times Square to queue at Actors' Equity for a coveted audition slot. I'd race back to Williamsburg, sleep for an hour, workout, do a vocal warm-up, practice my monologue, race back to Times Square, take my two minutes in the audition spotlight, and then scurry across Midtown to the tapas bar to wait another ten-hour shift. Rinse. Repeat. My actor's life had become as routine as my corporate one.

In 2005, through an aspiring playwright whose fiancée was best friends with the fiancée of the press secretary to then Secretary-General of the United Nations, Kofi Annan, I met Andrew Thomson, one of the *Emergency Sex* authors. One minute, the press secretary was offering me the chance to meet Andrew, and the next, Andrew and I were sitting in fellow *Emergency Sex* author Kenneth Cain's apartment, drinking beer as Andrew told me stories from the book, first-hand. When Andrew excused himself, I got up to peruse the titles on

Ken's bookshelf, where several personal photos reproduced in *Emergency Sex* were displayed. Standing in front of the real-life objects photographed in my favorite book was an Alice *Through the Looking Glass* moment which made the fantastical looking glass world of humanitarian aid real. Metaphorically, I had climbed onto the fireplace mantle at Looking Glass House and was poking the mirror behind it. That night propelled me to step through the mirror and enter an alternate world of expat, first as a teacher and later as an occasional humanitarian aid volunteer. I quit acting (no loss to the profession), certified to Teach English as a Second Language (TESL) because I thought teaching abroad could be a steppingstone to aid work, and didn't look back.

My first teaching assignments in the mid-aughts, in a tiny coal mining town in southwest Poland, in a cosmopolitan Turkish port city on the Aegean, and in Ukraine's capital as the country's currency plummeted, submerged me in tidal waves of culture shock. As I rode the learning curve of my first postings, logic often seemed reversed. On ice-covered, unsalted, and unshoveled sidewalks, young Polish women wore strappy high heels, which kept their ankles in a state of constant turmoil. In the Turkish language school where I taught, the director of studies reprimanded me for cleaning my own desk. I was *severely* reprimanded when I helped an older cleaning woman carry heavy grocery bags from the elevator we had just shared to the school's canteen. A 2008 tourist guidebook to Ukraine touted its women as its greatest commodity as the International Organization for Migration (IOM) started a country-wide, anti-trafficking initiative to help trafficking victims start small businesses. I felt sorry for the uncleverly proportioned eight- and nine-year-old girls I saw in Kyiv's city center, posing for pictures by a statue of Vladimir Lenin, instinctively knowing how to stand with their nascent breasts thrust forward and their lower backs arched out.

Before I went abroad, I hadn't thought much about the US's role in the world. I wanted to live outside of my culture for the same reasons I wanted an artist's life. Since I owned very little but books and designer clothing, I could easily pack up, ship out, and start over. Living abroad is more forgiving for those of us who have not found ourselves according to traditional American measures of success: spouse, children, and home ownership.

I took for granted my belief in American exceptionalism much the same way I took for granted my belief in God. I was baptized Catholic, grew up in Catholic household, went to a Catholic grade school, and graduated from a Jesuit university. Believing in God was as reflexive as breathing. Similarly, I was indoctrinated into American exceptionalism by American ideals-led school curricula and my father's lived experience.

He was a true by your bootstraps, from immigrant poverty to American middle class success story. Born in Berlin in 1933, he rarely spoke about his war-scarred childhood or how he and his mother had survived in bombed out Berlin during the war and in its immediate aftermath. One story rescued from the ashes of forgetting has my five-year-old father running through a field outside Berlin as Allied forces strafed it. I had a few stories about his journey to the US at age 14 and his first years in Chicago, from which I could extrapolate a life. He and my grandmother crossed the Atlantic aboard the *USAT General Henry Taylor,* a military transport ship, with support from the International Refugee Organization. Among their personal belongings, they had three US twenty-dollar bills, bought on the black market (Germany's monetary system had collapsed after the war.). Hoping they weren't counterfeit, my dad rolled them into the film compartment of a Leica camera while my grandmother packed a set of eight gold-rimmed dining plates. When they reached Chicago, they sold the camera and the plates to have money to live on. Learning English at night school, passing his GED, and earning a bachelor's degree from Northwestern, my father embodied the self-reliance and personal determination underpinning American exceptionalism, which heavily influenced my upbringing. Having attained the American Dream, he fervently believed the US was the best country in the world.

My first expat years coincided with the first WikiLeaks publications. *Standard Operating Procedures for Camp Delta* details US practices at Guantanamo Bay detention camp. I quietly doubted a Ukrainian student who told me about a US airstrike video in which two *Reuters* reporters were killed and two children were wounded in Baghdad until I went online and read about it for myself. The children had been travelling in a van which stopped to help the airstrike victims, and the US military fired on it. One pilot is heard saying, "Well, it's their fault for bringing their kids into battle." Reading the leaks was a *Wizard of Oz*, man behind the curtain moment. The government of the country my immigrant father credited for saving his life had violated prisoners' human rights and tried to cover up the killing of journalists and children. I was seeing the funhouse mirror image of the US that others already recognized. The realization was a cartoon steamrolling. Deflated, I read. Suzy Hansen's *Notebooks on a Foreign Country: An American Abroad in a Post-American World* is essential reading for believers in or those disabused of American exceptionalism.

At a book signing in New York City in 2011, I met journalist Jere Van Dyk, who had been kidnapped by the Taliban and held for 45 days. Once again, the power of stories set me on a new path. Jere talked about his time in Afghanistan, first in his youth in the 1960s, when Afghan women wore knee socks and mini-skirts in Kabul, and later in the 1980s, when Jere embedded with Jalaluddin Haqqani's *mujahideen* fighters as a stringer for *The New York Times.* He returned again in the mid-aughts, at which time he was taken. He was in his 60s.

"After I got out, the FBI told me that when I went home, there'd be messages from the Taliban on my answering machine. They wanted to know if I recognized the voices," Jere told me over dinner, recounting his first moments back on US soil in a little room off of passport control at the JFK airport.

Hummus clung to a pita chip suspended halfway between my plate and my open mouth. Jere and I were sharing a meze platter at a Balkan wine delicatessen in Hell's Kitchen, where I hung onto his every word. He paused, airing out anxiety before his story resumed, spreading and loitering. Afghanistan seemed to infuse him with an ecstasy of adrenaline, which was narcotic.

Thinking over his stories, I realized where I'd derailed. By the time I met Jere, I had already lived in Poland, Turkey, and Ukraine. Now, I was working as the director of marketing and operations for the man with the mammary fixation, trying to erect a superstructure of normal life. Haunted by the sense I was missing out on something, I decided to go abroad again and try on selves. Reading a job advertisement for an elite international school in Kurdistan, Iraq conjured the petal-soft notes of the oud, the pungent smell of sun-roasted desert sand, and the lambent glow of bustling streets teeming with errands of mystery. Naïve and fueled by the myth of intuition, I balanced on the edge of my courage and applied.

In a pre-ISIS world, my accepting a teaching position in Kurdistan, Iraq was to swing on a rope of convention and let go. Most people, including me, hadn't heard of the Kurds or Kurdistan. When I told my restaurant patrons I was moving to Kurdistan, they thought Kurdistan was "one of those stans over there, near Russia." When I said it was in northern Iraq, they would go all silent for a moment, look at their shoes sticking to the wine-soaked floor, assume I was military, and thank me for my service. My fellow servers thought I was "just plain crazy" when they saw the *Arabic for Dummies*, which I dutifully lugged on the subway for some light reading. A punk rocker who helped me break into my apartment when my key wouldn't work asked me if I was CIA before he promised not to come back later and steal our computers. Telling people about my impending move to Kurdistan was a dose of reality interrupting long blitzes of mental static. Beyond updating my vaccines and deciding which dresses to pack, I was flying blind. After all, Kurds speak Kurdish, not Arabic.

Reporting From Within

Christian Vazquez

I took myself out to go see *Dune: Part II*. It was after teaching a class on Zora Neale Hurston's work, her story "Sweat". After we pondered in class on how it was possible she took a radical conservative side in her career, a side which defended politician Spessard L. Holland's support for segregation at the time. She even opposed the 1954 desegregation decision. Perhaps it was just me who pondered. Well, the students who were mentally present and I.

Shortly after another failed relationship with a man I thought I could grow to love, I decided to go watch the new Dune movie after work. The social drain from the entire relationship, like all relationships, took a while to regenerate from. It was not just that relationship but all my past relationships. It was time to look within.

But honestly, that seemed trivial. How could I look within when the world is burning. As I grieved my relationship, taught, wrote, and ultimately watched *Dune: Part II* on the Screen X at the Regal Edwards Greenway theatre, a bigger feeling of loss was taking over me.

Just days after the self-immolation of Aaron Bushnell at the Israeli Embassy in Washington (Buckingham) we all witnessed the most radical thing any of us could do. The rest of us who witnessed it, through our screens, saw him in us. That would have been us if we could have mustered that courage in our lifetimes. Crazy courage. Insane courage. And sacrifice.

It is what we would resort to do if we alone wanted to actually change the flow of our system, especially if we wanted it to immediately stop aiding and abetting a genocide. We don't belong to the "ruling class" as Bushnell put it. Our mundane actions alone cannot alter the course of history immediately unless we resort to destroying all the power we have. Watch it burn.

The rest of us still here, we saw what he caused. The attention it brought. We were grateful he did it so that we didn't have to continuously ponder if even that would change things. Dozens of Palestinians were killed in a food truck attack, adding to the growing death toll in Gaza (Almasy and Elassar). Israel murdered dozens of teenagers running for food to feed their starving selves and families just days after Bushnell. So yes, we saw what would happen if one of us self-emulated.

The rest of us had to accept, and continue to live within this system, this "machine" as he and many before have called it. And cope.

To continue. To live on.

I don't know why I thought I could escape into *Dune II*, even with the three giant screens.

As the US and our current administration continue to fund Israel, it demonstrates a sponsorship of GENOCIDE. Just like the past administrations, it follows like baby geese narrowly focused on their mother duck. Has been…for a long, long time.

It's good to mention before we continue, you reader and I, the writer, on this collective experience, that this is not a review, or advertisement for the movie *Dune II*. This will not be featured on Rotten Tomatoes. Even further, this will get published long after the movie has been released.

Honestly, I enjoyed seeing *All of Us Strangers* more, even if it had me crying at the movie theater. There's just something about the catharsis of a movie exposing old and fresh wounds that you didn't even know were open. It allows the sewing of them to be more accurate as they rise into our visibility. In doing so, I realized that it was time to take a break from looking for relationships.

In the *Dune* franchise, however, love interests are not so

much felt. We see instead more clearly both the state and the oppressed; the consequences of supporting them blindly.

As Paul Atreides, portrayed by Timothée Chalamet, screams "Long live the fighters!" I thought of October 7, 2023. In the film, Paul is leading a resistance that has culminated in an act of violence on the movie screens. Fiction in *Dune*, but in Israel, innocent people were murdered. I couldn't help but think both resistances found those assaults as the only way out of oppression. We are supposed to be captivated by the explosions, the giant worms tipping the balance of the battle, but I know I am not the only one unconsciously making the connections. I grow more uncomfortable as the violence increases.

While the audience around me was gripping their seats, the powerful vibrations from the immersive speakers continued. I bet I was not the only one remembering that earlier that week, the hospital in Gaza had been blown to rubble.

As the Arrakis finally destroy the status quo, the system in place, only to be replaced unfortunately (spoiler alert) by an even more destructive force, I caught myself thinking how the people of Palestine can escape the iron grip of Israel's government, which is run by a psychopathic president and administration, without having to go to that extreme. The Israeli government does not see the Palestinian people as human beings, but a nuisance in their objective to expand territory since 1948. Whether it is for money or religious fanaticism, that has been the objective.

After the movie ended, we all walked away thinking of what we could do to help against massive suffering. At least that is what I hoped we all thought, as I walked away from the theater, away from Artimis, into Earth, back to our reality, to the 10:00 P.M. Houston traffic.

I thought about ending it here. The essay. This essay, movie review, diary entry, ramblings—whatever you want to label this. I thought it would speak on how impotent we all feel, that at the end of the day there is nothing we can do but simply keep existing within the parameters of our reality, our system.

But no. That is not entirely true.

For some reason unbeknownst, I was born within this system of reality called America. In another multiverse, perhaps I was born in another system of reality that is currently being bombarded as we speak out of the sheer force of global dominance, colonialism, occupation, manifest destiny. Regardless of the why, the how, I am standing here today. A writer. A teacher. So I did what I could.

I wrote. I taught.

I incorporated "Gaza Writes Back: Short Stories from Young Writers in Gaza, Palestine" into my English II class syllabus. After I slept on the question, was their stories that captured what was happening in Gaza just like storytelling has always captured what is happening in our world, our collective consciousness. I asked ChatGPT if there was any collection of short stories, sure enough it pointed me to that book which anyone could buy on Amazon. The voices of the oppressed readily available for consumption. Only one of the handful of collections from Palestinian writers that are able to make their way on to us. Sometimes the machine works with us.

These stories were written in the backdrop of Operation Cast Lead, Israel's assault on Gaza that led to 1,400 deaths, more than 11,000 homes, and innumerable industrial buildings, shops, roads bridges, and other infrastructure destroyed.

This collection of stories was edited and made possible by Refaat Alareer, the prominent Palestinian poet who was himself murdered by an Israeli air strike in December 2023.

"These writers and activists are the ones who made this book a reality," Refaat Alareer writes (Alareer 2014). "And like any society, Palestine is not perfect, something the stories touch upon. In addition to addressing occupation issues, the stories also have social purposes, as they never fail to point the finger of accusations, usually symbolically, at aging Palestinian leadership and certain undesired social conventions…This is not to suggest that Palestinian fiction writing by emerging young writers is reactive; it's rather a very creative, proactive response: resist in words the horrible situations imposed upon them."

I taught it with care, careful to not direct hatred onto all the Jewish population as so many quickly turn to as they are informed of what happens in Gaza, even if the information had existed since decades before.

Everyone, yes especially Jewish people, can see the injustice of it all. The Israeli Government, though. Netanyahu. They have created an altogether different kind of blindness, one close to insanity and the settlers, people, who have followed join their ranks.

I stand here like anybody else doing whatever I can do to promote less suffering, even if it is within a system that has funded the very thing we oppose.

I was supposed to finish this here, but yet again something happened that immediately attaches itself to this. Another self-immolation.

Maxwell Azzarello set himself ablaze during the Trump trial at a courthouse (Parkinson). It's crazy because no mention of Israel or Palestine, but Ponzi Schemes. Now there is a question that rises in my head: does the act of self-immolation get automatic approval? Is the cause behind the intention justified because an individual paid the ultimate unbearable price? I am not posing you to compare both causes to see which one is "better" to self-emulate under but rather be able to think about these two self-immolations that happened close to each other in the distance of time.

Although Maxwell Azzarello did not mention Palestine or Israel, in both there is the real justified feeling of losing something, taken, by those who do have enough power and wealth to never have that feeling. Maxwell Azzarello is centered on the destructive, exploitive nature of capitalism that inevitably is designed to overcompensate the individuals who are already within the echelons of that hierarchical system.

But surrounding all of this are the other real signs of mental instability, of losing the trail, of focusing on too much all at once and getting lost in it all. In the pamphlets he threw out before the act, Maxwell adds without concrete evidence that shows and movies are brainwashing us (Azzarello Pamphlets) specifically shows like the Simpsons.

He implies that this brainwashing is part of the root cause of our problems, regardless of whether the entire populace is watching those specific shows. It is disheartening that both Maxwell and Bushnell could have been saved if they had talked to someone, if we as society could have breached their isolation and perhaps resorted to something else. Was there something else?

The immediacy to both must also be considered. On the one hand Aaron Bushnell is throwing himself upon the gears of the machine to stop that very machine from killing more children. Maxwell follows suit, in an attempt to expose the believed operations of the machine.

Does Maxwell's self-immolation get dismissed because the overcomplication became close to the fringes of schizophrenia and psychosis, arriving definitely at an unhealthy mind? Was Aaron's mind unstable as well?

These are questions perhaps someone else can answer, whether it is truthfully or manipulating, or erroneously. But I can't give you that answer.

But all of this feels like psychosis.

You blink, and you find yourself watching students all over the country protesting against the genocide on Palestine. You blink, and you hear people calling them antisemitic even

though many of them are Jewish. You blink again and you
see people complain about the ruckus, the mayhem they are
creating. You continue to blink and see the next day pro-Zionist
agitators finally brought violence on to these protests, starting
with UCLA. Police become the new school shooters, as they
storm through the campuses and shoot the students with rubber
bullets. You blink yet again, and see the explosions in the news,
explosions from the IDF drones and missiles, killing actual
babies in Palestine indiscriminately with the excuse of HAMAS.

You blink. Until you want to keep your eyes closed and
not blink again.

Shaima Refaat Alareer, the eldest daughter of Refaat
Alareer who edited the book I incorporated into my class that
I mentioned, has been killed along with her husband and
2-month-old son while sheltering in the building of internation-
al relief charity Global communities. Shortly before her death
she posted on Facebook.

"I have a beautiful news for you, I wish I could convey it
to you while you are in front of me, I present to you your first
grandchild. Do you know, my father, that you have become a
grandfather? This si your grandson Abd al-Rahman whom I
have long imagined you carrying, but I never imagined that I
would lose you early before you see him."

Bear witness. Do not look away. If the least we can do
to fight against genocide is witnessing, then we must remember
Paul Atreides' cry, 'Long live the fighters!' In order to witness we
must continue living.

As I catch my breath on my own suffering, my own
unique individual problems, I try to witness what I can because
if I am not careful it can consume me into annihilation. I will
not be of any use in any battle if that happens.

I am reminded of James Baldwin's words," It began to
seem that one would have to hold in the mind forever two ides
which seemed to be in opposition. The first idea was acceptance,

the acceptance totally without rancor, of life as it is, and men as they are: the light of this idea, it goes without saying that injustice is a common place. But this did not mean that one could be complacent, for the second idea was of equal power: that one must never, in one's own life, accept these injustices as commonplace but must fight them with all one's strength. The fight begins, however in the heart and it now had been laid to my charge to keep my own heart free of hatred and despair" (Baldwin 1963).

Take care.

Works Cited

1. Almasy, Steve, and Alaa Elassar. "Dozens of Palestinians Killed in Food Truck Attack." *CNN*, 29 Feb. 2024, www.cnn.com/2024/02/29/middlee-ast/gaza-food-truck-deaths-israel-wwk-intl/index.html.

2. Alareer, Refaat, editor. *Gaza Writes Back: Short Stories from Young Writers in Gaza, Palestine*. Just World Books, 2014.

3. "Azzarello Pamphlets." *TMZ*, 19 Apr. 2024, dam.tmz.com/docu-ment/69/o/2024/04/19/69afe52280de4e22a6a2675833729a01.pdf.

4. Buckingham, Marcus. "Man Sets Fire at Israeli Embassy in Washington, D.C." *NPR*, 25 Feb. 2024, www.npr.org/2024/02/25/1233810136/fire-man-israeli-embassy-washington.

5. Parkinson, John. "Man Sets Fire at Courthouse during Trump Trial." *ABC News*, 29 Feb. 2024, abcnews.go.com/US/man-apparently-sets-fire-court-house-trump-trial/story?id=109433903.

6. Baldwin, James. *The Fire Next Time*. Dial Press, 1963.

Daughters for Liberty

Jo Scott-Coe

20 September 1978, front page of *The Bismarck Tribune*: At top right, a three-column text box highlights a story about parental activists addressing a North Dakota task force to urge a return to basics in education. Superficially, basics meant writing, math, and especially reading. But multiple parents fixated on offensive books and teaching methods. The fourth graph of the article summarized another worry that one woman (who happened to be my mother) expressed: too much attention to the "social, cultural, and psychological well-being of children" was undermining the primary purpose of schools.

I do not think I saw the article back then. I do remember at this hearing—or at another one resembling it—my sister and I killed hours waiting outside a grand governmental chamber. I do not recall any bench in the hallway (though there must have been one). I recall silence (though we must have chattered). The dominant impression in my memory is a cold marble floor under our knees and elbows, the closed and majestic door, perhaps a coloring book splayed open, fingers pressing rounded crayons into the grains of soft paper.

***

1979 Minot, North Dakota: A desperate eavesdropper by age ten, I absorbed a very adult catechism of (capital T capital F) Threats to the Family in America: legalized abortion, the Equal Rights Amendment (aka ERA), pre-marital sex, divorce, gun control, homosexuals and their agenda, moral relativism, environmentalism (aka zero-population growth for white Christians), big government (e.g. the 55-mph speed limit, forced school busing, taxes), communism, sex education, evolution instead of creationism, Planned Parenthood, teachers' unions, and women who called themselves "Ms."

Most of these threats, I heard, were encouraged by the creeping intrusions of secular humanism, identified as a non-theistic religion by the United States Supreme Court in *Torcaso v. Watkins* (1961). The ruling had protected atheists' rights to run for, and hold, public office. But a narrow and determined bandwidth of conservatives like my parents latched onto a more important implication in the ruling: secular humanism was a religion camouflaged in plain sight. Secular humanists were passing off their own doctrines by shamelessly supplanting Judeo-Christian values in American cultural life. Secular humanists were imposing their religion everywhere and it was not a fair fight.

Starved for language, for consistency, I absorbed every word I overheard, hoping what I gathered would somehow help me map where to fit in this world, to anticipate and avoid its grievances. When adults gathered in my parents' living room to discuss strategy for school board meetings or city council elections, I would perch to listen after bedtime on a landing of grey carpeted stairs behind a banister and railing.

I surreptitiously scoured forbidden texts to understand the parental attention and energy they were commanding. There were stacks of offending paperbacks tabbed for dangerous passages on our dining room table. Toffler's *Future Shock*. McLuhan and Fiore's *The Medium is the Massage*. *I'm OK, You're OK*, with its sherbet-orange cover art. I remember many young adult titles repeated, a verboten litany: *The Chocolate War, The Outsiders, The Pigman*. Anything Judy Blume, especially *Wifey* or *Deenie* or *Are You There, God? It's Me, Margaret*.

There were cardboard cartons filled with pink broadsides for distribution from a group called Women Who Want to be Women: "Ladies! Have You Heard?" In opposing upper corners, the broadside featured line drawings of white women smiling into telephone receivers. Phone wires looped down the margins and around chunky paragraphs telling how women's liberation was a lie: wives would be forced to work outside the home, divorced women would lose alimony and child custody. Homosexuals, gasp, would marry. There would be co-ed military barracks, firehouses, and prisons. One heading inquired without irony: "Do you want to lose your right to privacy?"

We also received Eagle Forum newsletter, a separate mailer from Phyllis Schlafly herself, the blonde patron saint of the anti-abortion, anti-ERA movement, ubiquitous lady ambassador of Reaganism and the Moral Majority. She was Catholic like us and had six kids and a handsome husband and still became a lawyer without needing to be liberated. We never talked about how she had married into a wealthy family. I never knew whom she paid to clean her home, babysit her children, do shopping, or prepare meals.

I struggled to differentiate, to believe my own my voice. A first diary was small and block-shaped, blue-gingham vinyl with a latch and tiny key I thought I could trust. At some point after crabbing several entries onto the small lines, I re-read the first pages and tore them out from the spine because my own words had already offended me.

Remember that presentation about the basic repro-ductive system in fifth or sixth grade? I was brought to school late that day, or was picked up early, or was taken to sit in the library. Remember when your high school biology class had the awkward condom demo? That empty desk was mine.

***

1989 Los Angeles: I was a work-study undergrad at the University of Southern California when Phyllis Schlafly visited Bovard Auditorium to debate Sarah Weddington, the lawyer who had successfully argued *Roe v. Wade*. I went, I thought, to geek out on Schlafly.

Before the debate began, I waited near an open doorway outside the green room, in a corridor below the stage. I recall no swarm of fans. Schlafly sat in the dim but concentrated glow of lights from a mirror, a portrait of tight and perfect posture.

I recall someone near her shoulder with a comb or a lint roller, perhaps reaching for a can of Breck hairspray. Schlafly seemed to sense my presence, barely turning her chin in response to whatever greeting I mustered. "So," she asked, "are you a good conservative girl?"

I remember being appalled by the abrupt cross-examination, even though I should not have been surprised. I recall hastily communicating the affirmative, well-trained in the reflex. Good girls were supposed to say yes always, unless they were saying no to drugs, sex, pornographic literature, or Twisted Sister. Yes. Like the Virgin Mary, who was told rather than asked what she wanted and then praised for making the proper choice. The script had been easy to learn, a way to bargain for some illusion of protection inside a family that communicated my defects long before puberty: ankles too thick, thighs too heavy, feet too long, too many sensitive ideas in my head.

Schlafly may have sensed the lingering self-consciousness I likely radiated at age twenty. But I wonder now if she saw that I was lying. Whatever I did to betray myself in that moment (a soft word or smile, a nod) activated a jolt of physical revulsion that caught me off guard. I was starting to comprehend that what she and the people I lived with meant by those words so familiar to me—good, conservative, girl—was just a bully's code for permissible cruelty.

After thirty-five years, when I close my eyes, I still feel it in my younger self: the revolt kicking up from the deepest center of my body into my throat, a clutching resistance that was only beginning to break free.

The Gift of the Fire Lizards

Barbara Ellen Sorensen

The spirits of nature have their dwellings within us as well as outside of us.

-Paracelsus

When my brother Richie was nine-years old he collected newts, salamanders, snakes and turtles. He and I would spend hours by the creek, just down the hill from our backyard in Walnut Creek, California, our hands submerged in the shallow water, pulling up one smooth stone after another. The frigid water, scented with eucalyptus leaves, was a haven for watery newts and salamanders, the skittery creatures whose bellies pulsed in our palms. Who would have thought that some of those luminescent beings harbored bacteria such as salmonella? And did the bacteria somehow tuck its serpentine essence into my brother's brain, schizophrenia blooming in its wake? The summer before I was to enter the fifth grade these questions would incubate and eventually haunt my family for decades.

Though two years younger than me, Richie was able to describe the family of newts quite intelligently and I listened intently.

"Newts are the same species as salamanders," Richie instructed solemnly. "But newts are more flat-shaped and some of them are semi-aquatic."

He stuck his hand into an aquarium where he kept his most prized creatures and extracted a tiny newt. Richie opened his palm, one finger of his other hand pressed firmly down on the newt's tail. He blew gently on the newt's face until it tilted its head upward, gazing up at us bleakly. I looked over at my brother and he seemed to be talking to the newt. Richie's hair was auburn, his skin tanned umber, his eyes a dark blue. He was small and fiercely fast. He could out-run every other boy in our neighborhood and always found the best hiding places. "Hey, you!" he said softly to the newt. Always feeling pale and skinny next to Richie, my blonde hair constantly tangled and knotted, I desperately wanted to be a boy just like him.

Richie kept his creatures in the garage. Periodically, our mother called out warnings, "Those aquariums better have tight lids!" In response to these veiled threats from our truly indulgent mother, Richie collected creek rocks and piled them on top of the aquariums ensuring all of us there would be no unexpected creature escapes. In addition to rocks, Richie used random books, sets of encyclopedias, and magazines to weigh down the aquarium lids.

Richie loved to draw and found solace in the concentrated efforts to render his creatures imaginatively. In his drawings, giant newts swam across the paper in torrid shades of red or opalescent white, their webbed feet reaching out to engulf a smaller, sparkly-eyed turtle. Sometimes I wandered into Richie's room to see him perching a turtle on his desk. As the turtle made a steady, methodical path across the top of the paper, Richie sketched it calmly.

In June the woods surrounding the creek were dense, the bushes scraggly and thorny. There were patches of poison oak and ivy. A walnut tree had fallen across one end of the creek, and we straddled it, inching our way across, the insides of our thighs scraped and bruised. On the other side we caught sight of a salamander flashing its way beneath a rock. Down on all fours, we scrambled to catch it, but it darted through the leaves and into pockets of earth. "Never mind," Richie commanded, "we'll capture more further up the creek." I followed him for hours, as did all the boys in the neighborhood and including our little brother, George. We were all convinced he was the king of salamanders.

In July, the afternoons stretched out with cricket song and our mother gave us little, plastic yellow buckets in which to collect blackberries. The berries grew in abundance by the creek. The succulent pulp smudged our fingers as we picked them. We brought them back up to the house and our mother, smiling at the stains around our mouths and on our T-shirts, made pie with the remainder of the berries. Our parents were young parents. Our mother had long, slender legs and porcelain skin. Born and raised in Georgia, she still had a distinct southern accent that though not discernible to her own children was nevertheless noticeable by other children who asked, "Why does your mother talk so funny?"

Exhausted from picking berries and chasing salamanders, we lay on our backs in the clover-covered grass in the front yard. Turning over on our stomachs, we buried our faces in the cool clover, breathing in the pungent scent. Next to us, the branches of a huge walnut tree shaded us and we listened to the clacking of walnuts as they ceaselessly hit the cement pathway leading to the front door.

"What are you doing?" we heard our oldest sister, Laurel, asking, clearly annoyed with us. "Go find some newts or snakes." She thought we were much too close to her spot under the walnut tree, and as the oldest sibling, she assumed her rights. Laurel and her friend, Vivian, spent their summer hours playing endless rounds of the dice game Yahtzee. The clacking of the walnuts and dice mingling in the cool air became our intricate rhythm of summer.

Sometimes I wandered over to Laurel's spot beneath the tree. I wondered if I should really be with her and Vivian. I listened to them discuss dense English novels like *Wuthering Heights* and *Jane Eyre*, or describe romantic thrillers like *Rebecca*, by Daphne du Maurier. Bored with their endless analyzing, I'd soon find my way back to my brothers.

Richie shared a room with our younger brother, George. Their room was upstairs at the other end of the house, above the garage where the cloistered creatures lived. Summer nights always seemed tumultuous. Little earth tremors sometimes woke us, and my mother rushed from room to room checking to make sure her children had not been thrown from their beds.

Our father traveled for weeks at a time, and when he was home, he kept me and Laurel awake with his restless pacing and heavy nighttime drinking. Our bedroom was next to the living room, and we could hear my mother's high-pitched, agitated voice and my father roaring in response. I knew my mother was not happy in California, that she wanted to return to the East Coast from where we had just moved, or at least to live somewhere closer to her relatives. My father loved California and reveled in the fact that he had been transferred there for work. During their volatile arguments, I'd stumble over to my sister's bed and whisper, "Laurel?" She'd whisper back, "Shush," but would slide over to accommodate me. Sometimes my father would barge into our bedroom and stand over our beds. He would stand there for a long time looking down on us, presumably deciding whether or not to awaken us. We were so frightened of him that we held our breaths and pretended to be deeply asleep. Eventually, he would wander out and with my legs tightly pressed against my sister's body I'd finally fall asleep.

Once, I woke to the sound of bottles being smashed. It was my mother who, enraged by my father's drinking, was breaking all of the liquor bottles over the sink. Thinking that our mother needed help, Laurel and I rushed up from our beds, and stumbled into the kitchen. We watched in awe as our mother's quick hands snapped one liquor bottle after another against the edge of the porcelain sink as if she were cracking eggs. In the morning, I asked Richie if he had heard any commotion during the night and he replied that he hadn't. My sister looked at me sharply and I knew not to tell him.

Though Richie was spared night dramas and the accompanying sounds, he was not spared our father's wrath. Our father was especially strict with Richie. Once while eating dinner, Richie said something sarcastic that set all of us off laughing. My father was not amused, and he lifted his body up from his chair and with his hand flat and wide, he reached across the table and smacked Richie across the head. Our father must have forgotten that Richie's back was to a tile countertop. The back of Richie's head made a hard thudding sound against the tile. The contact took his breath away. Richie's face turned pale for an instant, then bright red as pain and humiliation set in. Crying silently, he stared down at his plate. I don't remember my father saying anything after that. I don't remember my mother doing anything to comfort my brother, or chastising my father. I do remember thinking how often my father would warn us, "I'll crack your head open if you do that again." Now I knew that perhaps he would.

Our father eventually traveled again, and the summer days wrapped us in a comforting expansiveness. In August, we found a steep hill near a cemetery, just up the street from our house. Slick with dried, late summer grasses, it was the perfect hill to careen down. We found flattened boxes in the garage and made them into sleds. Over and over again we scrambled up the hill, dragging the boxes behind us, falling, stumbling, our knees discolored with dirt and blood. We turned up the ends to the boxes to create a maneuvering device and sat cross-legged as we flew down the hill. Our sleds flattened the grasses, forming sleek speedways, and the brown brush took on a burning smell from the constant rubbing. The acrid smell wove into our hair and clung to our clothes.

Dusty and tired at the end of the day, we made our way back to the creek, slipped off our sneakers and sank our feet into the water. The slow August water was now tepid and cloudy with mud. Richie reached in and pulled out a small turtle. Its carapace glimmered green and black, and Richie cupped the turtle gently in his hands. He sat it down on the bank of the creek and we waited until its feet poked out, wavering in the early evening air. The turtle made its way up the bank and rustled languidly into the bushes. "It's looking for food now," Richie informed me.

One morning my mother came down from Richie's room and

told us that she was taking him to the doctor. Throughout the night he had been vomiting and his temperature had steadily risen. Richie and our mother were gone most of the morning and when they returned our mother helped Richie up to bed again. "He has salmonella," she explained to us. "It's probably from those creatures. And he doesn't wash his hands."

That night she slept on the floor next to his bed, "to listen to his breathing," she explained. I wanted to go see him, to ask Richie how if felt to have a disease derived from amphibians and reptiles, but our mother told me, "Let him sleep and don't make any loud noises. His head hurts." Because he was so young and the infection was severe, the doctor put Richie on antibiotics. Within a week he could play again but when he emerged from his room, he seemed distant and pale as if he had gone through a great battle.

Richie and I played in our yard and down by the creek for only one more summer. Suddenly and inexplicably, I began to feel more comfortable hanging out with Laurel and Vivian. And I began to read their books. I discovered girls my own age. Our family lived in Northern California for only a few more summers but during those hot months in late afternoons I preferred the cool of my room. Curled up on my bed, I read *Jane Eyre* and *Wuthering Heights*. Always running up and down hills, Richie and the neighborhood boys now seemed thickheaded and silly to me.

When Richie was fifteen, he began to show signs of schizophrenia although none of us recognized it at the time. Mental illness wasn't on anyone's radar and had we been told of it we wouldn't have believed it. We all thought his strange actions were somehow deliberate and done to irritate my father who Richie had grown so estranged from in his teen years. When teachers in our high school came up to me and sincerely inquired about Richie's behavior, I shrugged them off as being nosy and authoritarian. As an insecure teenager myself, I pretended to know nothing and tried to distance myself from my brother as best as I could. At home my whole family was struggling to make sense of why Richie would spend hours staring at a blank wall in his bedroom, emerging only to eat. Sometimes I walked into his room, and he didn't look up at me at all or even register that I was there. "Richie," I'd say, impatiently, "Answer me!" Non-communicative and severely catatonic, he stared straight ahead. It was as if something or someone had captured him, or stolen him away. I felt how fragile his spirit was and how it was slowly sinking down into a black and venomous hole. His spirit was scurrying away, an empty husk left behind. Richie barely made it through high school, flunked out of his first year in college, joined the army, then cut off all communication with our family for the three-year period he was stationed in Germany.

Richie tried to kill himself years later when I was pregnant with my second son. At the last minute his hand holding the gun shook so that the bullet missed its intended, lethal mark. The bullet lodged at a point in his brain that rendered the left side of his body partially paralyzed.

In the years following Richie's suicide attempt my mother and I poured over books and magazine articles and tuned into any television or radio broadcast that dealt with mental illness and specifically schizophrenia. Each time there was a new research study conducted or a new theory or discovery, however rudimentary, I'd phone my mother, and we'd discuss the possibilities of Richie getting better and how he may have developed the illness in the first place.

Some neuroscientists said schizophrenia might be inherited. Others argued that it could have been triggered by traumatic events, closely aligning it with post-traumatic stress disorder. I recall one article suggesting that bacteria could trigger schizophrenia, a bacteria that lurked in a childhood illness. I thought of the turtles my brother collected and the shimmery newts and salamanders scooting under the creek rocks. I remembered how Richie cradled them so lovingly in his little hands. "Salamanders can live through fire," Richie had once assured me.

I remember one Christmas when my sons were almost the same age as Richie had been when we played down by the creek. At that time, my parents still took care of him in their home, aided by VA hospital staff in the city of St. Louis. Emaciated by years of drug therapies and episodes of self-induced starvation, Richie sat in a leather chair and stared out the window. My mother had said he was better this particular Christmas, that he actually conversed with others and spent hours reading and studying the Farmer's Almanac, copying random facts down onto paper. "Hi, Richie," I said as I sat down on the edge of his bed. I looked at his dry, cracked hands always slightly blue with cold because he moved so little. I wanted to cover them gently with my own hands, but he did not like to be touched. In the stillness of the room, I asked him what I wanted so badly to know.

"Do you remember when we were children, and we played down by a creek?"

"Yes, I remember," he answered hoarsely.

"We used to collect salamanders and newts," I said.

We looked at each other for a minute and he didn't answer. He was watching me closely.

"Yes," he finally said, softly, "I remember all of those things."

I sat with him for a little while longer and struggled not to cry. I wanted him to describe salamanders to me again and how important they were in the lost sphere of a childhood world that could never be made perfect. The room was chilly and outside it was snowing. He turned away from me then, absorbed in his Farmer's Almanac. His thin fingers turned pages that rustled like leaves over a shallow creek.

We were far from that place where we first thought we could hear the ephemeral sound of fire lizards. Simple and resilient, those creatures were responsible only for nudging tiny, bright places in my brother's heart and my own. They would be with us forever.

Growing Up Brown

Flora Gamez Grateron

Mama's red front porch is surrounded by a little white picket fence. My two brothers cut and installed it for her, slat by slat, and my sister primed it in April 2022, but never painted it. The front of the house was once adorned with white lattice and my sister asked Papa for permission to remove it and replace it with a picket fence like the neighbors across the street. Her hands were tied in moving forward until the patriarch gave the ok. As soon as he agreed, she started tearing down the lattice with Papa assisting at 101 years old. In his house, he ruled the roost, so nothing was done without his final word. Mama also had to ask for his approval at times. One sister nicknamed him *El Rey*. On his 100th birthday, he wore a gold cardboard crown and celebrated with mariachis. Now, sitting in his wheelchair, he used a sledgehammer to break up a slab of concrete in the front yard even though my sister told him she wanted to use it to place pretty pots of flowers against the backdrop of the white fence. He said no, *and no was no*, so he proceeded to swing away against my sister's wishes. In the photo she took, he's wearing his favorite yellow plaid shirt and red suspenders. His legs didn't function anymore, but his arms, hands, mind, and stubbornness worked just fine.

Eight of us nine "children" are retired so we travel home to visit, help care for Mama and Papa and do as much as we can on our trips to South Texas. Papa usually sat on the porch in his wheelchair and waved to his friends until they were all dead and gone. Later, he just sat to enjoy nature, a man who could never be contained indoors. He was a self-made carpenter by trade who worked in the hot Texas sun building houses by the bay. He could build a house from the ground up and came home red as a lobster every day. He was never afraid of hard work.

Even after he retired, he always had a shovel, rake, hoe, electric saw, hammer or other tool in his hand and later worked from his wheelchair. Being idle was not an option. Papa appreciated the addition of the picket fence until he passed away at the age of 102 in December 2023. Mama finished painting the fence a few months after Papa died, working from a chair, paintbrush in hand, white paint in her hair. At the age of 98, work doesn't scare her either. We picture Papa busy raking leaves in the clouds after a life well led.

We were a poor family who lived south of the train tracks. We had just enough beans, rice, and tortillas to keep us going while we attended school on our side of town. Meat was a luxury we didn't enjoy often." Many of us brown families had a multitude of siblings and we slept three to a bed. Our home was small and cramped. Papa had built the house on an empty lot with his own hands, Mama at his side. A few blocks west from our home and across a main road was an even shabbier side of town known as *la oja de lata*, or tin town. Some of my friends lived there and our Catholic School was in that vicinity. Even though we walked to school every day, we didn't feel unsafe. However, now, it has become a drug infested part of our small hometown. My brothers who live in town warned us to stay away from there when we visit. It's much too dangerous, they say.

When the Catholic school closed due to lack of funds, we were integrated into the public school system. We invaded the schools in droves and walked north across the tracks to our new schools, East Elementary, North Elementary, junior high and high school. I entered 6th grade at North Elementary and was placed in a higher level. I had never seen so many blonde haired and blue eyed kids. And I soon realized teachers could be prejudiced. We had been whacked by the nuns at Catholic School for misbehavior. When the nun said, "*comenzando con Florita,*" as we lined up to receive the first blow, it meant trouble for the entire class, but I accepted it. We all did. This new school felt different. When Linda tattled on me to Ms. Perry that I had rolled my eyes at her, Ms. Perry was livid. How dare I, a small dark skinned new student, disrespect a white teacher like that. It was unconscionable. I felt like a worthless speck, a new experience for me. I wanted to be invisible at that moment. Ms. Perry gave me a lecture from which I don't recall one single word, except for how inferior it made me feel. And Linda sat there, smug as a bug, smirking at me.

My friends and I experienced getting whacked for speaking Spanish. One friend vividly recalls getting pulled from the hallway by our tobacco chewing History teacher to get whacked with a ruler because he heard her speaking Spanish in the hall. Our Math teacher was the worst. Brown faces seemed to trigger her. She dragged my crying friend to the office by the arm for copying on a test while turning a blind eye on white students copying answers scribbled under long-sleeved shirts and sweaters. The disparity was shocking.

Mama used to attend all parent teacher conferences at the Catholic School since all the nuns spoke Spanish. We sat in the convent's living room with Mama as she delivered money from candy sales, clean linens for the altar, even shared a cup of coffee with them, and we felt right at home. Now, because of the language barrier, she could no longer attend teacher conferences. She simply hoped for the best while all nine of us went through the public schools. And she prayed a lot.

Mama took us to the doctor only when the *curandera* had done all she could. I recall my sister being healed from *susto* by our *curandera, la madrina* Maria. My sister went into shock when a large dog in an alley stood up on its hind legs over her back. Mama gave her salt and Maria performed *una barrida* by sweeping healing herbs all over her small body, and prayer. And in time, she recovered. On other occasions, we sat in the colored waiting room apart from the white waiting room. One sister fantasized that the white waiting room consisted of people with blonde hair and blue eyes floating around and lounging on beautiful colorful sofas eating bunches of grapes while waiting to be seen by the doctor. I'm sure we were the last to be seen as we waited endlessly for our turns, coughing and feverish. We didn't seem to matter much.

Sometimes we attended church service across the tracks. The coldness of the white parishioners when we sat next to them was palpable. They refused to hold our hands during the recitation of the Our Father prayer, or shake hands during the offering of peace, or even acknowledge our existence. We were invisible to them. And it always ruined the sacred mood for me. In God's church, even on Christmas, we were not welcomed.

I recall one day as we prepared for an oncoming hurricane. I waited in the station wagon as Mama hurried into the HEB grocery store to get a few things while Papa boarded up the windows at home. I spotted my teacher, Mr. Abram, as he walked by on the sidewalk carrying his bag of groceries. My childish thought was, "He's so lucky. Nothing will happen to him because he's white." I had already been conditioned to feel inferior. I was beneath and made to feel less. And I was fearful of the wrath of an oncoming storm that could possibly demolish our fragile houses.

I became obsessed with doorbells. As my parents picked me up from band practice and other activities, doorbells glittered in the night. As we drove by, orange little orbs adorned each mysterious home. No one on our side of town had doorbells. No one had solid brick homes with manicured lawns, air-conditioning, glowing doorbells, streetlights, sidewalks or fire hydrants. I pictured myself living in one of those homes with the green yards and sleeping in humming air-conditioning instead of a hot fan. I wanted to experience the luxury of having my own bed inside a house forbidden to people like us. We could never set foot inside any house in that part of town. Never. But I could still dream.

Papa constructed majestic houses with doorbells and intercoms. He measured, sawed, and painted, as he climbed, nailed, hammered, and built the best homes money could buy. He spent hours, days, and months supervising everyone under him. He had managed to work himself to the top and even worked as a contractor. The bosses trusted him. They said, "Find Greg. Ask him how to do it right." And the workers addressed him by "*Maestro*." Imagine a man with a 5th grade education being called Teacher. He took pride in his work, and it showed. Nothing was done half-ass. He wouldn't allow it. He was treated with respect from both brown and white men.

He took us to see some of the houses. We raced around and inspected the lovely houses on Ocean Drive and called each other on the intercoms for fun. We slid across the shiny floors and inspected the gorgeous gardens and patios. They were a fantasy to us, nothing we could afford, nothing we could ever hope to own. We wondered who would end up buying those houses. Who would enjoy those carpeted bedrooms and marbled kitchens? We knew without a doubt that only white people would live inside those walls. But dammit, I wanted one of those houses to live in! I wanted my family to live happily ever after inside one of those grand homes right by the Atlantic Ocean, by the Gulf of Mexico, even though they usually took the brunt of hurricanes. I wanted an intercom. I wanted glittering doorbells. I wanted to run up and down those fancy stairs and say they belonged to my family. *Envidia*. Major *Envidia*. Of something I could not have. The fairy tale that was unreachable, the one that would make my large brown family 100% American.

Fresh out of high school, I couldn't wait to move as far away as possible. I moved to San Angelo where my college friends and I went out for pizza one night and were accosted by a knife wielding white man who didn't like brown people in the restaurant. The manager came to our rescue, kicked him out, and gave us free pizza. We weren't too hungry after that. I moved away and followed my sisters to Wisconsin. After a few years, the cold was unbearable, so I moved back to Texas, got married, and raised children. We lived by the borders, where both white and brown families hired Mexican maids. My young children's friends called them, "my maid." Imagine a preschooler saying, "my maid

…" in their everyday conversation. Everyone seemed to have a live-in maid. As a family, we lived in different parts of Texas: Arlington, Mission, and Austin, before moving to Arizona. No one I knew had maids in Arizona.

As an adult, I was learning about self-acceptance. I had gathered memories, moments, and snapshots across the states, workplaces, and life. Now that I had children, I made the decision not to teach them Spanish, remembering my painful experiences starting in grade school. My siblings did the exact same thing, worried their kids would have an accent and not fit into the American world. My kids have never forgiven me, and I now realize the mistake I made. I thought I was protecting them but in fact, they lost part of their culture because of my decision.

I searched for my identity, needing to understand myself. Who was I really? Where did I fit in? I was caught between two worlds. A world that had never accepted me with my Mexican American accent and color of my skin. Spanish was my first language and I spoke it fluently. Instead of taking pride in that, I worked on perfecting my English especially in Texas colleges during my teen years to sound more American. I still recall pronouncing pizza as pit-zah in front of my college friends and wanting to disappear in shame. I was aware I was a minority but I had never questioned my roots until my children came along.

Along the way, we rented or owned large two-story air-conditioned houses, big swimming pools, many doorbells, and even a horse corral. I enjoyed all the things I never had. I even admired and rang my own doorbell at times. I loved having lamp posts and sidewalks right outside my home. I experienced border life, city life, and rural life. But none of them saved my marriage. None of them made me feel superior. None of them made me feel white. In fact, it proved the opposite and coerced me to find myself, my own true identity. The identity of a second-generation Latina mother with four brown children who thankfully, don't question who they are. We follow Mexican traditions and cook traditional dishes, roll out tortillas and make tamales together, and put our *molcajetes* to use.

I returned to my hometown where Mama still lives and Papa is now buried. We cross the tracks where all the nice brick homes have been taken over by brown families. Almost all the white folks have sold their homes and moved away after more and more brown families took over their neighborhoods. Even the church on that side of town has a miniscule number of white parishioners left. They moved to the next town over. We drove them out! No, they chose to leave. They didn't want to deal with rubbing white elbows with brown elbows. I imagine they squirm knowing brown people are sleeping in their old bedrooms and cooking in their kitchens.

At times, I still run into a few in church in the next town over, and I know better than to extend my hand to them. I know now they will never change. They will always be prejudiced and narrow-minded and bigoted. But that is not my concern. I have learned to ignore it and accept it. I recognized from way back even in grade school that I did NOT want to grow up and be like them. I wanted to be nothing like Ms. Perry. Cold, judgmental, prejudiced teachers that had no place in the teaching field. They spewed their hatred on impressionable kids.

I have finally accepted who I am and owned it. Discrimination doesn't hurt my psyche anymore. I don't let it. Instead, it pisses me off and I think, "Just who do you suppose you are? In no way are you better than me. In no way are you superior. I speak two languages, do you? I have a large, loving brown family, how about you? My culture and traditions are rich and fulfilling, are yours?" We have so much to be proud of.

I visited my old high school with my brother who was employed there and gave me and my sister a tour. The old memories returned. The classrooms still exist where I felt the smallest and most invisible. But I return as a retired educator, closing in on seventy, still vulnerable but more durable than those tender years of school. Those experiences shaped me into who I am today. I speak Spanish everyday even if it's to my dog. I plan to teach it to my very first granddaughter, coming soon.

Papa was once a fixture on the front porch next to the white picket fence, drinking his Coronita beer from a glass bottle after he finished raking leaves. I don't think he ever realized he surpassed barriers. He never allowed his bosses to make him feel less than he was. He was on equal footing with them. They treated him with respect and sought him out because they knew he could get the job done. They knew he offered something they needed. He was content with the house he built himself, the career he chose that supported a large family of eleven, the wife who loved and cared for him until the end, and the fulfilling life he led.

I don't think Papa had any regrets. He never spoke of what ifs. He lived life with gusto. He ate, played his guitar and violin, and worked with gusto. His sturdy little house was his castle, with or without the picket fence. For him, this was the perfect American lifestyle and he reveled in it. He had achieved his dream. He didn't desire a grand house by the ocean, only security and a paycheck to provide for his family. It proved he had made it as an American whose roots were in San Luis Potosi, Mexico. He watched the great grandkids play and commented, "*que cosa es la juventud.*" As he grew more frail he would often say, "*estoy bien jodido.*" And he reminded us over and over again, "*este gallo era famoso pero ya no canta.*" We laughed but knew what he meant. Papa made his indelible mark in this world, but he was ready to depart. He died in his own bed, under his own roof, on his own terms, with peace in his heart, in the comfort of the sturdy home he had proudly built for all of us, especially his paloma, Mama.

Shame

Sylvia R. Merino

Shame began on my first day of school, when I was singled out by a nun who told me, "Your name will be spelled with a "y" like the other Sylvia." The feeling was that of confusion. *"Why wasn't the other Sylvia's name changed to Silvia?"* The reason was to "Americanize" it. I went along with it because just two years prior, my older sister's name was changed from Ana to Anna for the same reason. At this young age we accepted the changes made to our young, small, brown-skinned person without our consent, nor our parents, for that matter. Slowly we continued to allow the white world mold us to what they wanted us to be.

In high school I had a "boy" friend, not boyfriend but I was secretly in love with him. One day, when we were alone at my friend's home, he came out and told me that I wasn't American enough for him. It hurt and I felt shame the same shame I felt in first grade.

It wasn't until I was an adult, when I realized that I was more than what I was made to be. It was when I found myself at a mall, sitting on a fountain ledge, crying uncontrollably because I was just by-passed for a promotion that I was well qualified for. I felt shame for not knowing the reasons, nor did I want to believe that discrimination played a role. On that day, I vowed that I would climb the ladder as far as I comfortably could on my own terms. For the next 30+ years, I was regularly challenged by the corporate world. I became a top performer working twice as hard as my white peers to get there. Then I was criticized by them, some even hated me when I was promoted. I ignored them and continued moving up the intended path.

Success came with consequences. An accidental voicemail message was once left in response to a call I made to a person I supported. The person was speaking to someone in the background telling them who had called, "Oh it's from some Mexican that I don't like." The reason was that I was doing my job, and he didn't like when I reminded him of agreements signed by the customer and our company when he was trying to bend the rules. When I heard the message two things came to mind, *"Was he drunk?"* I could hear water splashing and people talking, like they were in a pool. Secondly, *"What a hypocrite, he never treated me badly face to face. I wonder who else hates me behind my back."*

My manager wasn't in the office that day, so my team lead passed it on to the director of our department. I was called into his office. He mentions that he was told of the incident and that he listened to the voicemail message. He said he would have a talk with this individual. Since I had already confronted the man that hates me and who had already apologized, I told the director that everything was okay now. His response was, "That's what all you people say." I wasn't quite clear as to what he meant by that. He motioned with his hands for me to leave his office. I was furious. I was sick to my stomach. I was shamed once again; I could feel my cheeks burning.

With this same group, the customers that we were working with were pleased with a new system we had just launched. A system that was an improvement and more user friendly than what we had. I was a big part of the development and testing of the program, so I was invited to a big dinner at an upscale restaurant to celebrate the success of this new system.

As we are leaving the building, we passed by offices. Out of one office, a woman stops me. She pulls me in to give me counsel. She tells me, "You know, you are going to a very, very fancy restaurant." She proceeds by making a big circle with her hands and continues. "The plate will be this big and the plate will be decorated with a sauce, and the food you order will be a small portion and it will be in the middle of the plate surround-ed by the decorative sauce. Use the big fork and you must eat slowly." I stood in amazement as she insulted me. I wanted to scream at her to tell her I wasn't born yesterday. I wanted to tell her that I've been to fancier restaurants that our Branch Manager in San Diego took us to. They were 5-star restaurants. I wanted to tell her that we didn't eat with our hands at home, nor that we ate like pigs. I was shamed, insulted, and I was angry, but I never showed it externally. I quickly turned around and walked away to catch up with the rest.

I was later promoted and moved to another office. It was slow and so I offered another group my help. It was work I was familiar with. Sometimes, I worked until late hours helping them. On Friday's I listened to the ladies planning happy hour gatherings. I was never invited, yet I was left completing their work. There was one young lady that was invited but she declined each time because she had young children at home. One day, this lady asked if I would show her how to make tortillas. I was delighted and so I invited her to my home. I saw her one day at my daughter's Brownie camp but never saw her again. *Why can't more people be kind?"* This is shame on them.

Then there were the external experiences. While looking for a venue for my 25th work anniversary, my manager asked I find a venue for the event. A friend (and her 3-year-old daughter), and I, went looking and found one that had a perfect room for our party. When speaking with the hostess about our appetizer options, I asked the questions, but her answers were always to my friend. We were both confused. I tried numerous times to get the hostess to look at me when answering. We reserved the venue and once in the car, I told my friend that the hostess probably thought I was the nanny. If this wasn't shame, it was humiliating.

Shopping at the only mall in this small town was always painful. The clerks didn't want to have anything to do with me. When I stood in line to try on a couple of pants and shirts, I waited as the people behind me were taken to a fitting room. After a few had gone ahead of me, I finally mentioned that I had been in line before the last three that they let in ahead of me. The response was, "Oh!" As I walked into the fitting room the clerk and her clerk friend began to snicker and then they laughed out loud. I was so hurt and felt shame this time for not speaking up after the first person that went ahead of me. I never tried on the clothes, I just walked out and never went back to that store.

It was a day before Cinco de Mayo. I was at King Sooper's in the same small town. There were at least six cash registers. I was at one end and then at the very far register, the cashier was a young blond boy, probably in his early twenties. In between us, there were some Hispanics checking out and me, of course, also a Hispanic. The young blond boy suddenly began shouting, "Why don't you all just go back to Mexico to celebrate!" We all looked at him and ignored him. I was steaming inside. The cashier assisting me, whispered, "Ignore him."

Once at home, I wrote a letter to the King Sooper's manager and explained the situation. I also gave him a lesson on how/when Cinco de Mayo originated and asked him to share it with his employee. First, it is the date of Mexico's victory over the second French Empire at the battle of Puebla back in 1862. Mexico recognizes this date, but they do not celebrate it. Their big celebration is on September 16th when they gained independence from the Spanish Empire. Secondly, the U. S. made it a Holiday, and has been celebrated for many years. Finally, I mentioned that I am not from Mexico and that I was born and raised here! No shame here.

When my daughter went to pre-school, we were asked to only speak in English to our daughter. It is because when the teacher asked the children what the names of their body parts were my daughter responded in Spanish. The funny thing is that the only time we spoke to her in Spanish was when we were playing with her and pointing out her "pancita" her belly, "ojitos" her eyes, "boquita" her mouth. The rest of our conversations were in English and to this day, I wish I had continued to speak to her in Spanish, rather than being shamed for teaching our daughter a few words.

Then came the day when my daughter's summer daycare called to tell me that my daughter had lice and they were sorry she couldn't go on the field trip. It turns out that she had no lice. What happened is that they miscounted, and they had one seat left on the bus, but two kids needing a seat. They chose the white boy over my daughter and used "lice" as an excuse. My daughter was shamed, and I was too.

The stories can go on forever. We deal with them and move on, or we dwell on the small and rare incidents to only hurt us mentally and emotionally. I choose to move on because it is not worth the pain.

Today, I look back with joy and some sadness, at the many barriers in my life that I struggled with to reach my journey and my goals without shame.

Beyond the Brick Walls

Sahara Williamson

The cab stops in front of a large red brick building. Like many apartment buildings in NYC, it resembles a prison, far from the Marriott Marquis in Midtown. I open my address book to ensure this isn't a mistake, but no, this is it. I enter the building and walk down a dark, chilly hallway to the elevator. The doors open, and the smell of urine assaults my nostrils. I step over a mysterious puddle to board the elevator and ride it to the 3rd floor. I hear voices echoing against the cement. Apt 330, this is it. I knock on the heavy door. Anticipation in the air, I hear footsteps approaching, then the dull scraping sound as the ancient deadbolt is unlocked.

A tall, statuesque woman in her seventies opens the door; wisps of silver highlight her freshly styled shoulder-length black hair, complementing her cinnamon complexion. In her ears, there are tiny pearl studs. She wears a tailored white blouse with high-waisted navy trousers. I look down at my jeans and Starter Jacket and feel underdressed. She exudes an effortless sophistication that I crave.

Margaret, my great-grandmother. I don't know her very well. She has lived in New York for 50 years. She would come to Pittsburgh sometimes and stay with her mom, Claire, my great-great-grandma, for a few weeks. But it always felt forced, like she was just checking off a list of duties.

I've never been to her apartment before. She gestures for me to come in. No hug, but a warm, inviting smile. I feel some of my nerves shed. Behind her is a short, balding chestnut skinned man. He wears a bright-colored cardigan, sweater, and slacks. He approaches and holds out his hand.

"Hi, I don't think we've ever met. I'm Scotty. It's Paula, right?"

"Yeah," I say and take his hand. He shakes it gently.

"She is named after my Pauly," Margaret says.

Technically, I'm named after my father, not my grandfather, but I know better than to say that. So, I just smile.

"Let me give you a tour," she says.

I leave my shoes at the door. On the floor is a fluffy beige shag carpet that tickles my toes. The apartment is larger than I expected and much more pleasant. It's warm and vibrant, unlike the hoary brick building I entered. A space meant for living in. Margaret has lived here for over 30 years and there is evidence in every room. I recall my grandfather saying that thanks to rent control.

Scotty is her boyfriend; life partner would be more accurate since they had been together for nearly 20 years. This mild-mannered middle-aged man hardly seemed scandalous, yet he had never accompanied her on any of her visits to Pittsburgh. In my family, he was unacceptable for two reasons: he was significantly younger than Margaret. But she is ageless, so the age difference is not noticeable, and I cannot see why it matters. The other is that he had never married her. After only a few minutes with them, it is clear to me who runs the show. He seems to adore her. This leads me to believe they are not married because she doesn't want to be.

Scotty is a Broadway musician and a teacher at the Manhattan School of Music. He leads us to the apartment's back bedroom, where his music studio is. Inside is a giant bass leaning against a wall, along with a keyboard and saxophone. A shelf in the corner displays several awards he has received for his work. After a few minutes, he explains he is working on a piece for one of his classes and needs to get to work. He kisses Margaret on the cheek.

We head to the living room. I notice a fat gray cat stretched out on the loveseat. It looks up at me, its round, plush body tensing as I approach. Its ears perk up, and the tail swishes left to right.

"Careful," Margaret says.

"Can I pet them?"

"You'll have to check with her?"

I move closer as she purrs and bumps her head against my hand.

Margaret watches our interaction with amusement.

"She likes you. Do you have a cat? "

"I wish. I love them, but there are no pets allowed at our house, especially not cats. My grandmother thinks they are sneaky."

"Earlene? Of course, she would know something about that."

"I think they are discerning, I say. I am shocked you let her on the furniture."

"It's her house too. My mom, your grandma Clara, grew up on a farm in North Carolina. There were always cats roaming around. That was the one thing she didn't leave behind when she moved up north. We always had one. My house doesn't feel right with one. Her name is Lilac."

I take the seat next to Lilac and continue petting my new friend. The walls in the living room are littered with framed prints by Jacob Lawrence Basquiat. The shelves are full of records of Aretha Franklin, Marvin Gaye, Poncho Sanchez, and Arturo Sandoval.

"You hungry?" she asks.

I am, but I am also not rushing to return to the streets below. My grandmother senses my trepidation. She smiles.

"I don't know what you're worried about. I know this neighbor-hood. No one bothers me here. And you better get used to it if you want to live here. This is what New York is like. Yes, there are fancier neighborhoods but at the core, it's all the same. There is a grittiness you either love or hate. it this city can eat you alive, but it can also bring you peace."

I am mortified that she might think I can't hack it here.

"I've been here before. I've always wanted to live her. I just…"

"You're not used to it. It's okay. Let's go for that walk. Get some food."

She walked off to let Scotty know we were heading out. She returns with a pair of leather loafers and a matching handbag. We put on our coats and head out.

I am here to audition for colleges. With 17 years of ballet, jazz, and modern dance experience, four years of theater training, and a lifetime of writing stories, I am ready to go wherever I am wanted. I have it all planned. But I can hear my grandmother's voice in my head.

"I don't know why the hell you want to ride them dirty ass subways. What you need to do is go get your license, and then you can just commute to CMU or Pitt. Who wants to do all that walking, climb all them steps?" and on and on.

I try to shake off my suburban middle-class sensibilities as we head out for brunch. I look past the grimy exterior of the Bronx streets and focus instead on the street vendors selling empanaditas and pastelitos. I hear the Salsa and Bamba blasting from the storefronts along the strip. By the time we get to the restaurant, I am feeling confident again. There is magic on these streets. Everyone in the diner knew my grandmother; they called her Mami. She ordered our food in Spanish. Everyone spoke Spanish.

"Do you want coffee?" she asked.

"Sure," I say. I don't drink coffee, but it's a good start time. Even though it is just a little Puerto Rican diner, I feel all grown up sipping coffee with Margaret.

There is a large window next to our table. I stare out at the hustle and bustle.

"Is it always this busy?" I ask.

"Yup," she says as she blows the still steaming hot liquid in her mug,

"You are a pretty girl," she says. But it didn't feel like a compliment.

"I was a pretty girl once."

"You're still pretty,"

"Well, thank you, but you know what I mean."

I don't, but I nod.

"If you want to make it in this city, you just have to remember one thing."

"What's that?" I am eager to hear the sage advice of a woman who has spent the last 50 years living in this city.

"KYPC," she says.

"Excuse me," I say, thinking maybe I misunderstood.

"KYPC,"

I look at her, still bewildered by the acronym.

"You don't know what that means?" she says.

"No idea."

She laughs, looks me in my eyes, and says,

"Keep your pussy clean."

I don't blush, but if I did…My god, this is my great-grandmother. She says nothing for a while, just stares out the window and stirs her coffee. While I fidget in my chair, pick at the hangnail on my thumb. My coffee is gone and I am not sure what to do with myself. To my relief, Margaret changes the subject to the theater and her favorite restaurants in the city. We finish our food and I realize it is time for me to head back to the hotel.

Margaret reaches in her purse for her wallet to pay the bill, then hands me a $50 bill.

"It's for the car ride back." Down the block, there's a car service.

"I can't just get a taxi."

She shakes her head and smiles.

"Honey, this is the Bronx."

She pulls out an envelope and hands it to me. Inside are front row seats to see "Cats."

"Have you seen it?" she says.

"No." Thanks so much.

"They are from Scotty. I hope you like it. I didn't know what you'd want to see. He said Rent, but…"

"I've seen that."

"Well, good! Then I was right. Well, enjoy. Don't be a stranger."

But I was. That's the last time I saw Margaret. Her funeral was in Harlem—the coldest day of an otherwise mild winter. Folks in fur coats were packed in the place, sobbing.

"She was like a mother to me." One woman stood up and said,

Our family seemed lost. She had made an impression on them, but not on us? Except for that day almost 25 years ago, she remained just a signature on a check in a card that arrived in the mail twice a year, for birthdays and Christmas. So, despite moving to New York six months later, I never found the time to hop on the two train and make my way up to the Bronx. Even when she lay in the hospital dying of leukemia two years later, it didn't occur to me to visit. She never called me, either. Had we both escaped to the city, desiring the anonymity that only a concrete jungle provides? An escape from prying eyes and criti-cal tongues. Now I think, "Holy shit, what a cool ass grandma,"

I wish I could call her. Learn more about her life—the things she must have seen. But our elders are so often wasted on the young.

Xihuan the Nahual

Tezozomoc

In the ancient Mexican civilization, nahuales were considered powerful and feared beings. Nahuales were believed to be individuals who had the ability to transform into animals or other supernatural creatures, harnessing their unique qualities and abilities. This transformation was not merely physical but also spiritual, as the nahuales would tap into the essence and energy of the animal or creature they transformed into.

The fear of nahuales stemmed from their association with dark magic and their potential to inflict harm on others. It was believed that nahuales had the ability to cast spells, manipulate elements, and even possess humans or animals. In Mexican folklore, it was believed that nahuales would often use their powers for malevolent purposes, causing havoc and misfortune in the lives of those who crossed their path.

The creation of a nahual was believed to require a pact with evil deities or spirits. It was said that a person seeking the powers of a nahual would make a blood pact with dark forces, offering their loyalty and obedience in exchange for the coveted ability to transform into an animal or creature. This pact was typically sealed in a dark ritual, involving sacrifice and the summoning of supernatural entities.

The fear of nahuales was deeply ingrained in Mexican society due to the potential dangers they posed. People feared encounters with them as it was believed that nahuales could harm or even kill their victims. Stories circulated of nahuales using their powers to inflict illness, disrupt crops, steal livestock, or cause natural disasters. The ability of nahuales to blend into society by assuming the form of animals made them elusive and difficult to identify, further instilling fear and paranoia within the community.

The Mexicans also believed that nahuales had the ability to curse individuals, causing them great suffering and misfortune. The fact that nahuales were associated with dark magic and dealt with malevolent spirits only fueled the fear and dread surrounding them.

Xihuan

Xihuan is a Mexican indigenous boy with a deep connection to his indigenous culture and heritage. Born in the highlands of Milpa Alta, he comes from a family of brujos, where magical traditions and ancient spiritual practices are passed down from generation to generation. His family's unique gift is the ability to transform into nahuales, mystical shape shifters who can take the form of animals.

Among his siblings, Xihuan is the only boy, surrounded by seven sisters who have all embraced their nahual abilities. While his sisters fully embrace their transformation, Xihuan feels a sense of unease and fear about his own potential to become a nahual. He doesn't mind the spell casting, or the binding practices, or the sacrificial acts. This fear lingers in his heart and mind, causing him to have a hard time sleeping at night.

Throughout his young life, Xihuan has observed the power and consequences that come with being a nahual. He has seen his sisters silently leave the house at night, their human forms melting away to reveal the beasts they become. They roam the land, hunting and preying upon unsuspecting creatures, leaving behind a feeling of both awe and trepidation within Xihuan.

Xihuan's greatest fear is losing control over his own identity and turning into an animal like his sisters. He dreads the notion of abandoning his human form, unsure if he would be capable of causing harm and destruction like the other nahuales. The possibility of harming innocent beings and losing touch with his own humanity haunts him, creating a constant battle between his desire to fit in with his family and his fear of becoming a nahual.

This conflict reflects in Xihuan's inability to sleep soundly, his restless nights tainted by a mix of worry and anticipation. Every time he drifts off to sleep, he envisions himself waking up as a creature of the night, forever isolated from the human world he cherishes. This fear has become a burdensome shadow that lingers over his daily life, relentlessly reminding him of the potential consequences of embracing his true nature.

In spite of his fear, Xihuan remains deeply connected to his indigenous heritage. He deeply respects the ancient traditions and spiritual practices passed down by his family of brujos. He seeks solace and guidance from elders and spiritual leaders who help him navigate his conflicting emotions. Xihuan's unwavering determination to face his fear head-on is evident in his continuous quest for self-discovery and understanding.

EXT. MOUNTAIN VILLAGE - DAY

The sun shines brightly over the humble mountain village of Milpa Alta. The sound of the wind rustling through the trees fills the air. Xihuan, a curious and determined young boy of twelve, makes his way through narrow paths towards the small hut of Don Tiburcio, a wise and renowned nahual of the region.

As Xihuan steps closer, the hut emerges from the dense forest, revealing a humble abode surrounded by mystical herbs and artifacts. As he walks the hairs on his neck rise as he feels that something is following him along the path. He quickly looks but only sees shadows. He takes a deep breath to calm his racing heart before knocking on the door.

DON TIBURCIO (FROM INSIDE)

Enter, young one.

Xihuan pushes open the creaky door and enters the dimly lit room. An aroma of herbs and sacred artifacts lingers in the air. Don Tiburcio, an elderly man with kind eyes and a weathered face, sits cross-legged on a worn-out mat. He motions for Xihuan to join him.

DON TIBURCIO

Come, Xihuan. Sit, my young friend.

Xihuan cautiously approaches and takes a seat, his eyes wandering over the peculiar objects adorning the room.

XIHUAN (NERVOUS)

Don Tiburcio, I... I seek your guidance. I come to you burdened with fear.

DON TIBURCIO (CALMLY)

Fear is a natural part of life, Xihuan. Share your concerns with me, and we shall find answers together.

XIHUAN (FRUSTRATED)

It's about my family tradition as nahuals. My father expects me to embrace this path, but the thought of it terrifies me. I cannot understand why I am consumed by such fear.

Don Tiburcio leans forward, his eyes full of understanding.

DON TIBURCIO

Ah, the journey of the heart is not always what we expect, young one. You possess a gift, a connection to the spiritual world. But fear is a hint, a message that needs deciphering.

XIHUAN (CONFUSED)

Deciphering? What do you mean?

DON TIBURCIO

Sometimes, our deepest fears are tied to our greatest strengths. Embracing who we are requires us to confront those fears head-on, to understand them intimately.

Xihuan nods, his eyes reflecting a mixture of determination and trepidation.

XIHUAN

But what if I fail? What if I disappoint my family and my ancestors?

DON TIBURCIO (SMILING GENTLY)

Failure is merely a stepping stone on the journey to success. Your family understands it too, Xihuan. They believe in you.

Xihuan takes a moment to absorb Don Tiburcio's words, drawing strength from them.

XIHUAN

What should I do, Don Tiburcio? How can I overcome this fear?

Don Tiburcio reaches out, placing a hand on Xihuan's shoulder, radiating warmth and wisdom.

DON TIBURCIO

Seek solace in the natural world around you, young one. The wind, the water, the earth - they are conduits to our ancestors. Allow their energy to guide you, to help you understand yourself.

Xihuan's eyes light up with newfound hope and determination.

XIHUAN

Thank you, Don Tiburcio. I will follow your advice and embrace my fears, for only then can I truly become a different kind of nahual I am meant to be.

They both rise from their seated positions, a sense of purpose filling the room.

DON TIBURCIO

Remember, Xihuan, your ancestors walk beside you. You are never alone on this path.

Xihuan takes a final look at Don Tiburcio, their eyes locking momentarily, and Xihuan slights a view of Don Tiburcio's nahual. He leaves the hut, ready to confront a different kind of family tradition as a nahual.

Silent Song

Angélica M. Yañez

My entire being is an act of rebellion, but my sexuality is a quiet riot. Together, she and I crawl into the sweat lodge, a small, dome-shaped structure—a symbolic womb where we are reborn. Inside, we sit on the earth, surrounded by the community, gathered in a circle around the glowing stones. The sweat leader welcomes us with a nod, sitting beside the water, prepared to pour life over the heated stones.

Shrouded in steam and darkness, our hands seek each other. Fingers intertwined, and gentle glances meet; our feet touch, grounding us. Her toenails, pink against the dirt, are like delicate blossoms in the wilderness. We sit and sing, our voices weaving prayers to each other and to our ancestors. We cry the way women do—deep, ancient, guttural—summoning our warrior spirits with an instinctual call, echoing my yearning for *her*.

I'm mesmerized by the way her full lips move, her voice silky and smooth, and how her cacao-covered skin glistens under the heat, catching the soft shine of the lava stones. There is a fire within me that can only be stoked by her. After everyone is gone, we bend like willows, reaching for the tender sky. I can taste the sweetness of honeysuckles as my tongue explores the softness between her thighs. She sighs, and the stars cascade upon us, illuminating our bodies. She lights up and darkness fades, as we merge into one atop a bed of sage and flowers. At daybreak, the soft chirping of birds serves as a gentle alarm, and her hair brushing my face reminds me that the sun's rays betray me, exposing my naked body, along with all my secrets, and the raw desire I feel for this woman.

Carly Creley, *Farm Worker's in Coachella Valley*, Undated. Digital photography.

The day and patriarchal dictates demand our distance.
I gaze at her and ask if she'll be at the lodge next week. With a
smile, she replies, "Yeah, my dad will be pouring water. See you
there," as she gathers her clothes and flicks her braid. I watch her
silhouette fade into the warmth of the morning sun.

The drying of the Salton Sea and the industrial waste that
runs through the New River creates some of the unhealthiest air
in the country in the Imperial Valley and neighboring Coachella
Valley. Record levels of asthma, bronchitis, and heart attacks go
unaddressed, and children as young as 11 die of cardiovascular
disease. Despite grave public concerns and mounting conse-
quences, there has been little effective effort by the government
or industry to address this confluence of crises.

House Divided

Maggie Nerz Iribarne

My sister said she wanted to *mend fences*, invited us for a Labor Day picnic. I didn't want to go, I really didn't, but we had nothing better to do, so I loaded the boys in the car.

Max was wearing his damn purple and white College shirt. I handed him the six-pack bought at the gas station and went straight through the house to the back patio.

Max followed me, carrying a plate of burgers and dogs.

I wished I wore my red and white State colors, but unlike him I tried to keep things cool.

"You get your season pass?" he asked.

I nodded, took a swig of beer.

"Looks like it'll be a good year," he said, flipping a burger.

I'd been staying out of trouble, keeping my trap shut.

"Any luck with the job?" he asked.

I swallowed the ball of spit forming in my mouth.

***

She didn't even wait for me to say hello.

"You cut our tires last night, Pat?"

"What you talking about, Sissy?"

"You got into something with Max about stupid State and you slashed our tires."

"Why would I-"

"Because you've pulled shit like that before. To other people. We know you have."

"C'mon," I said.

"We're not pressing charges and you know why?" she said. "Because we pity you. We *pity* you. You didn't even go to State. It's pathetic."

Pity, she spat the word like green poison.

Then, she hung up.

***

That night after the boys went to bed I grabbed my sharpest knife, jumped in the car, slashed every purple and white flag in town.

I did it good and quick, barely making a sound.

Not one of them College people love their team like I love State.

Not a single one.

Eyes

Kevin Carver

Son, you know me. Look. Find my eyes. Seek the truth and you will witness a miracle: your father. My big champ, I still desperately love you.

Forget the body.

That's not me, not anymore. All that time spent in cartilage and hair. I remember my skin stretching uncomfortably like a toddler fumbling into footie pajamas after a bath. You do remember, don't you? I suppose not. No man still feels his own boyhood. Yet through your journey I recalled my own forsaken youth, like some melancholic hologram, and it hurt me. I'm sorry I was so hard, so distant.

But how you grew!

We had a special bond, me and you. From your first breath to my last. It is simple to love a small child, just like it is effortless for a child to adore a giant, someone who carries them, tickles them, and feeds them candy when the other giant isn't looking. You grew tall and emotional and self-conscious and difficult, but you were always my son. Always.

Look at me. I implore you. See my face. Will you hold me, as I once held you?

I was skeptical of your idea. Your mother certainly didn't approve.

As I lay dying, wasting away like a lost worm sizzling on asphalt, I caught only glimpses, heard only snippets of the argument. Moments really.

Your mother yelling.

Not uncommon but certainly unusual in the room of a dying man.

"No, no. I will not stand for it," and so on and so forth. Something like that. At once I became afraid, not of death, of course. When you are dying, fear is but the water you swim in. You learn to float.

A new fear emerged. When my father, your grandfather, passed, a rift tore our family in two. You remember, you were young but not so young. You must remember. I love you too much, you see, and in these moments of lucidity I became increasingly startled at the idea that my death would engender another such rift. That your mother would be alone. That you would leave again. All that arguing. Mother's yelling would peak, and I would stir. You noticed and came to my side, grabbed my hand. You placed a cool washcloth on my brow. "And I believe in yesterday," you sang. You still knew all my favorite Beatles songs. Your mother stood behind you, red faced, and clenched her weathered, quivering jaw. The argument ceased. You two were whole again. All of us, a family. Just for a little while.

I was never brave enough to tell you I loved you even when you disappointed us. When you left college and disappeared. Your mother took it the hardest, I think. I insisted she let it go. "What does it matter? He is alive. He is our son." I said these words. You must understand, your mother loves you, of course, perhaps more than I, but she does not know how to heal. If she were shot by arrows, she would leave them in, I think, just so she could feel them scrape her bones. So, she wouldn't forget. Some people are defined by their wounds. You are like this too.

But all sons run back to their fathers. It doesn't matter how cruel we are, how reckless or uncaring or uninterested, and at times, I too was a monster. Yet you returned.

Some version of you, at least. You had changed. Thinner and paler. Your eyes were as red as poison ivy and empty, as if someone reached inside you and stole the spark. "Drugs," your mother said, and I agreed, but I suspected something else had happened to you out there. In the wilderness. "If you knew where to look..." you once started to tell me, one cold November morning, the quiet mist invading our private yard, not long after you fell back into our arms. You were drinking coffee. I was peeling a banana.

"Knew where to look for what?" I asked, but then you left the kitchen counter and fell onto the couch. You turned on the TV. That was all you said that day. I didn't press. I just wanted to be there for you, for once, like I was when you were little, before I became so sad and before you became so angry. Your dad is still your dad, even when he can no longer hold you.

Son, champ, can't you do something for me? Can't you pick me up and hold me?

My last moments were strikingly clear. I awoke to a pounding. I thought it a hammer and then realized it was someone at the door. Trying to get in. I saw you, of course, my busy boy, moving like a surgeon's assistant, folding and arranging and cleaning and pointing. Focused.
I didn't know the others. Climbing in through the fire escape.

A man much older than me but vigorous and stern. He chanted plangent words I didn't know. I could hardly hear it over the pounding. He held an ancient and irregular book.

Some woman sat in the chair where I used to tie your shoes — do you remember? — her age indistinguishable, her face hidden by a hood, her tongue moving with no sound.

A man lying on the floor. A naked corpse. Hands and feet stretched and tied with sage.

"Son," I moaned, and the pounding stopped as you drove

a dagger through my heart.

You didn't know. How could you?

You are my son, and I know you better than anyone, better than my wife, than myself. Never once have you properly handled a broom, wiped a counter, or cleared a spider's web.

Look into my eyes, all my eyes, and see your father, whose spirit fled its doomed body and found a vacant corpse, a new host, just not the body you had prepared.

It is me. Can't you tell? I see the tears in your eyes, son. The dagger in your hand. Raise this jar and release me. Please. The air is thin. I tap with my front legs, my longest. I will reach high and caress your face, if you will let me, like I did when I held you, when you were just a boy and when I was still a man.

Yes, that's it. You know m—

Blues Streak

Terry Sanville

Liliana Nguyen brushed her long black hair, braided it, and pinned it up with a silver and turquoise barrette. Her father wouldn't be home from work for maybe an hour. If everything went as planned, she'd have just enough time.

Dressed in her after-school scruffies, she hustled to the back porch of their California bungalow. With much banging and clanging, she dragged a rickety stepladder inside and positioned it in the hallway, below the ceiling trapdoor. The ladder shook as much as her knees as she climbed, pushed the door open and pulled herself into the stuffy attic. Dim sunlight filtered in through windows that hadn't been cleaned in decades. She bent at the waist to avoid conking her head on the slanted rafters. A thick dust layer covered everything.

Liliana and her parents had moved into the bungalow five years before, lucky to find an almost affordable place in Huntington Beach. None of them had checked out the attic. Her father told her it was too dangerous to go up there, she could topple off the ladder or fall through the old plaster ceiling. And besides, she was too little.

"Not any more," Liliana murmured to herself, pushing her middle school shoulders back, proud of her attributes.

The attic's dust caused her to sneeze a half dozen times and her eyes watered. She wiped her dripping nose on her sweatshirt sleeve. Moving toward the cluster of cardboard boxes along one slanted wall, she stepped carefully, only on the ceiling joists and not on the old style lath-and-plaster between them.

The first two boxes held clothes that looked like castoffs from the 1960s. *Who wears bellbottoms and paisley anymore,* she thought . . . *or those wide collars. These things might be good for a*

She checked her wristwatch, hurried to open another box, and pulled out a hard-shell case with tweed-colored sides and a hinged top. She opened it. The case contained six large phonograph records, each in their own felt-lined slot. They looked like nothing she'd ever seen – about a quarter-inch thick, heavy, and almost a foot across. She doubted whether they could be played on her father's turntable. Their labels said they were music by Bessie Smith. Liliana never heard of her.

She had time for one more box. It contained an old record player with the same tweed-colored cover, a braided and frayed electrical cord and an unsealed plug. The whole thing looked like an electrocution waiting to happen. She carried both items to the edge of the trapdoor. Then, one at a time, she hauled them down the ladder and hid them in her bedroom closet, out of sight behind her laundry basket.

She checked the time. *He'll be here any minute and wanna know why dinner isn't ready.*

Liliana struggled to replace the ladder on the porch. In the kitchen she prepared a fish, rice, and vegetable meal, working fast, each movement graceful and precise. Her mother had taught her well and she learned from her parents how to cook both Vietnamese and Mexican dishes, and sometimes mixing the two. Her mom had called them their "Green Card Specials." Sadly, her mother wasn't around to teach her more, cancer taking her the year before.

A car door slammed just as she turned off the heat under the rice. She raced to a sideboard and dumped ice cubes into a glass, added margarita mix and a shot of tequila. The front door swung open and her father, Son, entered.

"I'm beat. You have my drink?" he called, managing a weak smile.

"Sit on the sofa and I'll bring it to you."

He slumped onto the worn couch and sighed. "There was a bad wreck on the 405. Sorry I'm late."

"Dinner is just about ready. How was work?"

"Fall term is always hectic. The computer lab is hopping. I have to go back tonight and babysit the damn system."

"You have time for dinner?"

"Yes, I'm starved. Bring it here."

She fixed a tray with the food and his drink. When she returned to the living room, the TV mumbled in the background and her father lay snoring. She shook him awake gently and he took the tray, tasted the rice.

"You cooked it just like your mother. It's delicious."

Liliana's face burned with pleasure. "Thanks."

After listening to the Channel 4 news, Son gulped the remains of his drink, kissed his daughter on the cheek and headed back to work. "Don't wait up. I won't be back until past midnight."

Liliana listened to his car sounds fade then counted to one hundred slowly to make sure that he didn't return to fetch something he'd forgotten. She whipped out her cell and phoned her best friend, Sophia. Liliana's friends were Asian or Latina with a few black and white girls thrown in. Sophia liked to make fun of her. "You look like a China doll with a bad sunburn." It was true. But Liliana liked the way she looked and had already worked out the design of her first tattoo, something with an Asian grace mixed with a Mexican earthiness. But where to put it?

"Hey Sophia, what's up?" She held the phone flat in front of her face and sipped diet coke.

"*Nada mucho.*"

"You wanna come over? I found something cool."

"What."

"You gotta see it."

"Okay, okay. I'll be over in fifteen."

"See ya."

While waiting for her friend she grabbed her laptop, logged onto the Internet, and Googled Bessie Smith. The images of a smiling, almost-pretty black woman stared back. Wikipedia described her career as a blues singer in the 1920s and her untimely death at age 43 from a car crash. Blues, that old stuff from 100 years ago? She'd never listened to it and none of her friends did. K-pop, soundcloud rap, and various forms of EDM were her favorites.

Sophia banged loudly on the front door and she let her friend in.

"So what's this big secret?"

"I found something in the attic."

"So tell me, already."

"Some strange-looking vinyl from a hundred years ago."

"Cool. Can you play it?"

"Don't know. I also found an old turntable. Don't know if it works."

"Well, get it out here and let's try."

Liliana brought the player into the living room. She put on a pair of Mr. Clean rubber gloves that she used to hand-wash the dishes.

"What are they for?" Sophia asks.

"Look at the wiring to this thing. It could fry me."

"Great. I'll be ready to punch 9-1-1."

But when Liliana plugged the record player into a wall socket nothing happened. She pushed the little lever on the machine's front and the turntable began to spin.

"So let's listen," Sophia said, sounding impatient.

"Hang on, I gotta figure out what speed to play these things."

"Doesn't it say on the disc?"

"No."

Liliana studied the little knob that had three settings, 33⅓ , 45, and 78. Choosing the lowest, she blew dust from the needle, turned the volume and tone knobs to midway, and queued the record. A low moaning sound bleated from the machine's tiny speaker. She shifted the speed setting to 45 and the moaning continued, only higher. Finally she chose 78 and the voice coming out sounded scratchy and distant, but real.

"Who is that?" Sophia asked.

"Someone named Bessie Smith."

"Sounds like that old sleazy stuff to me."

Liliana nodded but stayed quiet. The woman's voice sounded like someone blowing a horn. It was mid-range, full bodied, slid from note to note with perfect pitch, without sound effects, straight without reverb but never flat. In the background a clunky piano played simple chord progressions and every once in a while a banjo and clarinet would add funny little notes. The lyrics were simple – some gal losing her good man; tunes that made no sense but felt like they were talking about sex; and most always lyrics that had something to do with dying. The record had only two songs on each side, each ending abruptly.

"Ya can't dance to that stuff," Sophia complained.

"No, guess not."

"And they're real downers."

"Hey, I think they're supposed to be. It's the blues."

Liliana queued the second record. She grabbed her pawnshop guitar from the corner and tried playing along with the songs. They proved more complicated than they sounded and she struggled to find the right key and keep up.

She queued a song called *Grave Digger Blues* and hummed along with the lyrics, singing the repeat lines, trying to slide her voice from note to note like Bessie, all the while controlling the vibrato.

"Your voice kinda goes with that shit," Sophia said and grinned. "Never thought you could sing Pop. You need a high squeaky voice like those white girls or skinny *chiquitas*."

Liliana grinned. "Yeah, this stuff feels good. But who's gonna listen to a yellow-brown girl sing black music?"

"Yeah, yeah. Jus keep playin'. I'm startin' to like it. And give me a little of your Pop's booze. It'll go good with it."

"Forget that. He keeps track . . . and I've seen you drunk . . . not pretty."

"You're no fun at all," Sophia said and stuck out her tongue.

That night, they played all six records and Liliana wrote down the names of the ones she liked the most. In the weeks that followed, before her father came home or when he worked nights, she'd haul out the record player and copy lyrics down in her spiral-bound notebook with the guitar chords above the words. At school Liliana didn't mention the music to anyone. But Sophia couldn't keep her mouth shut and bragged about her newly-discovered blues star who lived right there in conservative Huntington Beach. The next time Liliana asked her friend over, Sophia brought along four other girls and a six-pack of beer that one of them had lifted from their parents' fridge. They were eighth graders, the top of the heap in middle school. It was their last year, then onward to high school and big kid stuff. They had to get ready, toughen up, learn what was cool and discard the rest. And most thought their parents couldn't possibly help with cool.

***

Liliana got her first real boyfriend during sophomore year in high school.

When Sophia found out, she poked her in the ribs. "Jeez, that guy's so white he'll sunburn in a rainstorm."

"Ashley's cool, kinda nerdy, but I like him a lot."

"Yeah, I saw you two sucking face at the game."

"Shut up."

"So, what's he like. I want details."

Liliana sighed, "I don't know . . . kinda shy . . . but crazy smart. Takes all those AP classes. Helps me with chemistry. I really like chemistry."

"A good kisser?"

"Well, yeah!" Liliana giggled, showing off her Asian heritage. "But he's no horn-dog like the jocks. All we've done is held hands and kissed."

"You be careful," Sophia warned. "It's those quiet types that 'll get you pregnant."

"Is that what happened to your sister?" Liliana asked, smirking.

"Yeah, and now she expects me to babysit three times a week."

"So uncool."

Liliana continued to play and sing the blues, copying more and more tunes off the Internet. When she heard her first Chicago style blues album by Buddy Guy, she begged her father to buy her an electric guitar and amplifier.

"What for?" he asked. "You mostly play folk songs, don't you?"

Liliana sucked in a deep breath. "Well . . . not much anymore."

"All right, Liliana. What have you been up to?"

She retrieved her guitar, sat cross-legged on the living room carpet and played her favorite Bessie tunes. Her father listened intently and smiled when she finished.

"So, old black music is your thing now? Do you even know what the lyrics mean?"

She grinned. "You can find just about everything on the Internet."

"I have to admit, the blues goes along with your voice, better than those English songs you used to sing."

"Jeez, Dad, you really haven't heard me for a while. My voice has gotten even deeper. But I can still hit the high notes."

"Not that I've noticed. Sorry I haven't been around to listen more. But work . . ."

"I know, I know, you work too hard."

"Well, it helps fill the space after your Mom died."

"Yeah, maybe . . . maybe the blues does that for me. And my friends seem to like it. But I'm starting to listen to Chicago blues and—"

"Really? That stuff is hard core."

"Yeah, and it's electric. So can I get a guitar and small amp?"

"The neighbors will complain."

"I'll insulate my room."

Son grinned. "You've got it all figured out, don't you?"

"Not everything."

"I'll help."

By her senior year, Liliana's bedroom looked more like a sound studio with insulated walls and ceiling and an array of guitars, microphone stands, small amplifiers, effects pedals, and a tiny four-channel PA. Her father helped her set it up and bought the computer equipment needed to burn CDs and DVDs. The blues became their thing.

Near the end of her senior year, the high school held a talent contest. Sophia had introduced her boyfriend, Mateo, to her. He played bass and had a friend that pounded congas. Three times a week they rehearsed blues tunes, with each taking solos. Liliana's guitar work had gone from strumming simple chords to playing lightning-fast riffs, Chicago style. They had become a power trio.

But at the talent show, it was her vocals that caught the audience off guard. Liliana and her crew followed a hip-hop group that sang to a generic streamed background and an all-girls band that performed squeaky K-pop. So Liliana's wine-red throaty voice blasting over searing guitar riffs left the crowd stunned. The scattered applause that followed mostly came from their parents and friends.

"I don't think they got it," Liliana complained.

"I know, I know," Sophia said. "But you were great. I wish I could do that."

They didn't win the contest. The prizes went to one of the hip-hop groups, a nerdy guy who recited his own poetry, and an Iranian girl that played the cello well enough to audition for the New York Philharmonic.

Son took the band and friends out for pizza afterward and they talked about what to do over the summer before disappearing – Mateo to Arizona State on a football scholarship; Chad the conga player to work for his father's construction company; and Liliana to Stanford to study chemistry – she did well in chemistry.

"You guys have those CD's and zip drives with MP3 files," Son said. "You should try getting your songs on Spotify or YouTube, or maybe hook up with iTunes or Bandcampon. Make a little money."

But none of the band seemed that interested. Their minds were elsewhere. They continued to meet every couple of weeks to play music, just for the fun of it. But by summer's end they all were ready to move on.

Dripping tears, Liliana hugged Sophia goodbye, her friend destined to stay behind in Huntington Beach and work in her father's grocery.

Son drove his daughter to Stanford, their Toyota loaded with her clothes, books and one acoustic/electric guitar and a small amp. These latter two items gathered dust in her closet all through college and graduate school.

After earning her doctorate in Physical Chemistry, she got an excellent job with a large Bay Area research laboratory, married a physicist from Seattle, and had two children.

She would play her guitar at home and sing, mostly when no one was around. But over the years her blues streak faded slowly into oblivion, becoming stories Liliana told at family dinners or at cocktail parties with friends and colleagues, stories about the diverging road not taken and the life of music beyond the white picket fence. And she never did get a tattoo.

***

Manu and his wife Rangi sat in the living room of their newly purchased California Bungalow, one of the few almost affordable homes in Huntington Beach. The house sat on a tall foundation, high enough to keep it from flooding during king tides. The bungalow was the last one on the street; the other lots had been redeveloped with multi-story steel-and-glass condos with their ground levels left open to accommodate tidal surges, even during tropical storms. And a neighborhood parking structure with charging stations had been built to hold more than three hundred electric cars and trucks.

The couple gazed at the last remaining boxes that needed to be unpacked. They had worked throughout the week setting up their new home, including a nursery for their expected child. In the end, there were three boxes of old clothes and personal items that wouldn't fit anywhere.

"Why don't you put them in the attic?" Rangi said. "We can deal with them later."

"Sure. There's an old ladder on the back porch."

Manu positioned the ladder in the hallway, climbed it, pushed back the trap door and pulled himself into the attic.

"Hey, there's a whole bunch of crap up here. Been here awhile."

"What is it?"

"Don't know. I'll bring a box down."

The couple moved to the living room and opened the box. It held square plastic cases containing silver discs along with what looked like some kind of computer accessories.

Manu struggled to open one of the cases and removed

the disc. Across its surface was scrawled "Memories of Bessie."

"I wonder what's on this thing?" he murmured.

"My Grandfather's old laptop probably can play it. I know just where it is." Rangi hurried off and returned with the dusty MacBook.

Manu plugged it in and connected it to their entertainment center's sound system. He inserted the disc and fumbled with the keys until blue sounds from a wine-red voice poured from the large speakers. The couple leaned back on the sofa, held hands, closed their eyes and let the music wash over them. After three songs, they were hooked.

Open Mind

Tisha Marie Reichle-Aguilera

Valeria sits in a chaise lounge on the back patio of her modest home in West Los Angeles. It's a warm fall evening, so she's barefoot in loose pants and t-shirt. A glass of whiskey over ice sits on the side table, sweat dripping onto the ceramic coaster. She reads, ignores her cell phone's buzzing and beeping.

Francisco joins her with a beer, still wearing his slacks and button-up shirt from work.

Valeria lifts one cheek for a kiss and asks half-heartedly, "How was happy hour?"

Francisco kisses her and untucks his shirt. "Fine. Same. You know my co-workers. One complains about his wife. Another about their husband. And Sandra reminds us all why she's still single." He gulps the next swig hard.

Valeria puts a finger to hold her page and holds the book away. "She go home with someone new?"

"Every Friday."

"I hope she's protecting herself." Her phone buzzes and beeps. "You ever wish you could go home with someone new like Sandra?"

"Sandra? No. She's totally not my type."

"I meant the way she does." Valeria smirks. "But *someone* then?"

Francisco can't make eye contact. "No. No one." He sits at her feet, takes one absently in his not beer hand. "Why? Do you?"

Valeria bookmarks her page and puts the book in her lap. She takes a drink and sets the glass down half empty. Her phone buzzes and beeps again. She glances at it but doesn't pick up.

Francisco glares at it. "You gonna answer that?"

"I used to."

"Used to?" He drops her foot.

"Want someone new… Someone else … Someone less serious… Less… permanent."

"When?"

"A long time ago, like when we were first—doesn't matter."

"It does matter! Why didn't you tell me?"

She shrugs. "No need. I got over it. Let myself fall in love with you again."

"Again?" He gulps more beer. "When did you fall *out* of love with me?"

Valeria leans back in the chaise. "I really wasn't out-out, just curious about what else could happen, I guess. I saw our college friends break up and find new love, my coworkers were dating. It looked like fun. You were the only guy I'd ever been with. I was curious." She sits forward. "Haven't you ever been … curious?"

"What? Why would you ask that?"

"Because you've already been with a bunch of other women. Had your wild days. Guess I wondered what that'd be like."

He drinks the rest of his beer with a pained face. "I wasn't really all that 'wild.'"

Valeria's phone buzzes and beeps again. She picks it up, looks at the screen, grins, and puts it face down on table. "Maybe I wanna be wild."

"What? No."

Valeria takes a sip of whiskey, checks her phone, and replies. She slides her other foot in his not-beer hand.

He rubs absently and sips his beer. "Let's say I have."

She continues reading. "Have what?"

"Been curious." He gulps.

She takes a long drink. "Curious about what?"

He gulps again. "Like … I heard people … talk about … open marriage." He rubs her foot harder.

"Ouch!" Valeria jerks her foot back. "Heard who talk?" Her phone buzzes and beeps.

He side eyes it. "People. You know. Like at work. At the bar."

Valeria pours herself more whiskey and checks her phone. "What'd they say?"

"About what?"

"Open marriage. Like were they advocating for it or criticizing someone?"

Francisco gulps. "They asked if we ever considered it."

Valeria sits up and narrows her eyes at him. "Like I could have another man? Here?"

"No! Not here."

Valeria's phone buzzes and beeps. She checks it again. "Why not?"

"I don't know. Just not here."

"Would we only be with others in seedy motels like the Snooty Fox?"

"How do you know about that?"

"I drive around. See things. Plus, I like irony—how you get to be "snooty" when people pay by the hour?"

Francisco side eyes her again.

"Or we'd only do it on a dark street in the car real quick?"

"You make it sound dirty."

She sips. "Isn't that what you want?"

"No! Just thought you might want to consider it."

"Clearly *you've* considered it." She sips again. "Have you decided who you want to be 'open' with?"

"What? Seriously? No."

"It's the skinny blonde receptionist from that real estate office next door to you, isn't it?"

"What? Seriously? No."

"I can see why." Valeria looks the length of her own body, rubs a free hand over her abdomen and across her thighs. "She looks fragile. Needy."

Francisco gulps. "Why would you think that?"

"It's her voice." Valeria imitates her high nasal squeak. "Ooh, baby! Yes, baby! Like that, baby!"

"Stop!" Francisco chokes on his beer. "Why you do that?"

Valeria checks her phone again. "I'd ask … Davis."

"Davis? From freshman summer program?" He scoffs. "Is that who's been blowing up your phone?"

"No. He friended me on Facebook. Just moved back to LA and asked if I want to get coffee or something." She repeats suggestively, "Or something."

"No. Not that guy.

Valeria checks her phone again and smiles. "You don't get to choose who I 'open' with."

Francisco shifts like he wants to grab the phone and see who she's texting. "But I get a veto. We each get one veto."

Valeria laughs. "Okay. Then I veto the skinny blonde receptionist."

"Wait? What? No."

Valeria narrows her eyes. "You've already talked to her about this haven't you?" She stands up. "You are really thinking about cheating on me with another—a younger—woman. Aren't you?"

"What?" He says meekly, "No."

Valeria slips on her sandals. "No?"

He says more quietly, "It's not cheating if your marriage is open."

She pours another glass full of whiskey.

"So what— What do you think? Maybe we consider it?"

Valeria finishes her drink. "Maybe you need to consider giving me a reason to stay in this marriage at all."

Going South

Julio Puente García

It is 4:30 a.m. and nothing can beat the sweet sound of the alarm this Saturday morning. You better be ready, Chavelilla! Starting today, no more complaints because I'm too tired to take you out after my 10-hour shift packing cantaloupes under the sun. Forget about all those random cuts on my fingers, my palms, and my arms or the twangy voice of that idiot of Mando yelling at me: "Mueva las manos, Tortillera!" Our senior year is about to start; and then, I will see you every day, but even that can wait. As soon as I hold the check in my hand, I'll be on my way to collect those tickets and together we will go south.

—Concha, it's late, move it!

As usual, he got up earlier. I can feel the engine of his eighteen-wheeler shaking our entire mobile home. He's preparing for another long day at the transportation company. No more field work for the man of the house.

I jump out of bed and get dressed with the same clothes I've been wearing all summer; some faded blue jeans that used to be his and my Fresno State hoodie that I received for my middle school graduation three years ago.

My mom is back in bed, but my lunchbox is not covered in mud anymore. I can smell the two burritos con chorizo that she prepared for me while arguing with my dad. "Esa muchacha no va a ningún lado," I heard him saying. But he's wrong on this one. I'm going.

I knock on my mom's door twice as a way of saying thank you and see you later.

I open the door of the mobile home and ignore him.

My mighty Toyotita 78 is ready. I know it can make it through the mountains and take us to Los Angeles. I washed it real nice yesterday. Once the sun was down, I snuck out of the house to hide the things that I need for the weekend. There should be plenty of space for my girl's stuff. This morning I just need to make one last effort, pick up the ladies and drive to the cantaloupe field to finish packing those damned melons before noon. That way, we can make it to the concert on time.

I look at the rearview mirror and he's there blocking my exit. He doesn't want to move one inch, but he has to let me breathe. That's why I bought the car with half of the money I earned this summer. That money, he thinks, should have been used to pay the bills. He's still mad at me and it's not only because of the car. He can't forget what happened in the cotton fields during bloom season. I know that deep inside he's proud that I've made it through my first harvest, but he won't admit it. "His only daughter, how can I humiliate him in front of his comadre, my Nina Angie, and the rest of the crew?"

He finally gives up some space and I hurry to leave his property.

Like every morning for the past two and a half months, I drive towards Chavelilla's home in the outskirts of town. I can't stop in front of her house. I'm not welcome there. But I like to pass by and contemplate her fine figure through her bedroom window. She knows it. As soon as she hears the Toyotita, she turns on the lights, gets up from the bed and slowly drops her bathrobe; the one that I paid for with a third of my first paycheck. From over here she looks smaller; it might be the effect of her black hair going all the way down to her lower back, one of my favorite spots. This morning, she has her head-phones on. Dancing on top of the bed, she's showing me those slender legs of hers. "Carcacha, paso a pasito; ¡no nos vayas a dejar!" Oooh, yeah, Selena's waiting for us tonight, girl!

***

It's rush hour in Mendota, our hometown, the place where Joaquín Murrieta used to ride his mustang and terrify the bullies of the region. There are few horses left here, along with a bunch of beat-up trucks, large vans, and former school buses rolling in the dark in search of day laborers.

In about thirty minutes I drive around town and pick up Doña Miguelina, la Betty, and my cousin Sonia. My Nina is sick again and today she couldn't make it. She's been like that since the sunstroke. We stop for coffee and pan dulce at the only gas station in town. A few men standing on the curb with their baseball caps on and their watery red eyes looking at us ask in Spanish if we need a pair of extra hands. "Not right now, I say, we'll finish the field today." When we leave the place, Doña Miguelina and I stay behind and that's when she asks me if things are getting better at home. I smile to thank her for her concern, but I say no. "No importa, I tell her. I'm living my own life, and I won't apologize for what I feel."

The town lies behind us. On both sides of the one-lane road we can see the harvest coming to an end: the asparagus has been left to grow and each furrow looks like a tiny forest; in the tomato fields there is nothing but crushed plants piled on the corners, while the garlic sacks sit quietly waiting to be taken to the canneries.

We arrive fifteen minutes before we start working. Alongside the water canal, there have to be more than twelve cars waiting like us, like me. I can see a few men, the Tractoristas, most of them in their fifties, walking towards the section of the field that we're harvesting today. They're dragging their work boots on their way to the tractors that pull the Máquinas Meloneras where us, women, pack up the cantaloupes with rage. Below us, bend-down men pick up the fruit sometimes without saying a single word for hours.

216

It's not even 6 a.m., but I'm starting to sweat. The air in the car is getting heavier, too. All the ladies rest their heads against the windows, so I decide to open mine. Instead of enjoying fresh air, we all smell the rotten flavor of cantaloupes. Betty starts coughing hard and it seems like she might vomit again. She opens the door and goes to do her thing. That first trimester is treating her badly.

After a couple of minutes, Sonia speaks:

—Over there! He's driving that new Chevy truck.

—Yeah, I say, that's el pinche Mando. The contractor's older son. I wonder if the checks are already in the glovebox.

—Doubt it, says Sonia. I bet last night he went to the casino again.

—He better have had a lucky night, I reply.

Mando leaves as soon as the tractors move and the crew starts packing the cantaloupes, but not before yelling from his truck: "Make her *work*, let'er *earn it*! Yeah, *you* Tortillera!" "¡Cállate, animal!, I respond. Go sleep off your hangover with your daddy and your wuilas!"

***

It's 9 o'clock and everyone is sweating through their hoodies or bleeding from the cuts caused by the cardboard boxes where we pack the cantaloupes. I got a big one today on my left hand between my thumb and my index finger. It hurts every time I lift or push one of the boxes that contain seven or nine melons, depending on the size. I'm sure my Chavelilla will fix the cut tonight once we get to LA, maybe even before that.

The ladies, especially the older ones, wish to take a break. "Let's finish this thing, I say, and go home early. It's Saturday, Doña Migue, maybe you can make it to Madera to buy that rocking chair that you've been talking about." She tries to smile back, but going into her late sixties, she is too tired. She was a veteran already when my mom began working in the fields the first year my family arrived in the Central Valley and my dad did not have any other choice but to allow her to work among men.

The rest of the crew agrees, and we keep picking and packing without a break. We all lend Doña Miguelina a hand. Not that she gives up. Never does. But she appreciates it and lets us know by sharing a bunch of tamales con carne she brought for lunch. We eat them with one hand and pack with the other.

One, two, three, six full trucks carrying hundreds of cantaloupes leave the field with a cloud of dust behind. As planned, we finish the whole thing early. It's only 11:30 a.m. We made it. I made it. It's my last week before going back to finish high school. For most of the crew, however, this is just another harvest. The lucky ones who have their papers will apply for unemployment to make it through the winter. The rest will either go to Washington to harvest apples in the fall or go back south to visit their families before trying to cross the border one more time next year.

We wait for Mando first on the Máquina Melonera and then we get tired and sit down in the cars eating our lunches. Without trees around here, it's getting hotter; 106 degrees at noon on this shiny day. Some men leave their cars and walk to the field to lay down below the tractors. If my Chavelilla were here, we would already be there exchanging hugs and some besitos under the shade.

It takes five phone calls to find Mando, and when he shows up he tells us that he ran out of cash yesterday.

—You, bastard!

Tranquila, Tortillera. Why don't you ask Chavela for money? I heard she's getting some lately. And I don't think it's a compensation for the cotton field fiasco!

I want my money, cabrón! It's not like we're doing volunteer work here. I need it!

Everyone does. But don't worry, you can cash it in three days. Tuesday afternoon should be fine, mi gente!

Shit, three days? I can't wait that long.

***

I drop off the ladies at their homes and thank Doña Miguelina for allowing us to finish early. I drive with my cousin Sonia to La Tapatía, the supermarket and butcher's shop where I preordered the tickets to see Selena, my girl's beloved singer. The place is full of housewives carrying sacks of corn meal and potatoes or small quantities of meat and chiles secos. Almost none of them buy fruit or vegetables; they get them from their husbands or sons or the neighbors who harvest the entire Valley.

—¡Hey, Conchita, ahi tan sus boletos, mija!

—Gracias, Doña Mari. But first, I need you to cash me this check.

—Mando's? No, mija, that pinche guevón has no credit here. I'm thinking of hanging his ugly picture on that wall, along with that one of the ox, so people don't ask me to cash his checks anymore.

But I *really* need this money, Doña. Help me out only this one time. It's for the tickets.

Can't do it, mija. It'd be like throwing this meat in the dumpster.

Órale pues, I get it. Can I at least use your phone?

The phone rings several times and no one answers. My heartbeat rises. Where are you, babe? After the third try, I hear her voice, and my spirit is in good shape again.

I can't talk right now. Mom's here.

Are you ready though? I have a big surprise for you tonight.

Umm… yeah. What is it?

Can't tell you, but you'll enjoy it all night long.

Oh, that?

No, no. Well, that too, but it's something else.

Got to go now.

O.k., but promise that you'll be ready by 5 p.m. Pack your stuff for the weekend and I'll…

She hangs up. My cousin Sonia is staring at me.

—Are you sure about this, Conchita? You've been wasting all your money this summer. First, the golden necklace and the earrings, then the cowgirl outfit. Even the car that you bought was because of her. And, honestly, you don't see her that much lately.

I needed the car. A girl gotta move on her own. You think your mom could lend me the money?

Naaah, don't think so. My dad's working, but she's been on and off since she fainted in the field.

I drive Sonia to her home to see my Nina Angie. It's getting late, almost 3 p.m.

We open the door of the one-room apartment and see my Nina reclined on her three-legged sofa watching TV. Sonia and I broke the fourth leg when we were around nine. She got punished for that, but my Nina never mentioned it to my parents. I can smell the Hot Cheetos from the entrance. After the sunstroke, the doctor told my Nina that there wasn't much to do. That she just needed to drink lots of water and consume Cheetos to recover her salts and minerals. It's been almost two months, but my Nina keeps taking her medicine.

Sonia leaves us to take a shower and I sit down in a low wooden stool pretending to watch the TV. My Nina gets up from the sofa, turns on the fan and brings me a cold soda. She asks about the workday: "How did the ladies do, how many truckloads were we able to complete, did we beat the other Máquinas Meloneras?" I tell her about Mando's issues with cash, I tell her that I need the money, that I could pay her on Tuesday afternoon once I cash the check in the bank, but she says "sorry, mija; I've spent all my savings in the past two months."

I say goodbye and drive away.

Maybe my mom has money hidden somewhere or with some luck she can convince my dad.

On my way home, I'm tempted to stop at La Tapatía to call Chavelilla again. But without any good news, I don't see the purpose. It's almost 4 p.m. I'm not in a hurry anymore. Perhaps one day Selena will visit Fresno and then I'd take Chavelilla to dance some cumbias tejanas with me.

I arrive home, but the door is closed. It's over. My mom is probably visiting one of her friends before my dad comes back. He won't be here until 7 p.m.

Under the heat, I drive around town with the four windows of my Toyotita down. The streets are empty at this hour. The engine's temperature is rising. I have to slow down ten miles per hour. I decide to go to Chavelilla's house; she must be waiting under the shade of the old olive tree. I don't know what I'm gonna tell'er. I have no money in my pocket. Only this uncashable check. The car is going even slower now. I make the next turn and that's when I see her holding hands with Mando. That bitch! She's wearing the cowgirl clothes that I bought her. They're going to the Saturday Rodeo in Bakersfield! My hands are shaking, and it's not because my mighty Toyotita is falling apart. A stabbing pain moves through my fingers, my palms, and my arms as if all the summer work had accumulated, but that's nothing if you compare it with what I'm beginning to feel.

Satisfaction

Mary Camarillo

After teasing and spraying for what seemed like hours, the beautician finally turned the chair around so Olivia could see herself in the mirror. Instead, she saw her mother's face, surrounded by a shellacked helmet of hair, flipped at the ends in perfect symmetry. When she touched the side of her head her hand came away sticky, leaving a palm shaped indentation in the helmet.

"Leave it alone," the hairdresser warned, picking out the dent with a teasing comb.

"I like it," her mother said, hesitantly, when she came to pick her up. "You've been trying to get that style for years."

Which was true, Olivia thought. She finally looked like the popular girls back in Charlotte did two years ago, with their perfect bobs that she'd never been able to replicate on her own. The problem was they didn't live in Charlotte anymore. It was 1966, and they lived in California now, where girls wore their hair long and straight, and parted down the middle. She was pretty sure that even in Charlotte the girls were wearing their hair long and straight now too.

"It suits you," the hairdresser said.

"I hate it." She ripped off the black vinyl cape and ran out of the salon but her mother's car was locked. She waited in the strip mall parking lot while her mother paid. The asphalt stuck to the bottoms of her sandals and the sun was hot on her face. She'd laid out too long next to the pool yesterday, freckling and then frying her skin. Next, she would blister and after that, peel.

"Please don't tell your father how much this cost," her mother said when she finally unlocked the car. "Everything in California is so much more expensive."

Olivia sighed. Every single conversation in the Armstrong household revolved around what things cost, even though the move to California had supposedly meant a huge promotion for her father.

"I guess I'm going to have to make a left turn," her mother said as she backed the brand-new blue Bel Air out of the parking space, clenching the steering wheel even tighter. California had turned her into a timid driver. "Or maybe I'll just turn right and make a U-turn at the light.

"I hate it," Olivia said, again.

"The traffic? We'll get used to it, honey," her mother said, not taking her eyes off the road. "It's an adjustment, for all of us. Once school starts you and your brothers will make new friends. You'll settle right in." At the red light, her mother glanced over at her and attempted a hopeful smile, but there was nothing convincing in her haggard face. The light turned green and the car behind them honked.

Her mother stepped on the gas and the car jerked forward. "Why are people here so rude?

"I didn't mean that I hate California," Olivia said. "I hate my hair."

"I was only trying to do something nice for you." Her mother frowned. "I don't know why I even bother. No one appreciates anything I do."

Olivia knew an apology was expected but her mother wasn't being honest at all, she was playing the martyr role. Again. The trip to the hair salon wasn't meant as a treat for Olivia, it was her father's idea. Last night, she'd overheard him whispering to her mother in their bedroom adjacent to hers, asking if something couldn't be done about Olivia's hair.

It was a frequent complaint. Olivia's hair was fine and tangled easily and everyone had an opinion about what was wrong with it. She needed a perm. She needed to cut it. She should grow it out. She stared out the passenger window. Roy Orbison was on the radio, singing about a pretty woman walking down the street. That will never be me, she thought, although it was kind of creepy how Roy expected the woman to stay with him and be "his" tonight. Maybe she was better off not being pretty.

As soon as they were home she jumped out of the car and ran into the house, straight up the stairs to the bathroom. She knelt down next to the tub and turned the water on full blast, then stuck her head under the faucet.

Her mother was there immediately, screaming, "Olivia Byrd Armstrong! What are you doing? Your father hasn't even seen it yet."

"I don't care."

"I don't know what has come over you. All that money, straight down the drain."

"Literally," Olivia said.

Her mother slapped her hard, across the face. "Don't get smart with me, young lady."

They looked at each other, equally shocked. Her mother hadn't slapped her since she was six years old. She almost said she was sorry but her mother wheeled around and walked out of the bathroom, slamming the door behind her.

Olivia got a towel and dried her hair. When she opened the bathroom door her brother Harrison was standing there, waiting.

"You're in trouble," he said, impressed. She was never in trouble. She was the one who got him and Hank in trouble.

"Get out of my way," she said, brushing past him.

Harrison looked shocked, which made her feel good. She was tired of always being so predictable. This was new ground. She went into her bedroom and closed the door, her heart beating fast. She and her brothers were supposed to keep their bedroom doors open. She clicked on the tiny transistor radio next to her bed. "Satisfaction" was just starting, a song her mother hated, so she cranked up the volume.

Keith Richard's opening guitar riff repeated three times, so urgent and furious that she could not stand still. She dropped the wet towel to the floor and danced in front of the mirror, waving her arms overhead, imitating the kids on Soul Train. Someday, someone would ask her to dance and be amazed at her moves.

Her father's voice now, home from work, downstairs in the kitchen, talking to her mother, clearing his throat, something he did when he was angry. "A herd of elephants," he'd said before. She stopped dancing.

Mick Jagger sang "I can't get no," which didn't make sense. He was a rock star after all, flying around the world, making tons of money. He could get whatever he wanted. Maybe he was just the same as her father, never satisfied no matter what. Maybe all men were like that. And what exactly was *girly action*? She wasn't sure if she'd actually want to have it with Mick or Keith, but she doubted they'd want to have it with her anyway.

Her mother knocked on the door.

"What!" she said, knowing this tone would get her in even more trouble.

Her mother pushed the door open. "Please turn that down."

Olivia reached for the volume knob. Maybe the lyrics meant the exact opposite. It was a double negative after all. *Can't get no satisfaction* meant that Mick could get some.

Her mother sat down on Olivia's bed. "Your father never even got to see how pretty your hair looked."

"I looked like an old woman," Olivia said. "And I'm not pretty."

"Of course, you are," her mother said, because she had to, because it was a requirement for beautiful mothers to say that their daughters were pretty, especially when they weren't. "Sit down." She patted the comforter. "You're pretty and smart and funny and generous." Her mother put one arm around Olivia shoulder and hugged her close.

Olivia stiffened. She didn't feel any of those things and she really didn't feel like hugging anyone right now. Her mother's change in attitude was confusing. She obviously wanted something. "Next you'll be telling me I have a great personality."

"You do have a great personality."

"That's how boys talk about girls who were are less than average looking."

"I wish you wouldn't be so hard on yourself." Her mother pulled away and stood. "Meatloaf for dinner. Comb your hair and come set the table."

"I'll be there in a second." Olivia stood up and stared in the mirror over her dresser. She wasn't hard on herself, she was realistic. Her nose was already peeling which would either shrink up her pores or turn them into pimples. She wished she could shed all of her skin. Maybe there was someone smarter and bolder in the next epidermal layer. Maybe it would be dewy and fresh instead of full of blackheads. She combed her hair straight back off her face. Now she looked less like her mother and more like her dad.

Downstairs, her brothers and father were watching the Dodgers on the television in the living room. "What's the score?" she said.

"Tied up in the fourth," Hank said. He looked at her and cackled. "Your hair looks weird."

Her father took his eyes off the television and glanced at her briefly. She thought she saw a small spark of recognition in his eyes but it was gone before she was sure.

"Your mother needs help in the kitchen," he said.

Nuclear Family

Audrey Gains

The television vibrated with a mechanical fuzz that lingered through blackened screens and moments of silence. The electricity quietly popped and radiated from the box, heating her skin from her shag-carpeted front row seat. Darkness consumed the room, licking at the floor around her, stopping at the glow of the tube that painted her skin a green, a blue, a red with each flashing image. The all-consuming murk fought with the all-consuming television.

It comforted her in times like these, where the status of her parent's thin-threaded marriage reflected the state of the world. Who could care about death and defiance and that hussy of a secretary when you could drown yourself in the lives of others? Tuning out was a skill she developed quickly.

Her father had bought the television back in '68 when they moved into their Pillsbury Street house. It was a nice model for the time, fitting perfectly in their little house. Two bedrooms, a bathroom, living room, kitchen, garage, and quaint yards. That was before her before, of course, which was stressful and unplanned, when they only had the boy. Her brother was two when they moved in, a time when his fat little legs tumbled through the halls and his laughter echoed.

Her mother cried when she got the positive result two years later– her sister babysat as she snuck off to the doctor. The doctor (God Bless His Soul) told her the news and she smiled, thanking him for his help. He comfortably left her to her own bearings, wishing her a good day. As soon as the door clicked shut the tears fell, muffled and embarrassed and brief, then her mother left with a polite nod to the lady at the front desk.

The television, now outdated with scuffs like stretch marks across the edges, was her only friend at the ripe age of five. Five and three quarters, to be exact. They moved it from its firm place in the living room to the children's room because of her inability to leave it. Even through the loudest and mean-spirited fights, she sat, glued to the screen. Her father grumbled on and on about her unruly addiction, but rather explaining the swears he would say to his wife, he simply moved the box in between the two beds.

Sundays were a bittersweet day for her. They began without words, just the motions of a morning. Breakfast, which included wonderful political commentary on her fathers part ("Finally some fuckin' brains on Ford"), then church. Church dragged on, just a couple hours of sitting and rising, sitting and rising, some mumbling and stiff clothing. She never understood what the priest said, rather she focused on the projections of color dripping from the tall stained glass windows. Each panel painted scenes of the Man, the one with the great beard and sad eyes. Her favorite panel was after the one of the Man sprawled on the cross with a sullen face; it was the one of him in the arms of a woman. She cradled the Man, bright blue tears casted onto the dusty floor, and held his deadened body. If she was any closer the woman would kiss him. The Manwasweakenedandthinned over himself like a piece of paper folded multiple times. The woman, though, was covered severely, wrapped in white blankets, bundled like a baby. Their faces, long and conjoined, gushed through with morning light, so full of sorrow.

That must be love, she would think every week from the pews, they must be in love. When church ended her brother would disappear with other kids his age and she would stick with her parents, who always put on the best show ever. Even at five and three quarters, she knew it was all bullshit.

Her mother would chatter with the rest of the ladies in pencil skirt dresses, adorned with Jackie-O hats and baby powder perfume, boasting about how their husbands have everything right in the world. Her father would exchange whispers with the men, occasionally barking out with a deep-bodied laugh.

Together, the two would morph into each other. His hand adjusted just right on her hip, her head laying itself on his shoulder; both situating the girl in front of them, screwing her into place. It was as if she dared to leave, they would unravel on sight. That was the most physical contact she'd see them have all week.

"God Bless this Country" was a phrase passed around like "Amen," churchgoers seemingly more American than Christian. She assumed the Man was American.

Her brother would return and the whole family would bid farewells with smiles and laughs, piling into their car for a silent return home. Her brother, in his Napoleonesque rage, would storm out of the car and join up with his Pillsbury street gang to patrol the neighborhood for a smaller kid or an unfortunate black child to torment. Her mother would silently resign to the master bedroom. The girl never knew what her mother did for the rest of her Sunday mornings, but she never asked, knowing how precious that alone time must've been. Her father would hide out in the garage until the sun would set, sipping beers and listening to the radio before finding something to parade back into the house for. He'd pick on her mother for the food, the government, her lazy-good-for-nothing-communist father, sex, the neighbors, how long the grass was growing. Dinner was at six every Sunday night, some rendition of casserole. The time from noon to then was dedicated to the television. She loved it, craved it. It rotted her brain and she adored it.

Her favorite were the cartoons. She'd catch the tail end of a Scooby-Doo, and she remained infatuated with the womanly shape of Daphne. At commercial call she would race to the mirror to check if her breasts grew in yet. But she remained boxy, pudgy around the middle. Usually a new episode of The Jetsons would roll on after, zooming by with stainless wonder. She loved the idea of a future like that, so fixable and so clean.

In '88 she died, alone and away from the television set. She was on the cusp of adulthood, fresh with a license and a car her father bought to prove a point. The crash was swift and vibrant, and in the last hour of her life she immediately relapsed back into the innocence of five and three quarters. Her fancy new automobile wrapped itself around a tree eight miles away from Pillsbury street, and her position behind the steering wheel mangled her whole face into distortion.

It took the ambulance twenty-three minutes to arrive and in those twenty-three minutes the only thing she could think about were Sundays as she sat perched on top of the hood. She thought about the Man, only finding solace in her old interpretation as she realized the weight of a tree branch on her back and the pressure of the airbag against her abdomen. For a second she regretted all of the time she spent behind the screen, but that was only for a second. She then tried to recall the plot of a Disney flick she had seen in theaters earlier that week.

She was completely out when the rescue team listed the metal away from her, disrobing her from folds of bark and glass. Despite her lack of consciousness, she felt everything. Every tough, every needle prick, the compressions pushing her frail ribs. At one point she could feel the inner workings of her frantic organs; her lungs barely being able to expand, her heart pumping urgently, attempting to revive something. There was a sharp pain where reasoned was her liver, something flowing out of the area like water through a broken dam.

They found her license long after her heart stopped, nestled between a compact and a TV guide in the glovebox. Around eight in the morning, her mother and father scurried into the hospital to see her tied to machines, the flatline's volume turned off out of respect. They sobbed, as you would assume, knitted together for the first genuine time. Her mother was most disturbed by the fact she couldn't recognize her, and her father was mostly angry that all the time he spent teaching her to drive was a waste.

Eventually the hospital had to move her body to the morgue, as there were alive people who needed the room, and the ceremony for her life was sweet; a mourning ritual any Roman would've been proud of. Her dad threw out the television a month later, which had since been retired deep in the garage when a new one was bought. And their lives went on.

Girl Power

Regina Garza Mitchell

She was probably more surprised than anyone to learn at the age of sixteen that she could say no.

She was not surprised to realize that nobody wanted to hear that from her.

"You'll have to get," her mother paused before whispering, "an abortion."

She shook her head slowly, trying to process that her mother said that word. Her mother had been raised Catholic and was very against abortion. "No." She had not planned to say the word. Had not planned to find herself in this position. She knew several girls who had gotten abortions, had even loaned some of them money to help them afford it. Although she hadn't expected to find herself pregnant at sixteen, she had somehow assumed that she would simply be able to get an abortion if she found herself in that unwanted position. Never wanted kids or marriage. Never wanted to wind up like her parents or to add more people to a planet filled with people who seemed intent on destroying it.

But when she figured out that the nausea was not a stomach virus, that something was growing inside of her, abortion wasn't an option. Her decision had nothing to do with her Catholic upbringing or Abuela's insistence that her grandchildren have lots of babies when they grew up. Sixteen wasn't grown up. She still had a year of high school left and college applications to fill out. But she felt a protective responsibility for the creature developing inside of her. Was awed that something so marvelous could be happening when everything else was shit.

"What do you mean 'no'?"

She took a deep breath. "No, I will not have an

abortion."

"Who's the father?"

"It doesn't matter."

Her mother gasped. "You don't know, do you?" She crossed herself. "You're no better than the women on the corner downtown."

Tears sprung to her eyes, but she said nothing. She knew who the father was, but he was too much a kid himself. She didn't want him in the picture. This was the nineties. Girls—women, she reminded herself—could raise a child on their own. Girl power and all that shit.

She held firm, saying "no" whenever her mom told her she was getting an abortion or asked who the baby's father was. Her friend Carmen once told her it would get easier to say no after the first time, but it didn't. She didn't tell Carmen or any of her other friends about it. She did not trust them not to spread it around the school. She knew how it went. Even your friends would call you names.

Her mother insisted she go to the doctor. She knew what a gynecologist was but had never had an exam. It was a nightmare.

The doctor was about her mother's age, an old white guy in his forties. He let her mom stay in the room even though she told her mom to go. The doctor said she was a minor, so her mom could be there. When she cried at the pain he seemed to deliberately cause in the exam, he said, "Shut up and stop over-reacting. It's not that painful. Maybe you shouldn't have gotten pregnant if you didn't want to deal with the consequences." She looked to her mom who looked straight ahead, pretending this was not happening. The way she always had. So she retreated into her own head, the way she did when her dad used to hit her, or that time she woke up after a party to find that older guy doing it to her, the way she did when her mom berated and belittled her. But she still felt the pain when the doctor shoved his hand inside.

"Can I make her have an abortion?" her mother asked.

"I don't believe in abortion," the doctor replied, "but—"

"Neither do I," her mother said.

"But," he continued, "in this case, if I had my way I would force her to have one right now. Unfortunately, the law does not allow me to do that." He looked away from her mother and at her. "Women should not get abortions, but you are not a woman and you should not be allowed to have a baby." He mumbled something about welfare under his breath.

She lay there on the table, legs open with her private parts exposed to the doctor and her mother, and smiled. The doctor did not realize it, but he had given her what she needed. There was nothing they could do. She had said no to her mom, and even though the doctor thought she was scum and her mother thought she was a slut, this was her choice.

"No," she said. "We're done." She got up and put her clothes on.

Her mother talked all the way home about how she used to be so smart, had been skipped up a grade, was an honor student on the college track. Now she was throwing it all away. She couldn't take a baby to college.

"Then you at least have to marry him," her mother said. "Or give it up for adoption."

She looked at her mother and shook her head again. "No." And went inside to pack her clothes.

She still did not know what she would do, but she had a long bus ride to Abuela's house to figure it out.

Nocturne

Nick Young

It had come again, rising from within, a murmur—the awful scrabbling, the horrid *scritch, scritch, scritch*—a rat between the walls, desperate for a way out.

No exit.

No respite.

Only louder. And, as night descended, more relentless.

He had crouched for long minutes, gathering himself within the lingering, oppressive heat. The world was still. Silent. Expectant.

Then came the wind. At first a whisper before growing to a low moan up through the gully, driving the sere leaves beneath and the dead branches above to stir. Only the ivory rind of August moon caught their naked dance. He paused at the lip of the slope and turned his head back in the direction he'd come, back toward the yard with its deep grass that did not chafe and needle his feet.

He looked across the broad expanse of lawn, beyond the haphazardly tended garden and smooth stone of the patio to the house, its brick walls veined over by a thick ivy that rose from shadow and was engulfed by the gloom above the trees that shrouded it. He cocked his gaze higher, to an open second-story window and the dull glow of the bedside lamp within, its light muted by a scrim..

Pivoting to his left he turned away and began inching down the slope. A few feet, and then he twitched at a stab of pain, his right hand reflexively clutching at the brambles that ensnared his feet. His fingers felt the slick trickle of blood that oozed from an ankle. He brought it to his chapped lips, an elixir.

And an excitant, mingling with his sweat, glistening, oleaginous, his pores alive with its musk. He drew a deep lungful, then froze, senses alive.

A muffled snuffle. To his left. Near. His breath stopped. Nothing moved save the *scritch, scritch, scritch* inside his head. The rat never ceased.

Never ceased.

Never ceased.

Never.

It moved again…small, furtive, it moved. A slight shuffle of leaves, and the snuffle. His ear attuned, following, calculating. Soon it would be his. But he dare not move. Not now. Not this close. The snuffle…rustle of the sere leaves. A freshening of the wind brought the scent to him while overhead the naked dance of dead branches resumed below the ivory rind of August moon. Eyes darted down, left. Blackness too deep to see. Only feel. Closer. Slight shuffle…tiny snuffle—*now*!

Snakelike, the left hand struck, fingers clutching as his cracked, jagged nails bit into the soft flesh of the thing. It twisted, tiny clawed feet madly scraping against his tightening grasp. In its throat, a gurgle, whimpering terror.

Soon enough, it was over.

Its lifeless body hung limp, moist, still warm. But now it was of no interest. With its vital force crushed away, he cast it aside. They might find it, the men who had come searching for signs of him before, crashing through these woods with their shouts and dogs, but they would not find him.

A wraith.

The itch to move flared. Rising to a half-crouch, he let his eyes seek their way through the gloom. His felt the ache in his legs from immobility but shook it off as he picked his way through the underbrush that choked the rim of the gully.

He worked west, pausing every few feet to listen, ears keen to the vibrations of the night. But there was nothing, save the sigh and ebb of the wind and the distant yap of an old hound somewhere far beyond where the road wound serpentine among the big houses on spacious grounds cut from thick stands of oak and maple and ironwood.

He moved forward, bent, pausing, ears keen, the soles of his feet stung by nettles and the points of sharp sticks among the sere leaves. Twenty-five yards more, he halted, nostrils filled with the sour odor of his ragged breath.

Just ahead—there.

At a lonely corner where a wide lawn gave way to the wildness of the gully slope, a white pine grown to a height just above his head, lower branches pruned away. Beneath, cedar mulch overspread with long needles. He had come there before and now sought its shelter again, an oasis from his anguish, if only fleeting.

He crept under and curled himself onto the gentle bed, easing into the soft push of the needles against his moist skin. His breathing smoothed its tempo. He allowed his eyelids, sweat-crusted at the lashes, to flicker shut. Now came a zephyr, stirring to murmur the boughs above, coaxing him back through time.

Days of summer, the sun searing the back of his neck as he roamed the farmer's field that lay beyond his house, deep into the green July corn, rising to his thirteen-year-old waist. Tall enough. Finding his hallowed, hollowed spot far from the dusty farm lane, he laid himself down between the rows, burrowing his bare back against the rough soil, cool in the shade of the plants' broad leaves. Sheltered, he lay, lulled by the gentle rustle of the leaves and the pungent smell of earth. He could not be found now. He would stay hidden, safe from the thousand cuts of their world, the suffocation of its conformity.

His eyes closed. He drifted. An ant climbed noiselessly

over a ridge of dried clods, up onto the crook of his arm. With an idle hand he brushed it, flying, to land at the base of a nearby stalk, there to resume its meandering. He laid his hand on his chest and gave himself up to the doldrums.

There, in those moments, his mind quieted. The murmuring, the faint, insistent scrape of fingernails across sandpaper, sank back into uneasy silence. There his guard, so carefully cultivated and deployed, melted away. They did not know him—how could they? What would he tell them? How to begin to describe what he himself wrestled to comprehend? He only knew in his depths that he was dislocated from their world, driven to flee, to lose himself, to find a measure of serenity in brooding solitude.

But this night his respite was short.

The night was beginning to bend its arc back toward daybreak. His reverie was ending despite the inner yearning that somehow it could be stretched into eternity.

From down below, in the belly of the gully he heard scuffling…tiny yips.

Coyotes.

He knew them, had heard them many times as they ran down small prey in these woods, crying out in hunger lust and bloody triumph.

He must move. Stealth.

From beneath the pine, he emerged slowly. He listened keenly to their passage, below, heading east. Scuffling…tiny yips. He swiveled on the balls of his feet, steadied by his left hand, knuckles braced against sere leaves, raw earth. And when the pack had moved safely beyond, he resumed his creep.

He worked his way through the tangle of overgrown weeds and vines that raked his flesh and over fallen and rotting tree limbs just below the rim of the gully. Turning his head, he could see through the strands of sweat-matted hair dangling over his forehead that the ivory rind of August moon had slipped lower in the sky. The wind had fallen away to no more than a fitful murmur. Now the heat would begin to uncoil again and to stifle.

His time was growing short.

The house he sought came into view, across the gully, fifty yards. Swiveling, rising part way from his crouch, he started down the embankment, right foot leading to brake against the slope, against the steady pull of gravity. At the bottom, his feet sank in the muck of rotted leaves and runoff mud. Quickly through, and leaning into the upward angle of the opposite embankment, he scrabbled to the gully rim, over the rough planks of a low fence and onto fresh-cut grass, stirred by his quickening steps as he traversed the yard, bounding quietly onto the wide deck of the house, a single-story sprawl of weathered shake shingle.

This was the place.

Inside was his tormentor. The one who held sway over his daily existence. The one who exhorted, who cajoled, who squeezed. The one who decreed conformity. Between the corporate white lines. No deviation.. Do not stray. Do not *think* of straying.

And so it was, this asphyxiation . . . until the shroud of night fell and the whisper of the scritch, scritch, scritch became a shriek, compelling his transformation, driving him to crouch beneath the ivory rind of August moon near the glass doors of the perfect house with the perfect wife and the perfect life.

There he would make his response, wrapped within the indigo heat, a crude defilement. So, rising up slightly, he squatted and emptied himself onto the smooth wood.

It was done.

His lips curled into a faint smile, tongue raking over the

scum coating his teeth. He knew his time was short, attuned as he was to the subtle character of the darkness. And the dog, far off, took up his bark again, a sure sign of the new day's advance.

He did not linger, nor cast a second glance behind, letting the reek that filled his nostrils suffice as coda. Quickly, with practiced stealth and agility, he loped back across the lawn, over the low fence and into the trees. With no time to pause, he moved swiftly to retrace his steps, returning to the lip of the gully beyond which the big house stood. Then, amid the murk that separated night from day, he raced through the gathering dew, his feet threatening to lose their purchase on the slick grass, until he reached the base of the house. With a glance up toward the dull light that shone from the second-floor bedroom, he seized the thick tangle of ivy covering the brick wall, and he began to climb.

Dawn was coming soon enough, but there would be time to cleanse himself, to allow a few fitful minutes upon the pillow where the rat's incessant scrabble would ebb. And time to steel himself before he donned the accouterments of the day and fell in with the others as they shuffled numbly to their seats for the long train ride to the teeming city. He would find his way among the jostling throng to the sleek glass-and-steel tower, upward to the appointed floor and inside the cold fluorescence of the sprawling office where he would smile and nod at the banalities of the others, take his place inside his cubicle…and begin again.

The Hard Ass

Ute Orgassa

Arthur Holbroke closed his genuine leather teacher's bag with a satisfying snap. He had done it. Forty-five years of a successful teaching career. They had celebrated him earlier in the lounge with one of those unbearably sweet, cheap sheet cakes. He had taken two bites to be polite.

They meant well. He didn't care. Those teachers were not like him. They were weak, had frazzled looks, easy smiles, and were on their phones too much. 'They relied too much on wishy-washy waffling and had no idea how to keep order in the classroom. None of his former stalwart colleagues had made it as long as he had. He was the last remaining dinosaur, surrounded by all new people. He doubted that they would miss him. Well, the feeling was mutual.

Now he was leaving his classroom for the very last time. It was not even that late in the afternoon yet, 5:47 to be exact, and yet the sun had gone down already, and the streetlamps had buzzed into orange wakefulness. Those winter months never let him see sunlight. Arrive in the dark, leave in the dark. That would change now. Sweet retirement was calling for him.

He was happy that it was only the one bag on his last trip. He had already moved books and maps and boxes into his sedan earlier. First, he had offered them to his replacements. They didn't want them. They called his tools outdated. *It's all online now,* was the refrain he had heard.

Arthur Holbroke had no use for that. He had taught math and history, both foreign and American, for decades with these materials and he had refused to deal with these newfangled computer things since they first showed up and had caused waves of excitement among his colleagues.

He sighed, walked to the door, turned out the lights, and closed the door behind him. The hallway was empty, but lit. He walked it with measured steps and mixed feelings. Somewhere off, he heard music. Who was playing rock music now? I came from the direction of the gym. Was that seventies pop? Arthur couldn't stop himself. He went to investigate.

The hallway pulsed with the sounds of the long-forgotten band. They were crooning their farewells to some lovers. The bass thundering and reverbing all around Arthur, making his hair stand on edge.

The last door on the left of the hallway was practically pounding with the rhythm of the song. He marched resolutely towards it, got ready to yell, and opened the door. He was greeted by resounding quietness. After the earlier blast of noise, it felt like falling into a vacuum.

He lowered his accusing finger and let out the breath he had taken in anticipation. There was nobody there. Silence and empty chairs mocked him. He shook his head and turned.

"You're still the same hard ass you've always been," said a girl's voice.

Arthur swiveled his head and stared back into the class-room. There she sat, backwards on a desk, wearing ratty bell bottom jeans and a striped T-shirt with sunflowers appliqued on it. He turned to face her fully.

"Who are you? Where did you come from?" Arthur could have sworn there had been nobody there just seconds before.

"Don't you remember me? Come on."

She was so thin, her hair was lanky, falling to either side of her face. Her eyes had dark circles and were piercing him now. She was dangling her legs, and her face turned into a superior smile.

Arthur had no idea who she was, but that was no way a student was supposed to treat him. Last day or not. He was going to set her straight.

"Young lady, what are you doing here after hours?" he boomed. He took a step forward when she did not respond to this at all. Behind him the door snapped shut with a bang. Arthur startled but regained his composure.

"I'm here all the time," she said. "Because of your doing." She lit a joint and blew the smoke in his direction. It smelled of decay.

"Put that out immediately!"

"Still up to your old tricks, I see." The joint vanished. Then the girl did. Only to reappear a few desks closer to Arthur.

"Who are you? What are you?"

"I used to be Charlene Becker. You made sure I got in trouble for one lousy joint I smoked in the bathroom."

Charlene Becker, yes, he remembered her. Obnoxious, loud, and contrary. She never turned her homework in on time. Disrespectful brat who could not follow the rules. The kind of girl who could never fulfill the definition of ladylike. But that was decades ago. She would be in her fifties now. Not a teenager with a bad attitude and worse skin. Arthur's heart began to hammer. Something was definitely wrong here.

"What was it you wanted in the girl's bathroom anyway, Artie fartie? Hm? A bit of a looky look, a bit of a copping a feel?" she teased.

Arthur took a step back. There was a word forming in his mind and that word was hostile. He had never even thought of a girl bathroom like that. He only ever wanted to keep order and curtail the criminal element. The girl hopped off the desk and walked forward.

"You killed me! You sent me on the road to destruction that ended like this!"

She held out her arm, which was bound with a string at the biceps and had a syringe still stuck with a needle in the vein. Crusty blood surrounded the hole. Arthur stared at the arm for a split second, then fled the classroom.

"Run all you want," he heard her call after him.

This could not be real. No, this was a prank, someone was playing a prank on him. He held onto the hallway wall and took a couple of deep breaths. He wiped the cold sweat off his neck with his handkerchief. The physical world did not work like this. Logic dictated the girl could not be there. Best to ignore this and to just go to his car and go home. He walked a few steps and let out a big sigh. And Charlene was wrong anyway. What he had done was standard procedure, he told himself. It wasn't his fault she went off the straight and narrow. His breathing normalized; his heart rate went down.

A different sound reached his ear. An eighties one hit wonder climbed through the refrain into falsetto heights. This time his old classroom door opened by itself with a low creak. He went to close it again. Another girl stood in front of him. He yelped as he retreated from her. She wore ice cream pants and a Wham sweater. Her ponytail had at least one can of hairspray in it. He recognized her. Beth Miller.

"Hello Mr. Holbroke", she said. "Long time no see."

She held a notebook close to her body and walked towards him. He walked backwards; his eyes fixed on her piercing stare.

"Do you know what you did to me?" she asked.

He tried to think. She had always been a great student. Never had she given him any trouble. He even remembered her fondly. If he didn't hate the term teacher's pet, he would have sorted her into that category. But he must have done something wrong, he deduced by her still unrelenting accusatory stare. What was it?

"You don't even know how you ruined my life," she stated. He had no choice but to silently agree. He did not remember doing anything wrong.

"Three hours," she said. "My paper was three hours late and you refused to accept it. It ruined my grade. That brought down my GPA and that made me miss the cut-off point for the scholarship I needed. All of that for a lousy three hours. You could have just let it slide. But you didn't."

"One scholarship missed is not the end of the world," he countered. "I just followed the standard rules."

"Maybe not for you, but in my house with my parents, it was. The end of the world, my world. I was a loser, a failure, not worth it. Do you recall now?" Her sweet voice had turned icy.

"You didn't come back the next year."

Beth Miller marched forward, but her body twisted in strange ways, her legs turned outward, and her neck twisted at a forty-five-degree angle. Bruises bloomed all over her skin. Yet she still came closer. Arthur fled from her.

"I didn't do anything wrong," he uttered.

I ran into traffic," she yelled after him. "They pretended it was an unfortunate accident. It was easier for my parents that way. And nobody ever held you accountable, but it was your fault."

He ran all the way to the double front doors of the school. Against them leaned a boy wearing ripped jeans, a band shirt, and a red flannel. His blue converse had been written on in permanent marker.

"Where do you think you're going?" he asked. Then he sang along to the music blasting through the hallways. The band lyrics were wondering violently about what was happening.

Arthur would have liked to know that very much as well. The reality he was observing did not correspond to anything that was logical or made sense. And the fact of the matter that this had been going on for quite a while now, did not help. What he did know was that he knew the kid. He recognized the dark hair that fell across his face. The big eyes. Yes, it was Josh, what was his last name again? Whitmer? Yes, the Whitmer kid. An ice-cold shiver ran down Arthur's spine. He remembered what had happened to that boy. It had made the news back then and it had led to teacher training sessions he had hated.

"You killed yourself, didn't you?" he asked.

"No," Josh said. "You killed me. You got the ball rolling. I just finished what you started and brought it to its natural conclusion."

"I didn't kill you!"

"You saw me and Mark. We thought we were alone, but you saw us kissing and you reported it. You could have just forgotten about it. But no. You had to butt in and make our lives miserable. Do you have any idea what that meant? Being exposed like that? Having to go to confession about that? Being hounded, watched endlessly, and maligned and beat up about that? And for what? One kiss?"

Arthur thought about defending himself. About how reporting that had also been standard procedure. How it had been his responsibility to ensure morality at school. His duty to the parents. But he felt a lump in his throat that he could not speak around.

The strangulation marks on Josh's neck were now visible, angry, and red. He moved deliberately towards Arthur.

"If you had only minded your own business," he said. "Just let it go."

Arthur looked for a way out, his panic making everything spin and slow down at the same time. There was no way out. Beth came down the hallway from the left, Charlene from the right. Together with Josh, they formed a perfect triangle around him. The word equilateral flit through his mind for a split second.

"But you can't do that, now can you? Let students get away with things?" said Beth.

"Because you're a hard ass," added Charlene. "A boring, dull, unimaginative hard ass who only gets pleasure out of harassing the kids you were supposed to care about."

"Fitting everyone in a neat little box and cutting off all the parts that you don't think fit," added Josh.

"That's, that's not true," Arthur cried. "There are rules! We all must follow the rules. If we don't, everything crumbles. You all broke those rules and that is not my doing!"

They circled him now, coming closer and closer.

"One joint," said Charlene.

"Three hours", said Beth.

"One kiss," said Josh.

"One joint."

"Three hours."

"One kiss."

"One joint."

"Three hours."

"One kiss."

***

Ruby Meyers heard a shrill scream. The mop fell from her hands and clanged to the gym floor as she ran down the hallway. She found Mr. Holbroke lying in a heap on the floor by the front exit. His bag twisted around his arm and blood flowed freely from his ears. His face was a grimace of fright. He was also very much dead. Ruby shook her head and called it in.

Reduction

Bonnie Hearn Hill

"If you lost five pounds, you'd be perfect."

They stood nude on the balcony the morning after their wedding, overlooking the empty beach of San Quintín.

Maddie squared her shoulders, clenched her stomach even tighter, and reached for her robe.

That night, she and Arthur sat at one of the few occupied tables in the chilly, almost empty hotel dining room while mariachis serenaded them. Maddie picked at a bread stuffed clam while Arthur nodded to the strains of "Cielito Lindo" as if conducting.

She had won him over with food. When he and his then-girlfriend attended a class called Date Night Dining that Maddie taught at Sur La Table, Arthur had watched intensely as she explained that a reduction sauce was simply boiling down each ingredient—the herbs, the butter, the broth, the wine—to its essence. Feeling his gaze on her, she artfully spread crostini with goat cheese and chopped cherries. Then, she drizzled on the zinfandel sauce, its smell like fragrant needles stinging her nose.

His girlfriend, an almost invisible brunette, giggled, and Arthur gave her the kind of questioning look you might give an annoying stranger in a crowd.

"Unless you learn how to cook like that," he told the girlfriend, and motioned to the crostini, "I'm going to have to marry this woman."

Now, he had. Maddie quit the job at the store because he said they didn't need the money. Every weekend, they ate lunch on their patio, beside the Paradise manzanita with its shaggy bark of cinnamon red.

"Laugh lines," Arthur told her, studying her face under the lurking Santa Barbara sun. "They do age you."

After the surgery, she wanted only rest, that deep kind of sleep where you just ooze away into nothing.

Arthur heated some broth and told her she looked almost perfect.

More cuts. More stitches. Her eyes, her neck, her cheeks, parts of herself she could not see and he could not abide, all of them gone.

One day in early fall, Arthur sat across from her at the kitchen table, neat as the begonia plant on the stand beside him. He had steamed crab legs, set out the tiny mallet and gleaming stainless-steel picks.

Although Maddie could feel her arms, she could no longer see them. Only her mouth remained, a shrinking circle between them.

"That's it," Arthur said. "That's what was wrong all along."

And then, she realized there was only one way she could begin putting herself back together. She went for his eyes.

Rules Are Rules

Roberta H. Martínez

<u>CHARACTERS</u>

Victoria "Vickie" Ramos, Mexican-American, early elementary, clean and crisp "after school" clothes

Teresa "Terry" Vigil Ramos, Mexican American, early 30s, housedress & apron

Eduardo "Eddie" Ramos, Mexican American, early 30s, uniform work clothes

Paulita Vigil, older Mexicana, originally from Cd. Juarez, modest, well-worn house dress, dark sweater, glasses

<u>TIME</u>

1953, Fall

<u>PLACE</u>

Pasadena, California

<u>SETTING</u>

A modest and comfortable well-kept home. Household is established blue collar.

ALL RIGHTS RESERVED

SCENE I

AT RISE:

CHILDREN HEARD - "PATO, PATO, GANZO".

(VICKIE PLAYS PATO ON STAGE WITH CHAIRS).

VICKIE

I'm done.

TERRY

(off stage) Okay.

VICKIE

Hey, Mom... is it okay if I go and play with...

TERRY

(Enters) What've I told you about using the word "hey".

VICKIE

(Sighs) "Hay is for horses". (beat) Mom, I'm going to go and play with Margarita.

TERRY

Who?

253

VICKIE

Mar...Mar...ga-ret. We're gonna play jump rope and uh, duck, duck, goose.

TERRY

Okay. Stay by the house. Dinner'll be ready pretty soon.

(Vickie exits, phone rings,)

I hope that's not Wanda. I can't teach another class of catechism.

(Sweetly on phone)

Ramos residence. Oh, hi, Sally. Whew.   Glad it's you, I thought the call might be Wanda. (Short beat). We couldn't make the group meeting. I know it was important...Vickie did what?...Thanks for the call. I'll make sure she understands.

(TERRY hangs up as EDDIE enters with lunch pail)

EDDIE

Who was that?

TERRY

(OS) Sally. (Enters with coffee) She was giving me a head's up.

EDDIE

About what?

TERRY

Her son's in Vickie's classroom. She's also the Vice Principal's secretary.

(Terry shakes her head and sighs).

EDDIE

What'd she do?

TERRY

Vickie was caught speaking Spanish again...to Margaret...in the classroom. They both had to sit in the dumb-dumb corner today.

EDDIE

You told me you talked to her.

TERRY

I have. I told her if she gets in trouble in school for speaking Spanish again, she's going to get it even worse when you come home.

EDDIE

Why can't she be more like Jr.? None of his teachers have ever complained about him and Spanish. She understands, doesn't she?

TERRY

I don't think she knows how embarrassing this is. How it could hurt her grades.

EDDIE

Then why is she being so stubborn?

TERRY

I don't think she's trying to be stubborn. The kids who speak Spanish they're the ones who play jacks and jump rope. She loves to play those games with them. You, of all people, should understand how she feels. How many times have you told me how you hated having to move to Mexico and feeling like you didn't fit in.

EDDIE

Damn right I hated it. Didn't want to go. I'm American. What did I know about Mexico. I'd never been there. And Dad said we'd have to learn Spanish. None of us kids knew Spanish only my mom and Dad. And they always talked to us in English.

TERRY

Wasn't Casimira born in Mexico? Didn't you tell me she was your dad's favorite? She could have helped you younger kids!

EDDIE

Casimira, Nah, she'd been here so long she didn't remember Spanish or anything about Mexico.

TERRY

Come on, she was born in Mexico!

EDDIE

Casimira was a baby when they came here. She didn't want
to go. I heard her tell Dad...but Dad said we had no choice.
So, we packed up a few suitcases and there we went to Union
Station. It was really dark, and it was so packed with people.
There were so many people there you could barely move. I kept
bumping into people I didn't know.   I was afraid I'd get separat-
ed from my folks and get lost. And then there were the soldiers
with their guns. I cried when the soldiers put us on the train.
Shit, my mom and dad cried, too. My folks were afraid of what
might happen because Mom was pregnant.

TERRY

How could they do that to your mom? They forced her?

EDDIE

Maybe, maybe not. But what was she going to do? Stay here
and raise a baby all by herself and hope the rest of us would be
okay without her?

TERRY

I didn't know.

EDDIE

No, she had Jaime on the train...after it crossed the border. And even after that It took days before we finally got to Gomez Palacio. We weren't there long and then we had to go to school. Kids made fun of me. The way I dressed, the way I talked. I tried to learn Spanish and they'd laugh at me. They called me Pocho or worse, "Repatriado". The way they said it was like calling me "Gringo". They said it was just their way of being funny. Really their way of being mean. And then Casimira died. And my folks had to leave her there. It broke my mom's heart.

TERRY

Your poor mom.

EDDIE

Yeah, and then, when my folks tried to come back they had to do months and months of paperwork just to prove Jaime was their child. That they weren't sneaking him into the States.

TERRY

That makes no sense.

EDDIE

Then we end up coming back to the States and here we go again. No Spanish permitted. If they catch you...

TERRY

Dunce hat.

EDDIE

And smacked with a ruler or...slapped across your mouth.
Damn it, I'd been thinking in Spanish for years. I was 8 when I
left and 12 when we got back. What was I supposed to do...push
some magic button and speak good English?

And how they chose us wasn't fair! I mean, how come our
family got shipped off and your family stayed?

TERRY

I don't know! I've asked my mom; she switches the subject. Alls
I know is she's determined to only speak Spanish; keeps her
from being "tan Americano".

EDDIE

Esta señora, with her "tan Americano" ...You don't think...She
better not be speaking Spanish to the kids.

TERRY

She doesn't. We speak in Spanish, but only when Vickie and Jr.
are out of the house.

EDDIE

You're sure?

259

TERRY

She says she doesn't.

EDDIE

How can you be sure?

TERRY

I'm sure. Do you think I want Vickie to be held back or be sent to a school like the one you went to…

EDDIE

No, no, no Junipero Serra Mexican School for our kids.

TERRY

It's 1953! They don't call them Mexican Schools anymore!

EDDIE

Yeah, they don't call'em that anymore, not since that Mendez family made that stink. But those schools get Mexicans ready to work "with their arms, not their brains". Don't ask questions. Don't think! It was awful! I hated being treated that way. That was why I dropped out of school! [beat] I want better for them.

TERRY

I do, too! But sometimes when I'm talking with my mom, I wonder, well, what problem could there be in knowing Spanish?

260

EDDIE

Do you think I'll ever get to be a foreman or a supervisor at work? Nah, I don't sound smart because of my accent. I don't sound like an "American".

TERRY

She doesn't have an accent. What's the harm?

EDDIE

What's the harm? The harm is someone will hear her speaking Spanish and decide her life for her. I want more for her! Don't you?

TERRY

Of course, I do! How can you even question that?

(Exits; yelling)

Vickie!

(Paulita enters, rosary in hand, concerned).

PAULITA

¿Qué pasa? Los escuché en mi cuarto. ¿Por qué gritaban?

EDDIE

Dispense, Señora, pero Terry no ve el problema.

PAULITA

¿Gritarse unos a otros le mostraré el problema??

EDDIE

No, pero Vickie está hablando en español en tu escuela.

PAULITA

¿Qué, qué?

EDDIE

Es contra las reglas…for her to talk in Spanish. Está rompiendo
una regla.

PAULITA

(Becoming irate.) ¿Hablar español es contra la ley en Los
Estados Unidos? ¿Me llevarán a la cárcel porque hablo español
en nuestra casa? ¿O en el mercado? ¿O en la iglesia?

EDDIE

(Through his teeth) No, Señora. But it's not that easy. No es
tan…oh, shit, what's the word for easy.

PAULITA

Fácil!

EDDIE

Fácil! No es tan fácil. Damnit. I love my kids. I don't want them to go through the same things I did.

PAULITA

¿Tienes vergüenza del idioma que te hablaba tu mamá? ¿Los sacrificios que hicieron por ti?

EDDIE

I know the sacrifices they made.

PAULITA

¿Quieres enterrar eso? ¿No tienes orgullo de quien vienes?

EDDIE

I am proud of them!

PAULITA

Debería ser. Fueron inteligentes, trabajaron juntos. Tú y Teresa puedes hacer lo mismo por la Vickie. Enséñele cuándo puede o no puede hablar español. Ella aprenderá.

EDDIE

(Beat) Maybe...maybe...

263

PAULITA

Si no lo tratas, eres menos hombre de lo que pensaba.

EDDIE

Señora, Señora, no puedo permitir...

PAULITA

Eduardo, hay reglas y hay reglas. Y a veces, si necesitas seguir las reglas, debes doblarlas un poco. Descubre como. ¡Y ya, nada mas de gritos!

(Paulita to table. Terry, Vickie enter. Vickie goes to Paulita)

EDDIE

Terry, I think I know what we need to do.

TERRY

I'm glad you do. What might that be.

EDDIE

Your mom said something that got me thinking. I know you'll be okay with it.

VICKIE

(To Paulita) ¿Qué pasó?

PAULITA

(To Vickie) Sabrá Díos.

EDDIE

Get over here. (Vickie hesitates.)   Now.

(Vickie between Eddie and Terry.)

EDDIE

I heard about school…

VICKIE

But, we were only playing…

EDDIE

You can't do that at school.

VICKIE

But, Dad…

EDDIE

If you do, you'll be punished and you won't be permitted to go outside and play with any of the kids who talk Spanish.

VICKIE

Why? Is Spanish bad?

EDDIE

It's not bad and (to Paulita) English isn't bad, either.

No one should be ashamed of talking in either language. So at school, you need to talk in English.   En la casa - puedes hablar Español con tu mamá o conmigo o con tu abuela.

TERRY

Well, that makes sense.

EDDIE

Por qué…como dice tu abuelita, sometimes you just need to bend the rules.

VICKIE

Ok.

(They hug)

TERRY

Okay.

PAULITA

Eso.

END OF PLAY

Por mi madre yo soy Mexicano, por destino soy Americano, Yo soy de la Raza de Oro, Yo soy México Americano. Dos idiomas y dos países, dos culturas tengo yo, Es mi suerte, tengo orgullo, por que así lo mande Díos.

The Walls You Cannot See

Rosemary Frisino Toohey

CHARACTERS

ANNA…female, any race, 20s-30s.

DREW…male, any race, 20s-30s.

TIME

The present.

SETTING

A living room.

SYNOPSIS

Falling into bed together has become too easy...so a couple decides to put some distance between themselves to discover whether there's anything to their relationship beyond the sex. Will it work? Will this bring them closer? Or will it kill what they thought they had?

It says here that the artist sipped absinthe before he picked up
his brush, that he frequently went without food for days before
attempting to paint.

                        ANNA
He should have eaten.

                        DREW
Anna, you could try to look for---

                        ANNA
I can't go there.

                        DREW
I'm only suggesting that you try. That you begin the journey.
After that, who knows? You might find your way.

                        ANNA
I just don't want to go through the trouble.

                        DREW
Okay. But that's kind of lazy.

                        ANNA
All right then, I'm lazy.

                        DREW
But you're really not. Not at all. You're ambitious and intelligent
and goal-oriented and…I just don't see why you don't want to---

                        ANNA
I don't want to be bothered, Drew. It doesn't interest me enough
to look at it the way you do.

                        DREW
With some art you have to work at it. Wade into it, stroll

around in the piece and try to determine---

ANNA

It reminds me of church.

DREW

Church? Who said anything about church?

ANNA

I did. I don't like work that is such…hard work.

DREW

But to find the relevance, the beauty of it…those things take time. You need to give yourself that time. Not everything can just be handed to you. Some stuff you have to work for. So. What did you think of that other lecture?

ANNA

I thought him well-educated, I suppose.

DREW

But you didn't like what he had to say?

ANNA

Not so much.

DREW

Because?

ANNA

It was dreary. The world is dreary enough without more dreariness in it.

DREW

My, we are melancholy tonight.

ANNA

Only trying to get it right.

DREW

It?

ANNA

What I want to say. I'm trying to express myself.

Pause.

ANNA

You sure you don't want to play cards?

DREW

Not if I'm going to lose again. Yeah, I know. That makes me a poor sport.

ANNA

You don't want me to give you the game, do you?

DREW

Of course not. I just want to feel not stupid when it comes to card games.

ANNA

You're not stupid, just…unlucky. The cards have their friends.

DREW

And I'm not one of them?

ANNA

Apparently not.

DREW

Well, the hell with it then.

ANNA

We could try to find a different game.

DREW

Maybe. Maybe tomorrow. Or later on tonight.

ANNA

You mean when we're both tired.

                                                              Pause.

Oh, look outside. The birds.

DREW

Those? They're just starlings. Nasty birds.

ANNA

I don't understand why you say that. Birds are only birds, right?
How can you say that some creatures are nastier than others?

DREW

Because they are. Starlings are. They steal other birds' nests, they
eat other birds' eggs. They're vicious.

ANNA

But they're just little birds.

DREW

Okay. You want to like starlings, go ahead. I just…well, I don't.

ANNA

I don't understand you on that. To me that's like saying you
don't like a certain kind of grass or tree or something. I mean,
birds are just part of nature, right?

DREW

Well, flocks of starlings can be---

ANNA

And they don't fly in "flocks." It's a "murmuration." I looked it up. What do you think of that?

DREW

Somebody sat around and thought all those names up.

ANNA

Right. A muster of peacocks, a parliament of owls…

DREW

Well, the word "murmuration" doesn't make starlings any less vicious.

ANNA

I think it's all in how you look at them.

DREW

Okay, okay, it's all in how you see them. Vision is a gift, they say.

Pause.

ANNA

And what about this? This…space between us. I'm having a hard time seeing it.

DREW

You're not supposed to see it. It's meant to keep us apart.

ANNA

And this is helping how?

DREW

Maybe we need to isolate. For a while anyway. We agreed we were on thin ice, Anna. You were the one who said---

ANNA

I know what I said.

DREW

Have you changed your mind then?

ANNA

No. Not on that. The fact that we so casually fell into each other's arms. It had gotten dead easy. And I didn't think it was…well…you saw it, too, didn't you? You felt it too, right?

DREW

Yeah, kind of. But I…I wasn't as brave as you. I didn't want to say it.

ANNA

I'm not complaining about the sex, you understand. I'm just saying, if that's all there is…

DREW

And I respect that. You know I respect your opinions, your thoughts. You're so solid, so precise about what you think, how you feel.

ANNA

It was your idea to put the distance between us.

DREW

I thought it would help us figure it out…whether we're meant to be together. That's why I suggested this…physical retreat.

ANNA

Because not recognizing the problem is like denying it.

DREW

And denying it won't take us to the new place. The place we
have to go. The place from where we can maybe…

ANNA

Get back. I know.

DREW

If we can get back.

ANNA

Talk out being precise.

DREW

Yes, I know. But what's more important than this? All the other
stuff…like whether we move to the coast or stay here…

ANNA

Or whether I stay with the publishing company or not…you're
right. It's not critical.

DREW

Exactly. None of it's critical. It's kind of like deciding what to
have for dinner. We're agreed on that, right?

ANNA

Yes. But this, the feelings between us…they should be all in all.
That's why I spoke up. That's why we have to know.

DREW

You're hard, lady.

ANNA

I don't know how to be anything else.

DREW

Anyway, the isolation…I guess I think that's the only way we
can see whether it makes a difference. And you agreed. Have you

changed your mind? Are you now saying you don't want to---

ANNA

No. I know what we said and I know why we're doing it. But the reality…I'm just not sure it's going to work.

DREW

This could do it for us, Anna. It could make the difference. Bring us back to a place where---

ANNA

But what if it doesn't? What if, instead of doing it for a while, what if…what if this ends it for us?

Pause.

DREW

You think we're that close to an ending?

ANNA

I don't know. I just think we could self-isolate in separate rooms.

DREW

Because?

ANNA

Because the walls you can see are not as scary as the ones you can't see.

DREW

So this…this space between us…is scary to you?

ANNA

Kind of.

Pause.

And I wonder if we saw each other less…maybe we would love each other more?

276

Pause.

DREW

I don't know. I just don't know. And that's really scary.

END OF PLAY

Menopausally Ever After

A Play in Two Acts

Sunee Lyn Foley

SNEEZY 49, Female, neurotic, with tissues coming out of her pockets, her cleavage and her purse. Also in her purse are a bunch of allergy medications, a full box of tissues, sunscreen, bug spray, and a full-size can of LYSOL.

HAPPY, 62, Female, dressed in bright gardening clothes, a big, floppy hat, and carrying a tote bag with her knitting supplies. Noticeably sticking out of HAPPY's tote bag is a simple happy face mask on a stick, like the ones on commercials for an add-on treatment when antidepressants aren't enough.

DOPEY, 51, Female, stoner, in a hoodie and jeans with a large Guatemalan "Mary Poppins" bag.

DOC, 59, Female, wearing a white lab coat and chunky black glasses, looks up from her phone.

SNOW, 55, Female, a modern-day Snow White- still sporting black hair and ruby lips- but her princess dress has been replaced by a blue moto jacket, slim yellow t-shirt, skinny red pants, and carrying a large red apple.

BASHFUL, 58, Female, in skin-tight camouflage with perfect makeup and hair.

GRUMPY, 45, Female, grouchy and sarcastic with a huge heart, dressed in sweats, messy hair, etcetera.

GRUMPY

When I went to Dr. Katz, my gynecologist, in search of relief
from some of my more severe symptoms, this little wimp of
a man was so condescending it took everything in me not to
smack the smug expression right off his face. Ira got this patron-
izing tone and said,

(in a condescending baby voice)

"Are the itty-bitty hot flashes bothering you?" The man wouldn't
make it through a day of menopause. You know what I'd love?
To watch Dr. Katz, or anyone who says things like, "It's just
menopause," try to navigate feeling like you can't control what's
happening to your body, your mind, and your emotions all at
the same time. One thing's for sure, he'd be sniveling like a little
bitch after just one hot flash, begging for some goddamn relief.

(mimicking the doctor sniveling)

"Please, give me something to make them stop! I haven't slept in
days and my body's burning up. I can't maintain a single train
of thought and I cry all the time. I can't take it anymore!" Wah
wah wah.

(in her regular voice)

After I watched him whine for a good while, I would do for
him exactly what he did for me. Nothing. Zip. Zero. Zilch. I'd
tell him to dress in layers, keep baby wipes in the fridge, and
avoid caffeine and spicy foods. And alcohol. I know, right?
No alcohol? Is the medical community so delusional that they
expect me to feel this shitty and NOT have a drink?

HAPPY

I've been going to the same nail salon, around the corner from my house, every three weeks since they opened 10 years ago. Lucky Nails. It's familiar. It's comfortable. I like going there… But when I get anxious, even something comfortable and familiar feels scary.

(beat)

Cindy was doing my pedicure first like she always does. I turned on the massage chair and prepared to relax, maybe play Candy Crush on my phone. What can I say, it relaxes me. But right away I started feeling claustrophobic. Which doesn't make any sense. I mean, it's a large, wide-open salon, not crowded with too many stations or pedicure chairs. And it never gets loud. Never. There's just the low hum of conversations and perfunctory pop music.

(beat)

Suddenly, it was hard to sit there, because I felt trapped, but one foot was soaking, and Cindy was holding the other. I started to sweat and breathe way too quickly for my own comfort. My mind started to race, trying to figure out how to get out of there, get to somewhere that didn't feel like… like it was closing in on me. I was like Han Solo in the trash compactor and the walls were closing in and I couldn't get out. Then the list of all of the things I hadn't finished on my to-do list started looping around and around and my pulse was beating faster. It was out of control. I thought maybe some deep breaths would calm me down, but I couldn't get enough air in my lungs, and it felt like the collar of my t-shirt was choking me. All I could manage to do was take short, shallow sips of air. I felt like everyone was staring at me and that made the space feel even smaller. I was ashamed that I couldn't just be present and enjoy this experience, be grateful I was privileged enough to have regular nail appointments. Something that usually calmed me down. Ironic.

(beat)

So, I was moving around so much I have no clue how she did such a beautiful job on my pedicure. I had chosen the OPI color "Let me Bayou a Drink." I needed a drink. Time seemed to be going in slow-motion and I felt so overwhelmed I was on the verge of tears. And of course, I had a hot flash. You could hear the shaking in my voice when I told her, "I CAN'T DO THE MANICURE TODAY" Cindy was very sweet about it. She could clearly see that something was wrong. She wanted to walk me home, she even tried insisting. I thanked her and assured her I'd be okay. Honestly, I just wanted to be home with my dogs.

(beat)

When I got home I cried like a baby, which did release some of the anxiety, but I still had to take a Xanax. Then I put on that baking competition that always relaxes me and listened to Mary Berry talk in her soothing voice and I pet the dogs until I fell asleep.

(beat)

Anxiety is a bitch.

BASHFUL

The reason I talk about sex so much is because I think about sex so much. Before I started wearing this little miracle of an estrogen patch, I had no desire for sex. None whatsoever. Like, a don't-touch-me-I-might-hit-you kind of thing. And this is a relatively new feeling for me. I mean, I've always enjoyed sex. In fact, we always had a very healthy sex life, hence the five children. Adam was a beast in the bedroom with this beauty.

(beat)

Before I even found out I was in menopause, my sex drive plummeted. I was in perimenopause, I suppose, and the thought of someone touching me made my skin crawl. Now that I'm on the other side, the only thing I want is for someone to touch me. I… can't have enough sex. Seriously, I'm horny All. The. Time. I'm in the mood the second I open my eyes in the morning and

I'm insatiable all day. You know how they say gonorrhea, chla-mydia, and syphilis are often found in nursing homes? That's because SENIORS ARE HORNY AS HELL. Stop marketing us with products like "I've fallen and I can't get up." Market lube to the over 60's. We have disposable income and we *will* spend it.

(beat)

You'd think my husband would be ecstatic that I wanted to make love so often, that I'd gotten more adventurous. But he started complaining, actually complaining, like I was asking him to mow the lawn or clean out the garage or something while the game was on. What the Fuck?

(beat)

When I tried to make love he actually said that he wanted to watch the Office. I mean, he's choosing fucking Steve Carell over me? The truth was: He was tired. He was embarrassed. His libido had not had a spring awakening like mine had. Finally, he told me to get a lover because he didn't have the stamina to satisfy me.

(beat)

God, I hope he was serious.

SNEEZY

I wish my husband would tell me to get a lover.

(sneezes repeatedly)

When I was pregnant, I had the most vivid, sexy dreams. Well, vivid sex dreams. The first time it happened I was shocked. I dreamt about a professor I had a crush on in college. He taught Statistics and his classes were total snooze-fests, but he was hot, like Paul Rudd hot,

(to audience)

Right? I mean, who DOESN'T fantasize about Paul Rudd?

(to the group)

Anyway, after I gave birth, the dreams stopped, though I tried everything I could think of to have them again. I tried reading erotica or thinking dirty thoughts before I went to sleep. I watched every Paul Rudd movie out there, even Ant-Man Quantumania. But nothing. Eventually, I gave up. Flash forward 30 years, I'm in menopause and I've been on hormone replacement therapy for a few weeks when I start having really sexy, vivid dreams again. But, this time around they don't involve a professor I haven't seen in over three decades or an unattainable actor. This time it's my allergist. Vanessa. Dr. Vanessa Eisenberg.

(sneeze)

I'm absolutely positive I blush ten shades of red every time I have an appointment with her.

HAPPY

Don't overanalyze it, dear, just do whatever makes you happy. I have spent far too long making everyone else happy, doing only what was *expected* of me. Now with a little help from Lexapro, okay, maybe a lot of help, I'm working on making myself happy.

(beat)

Instead of worrying about what people think or bitching and moaning about hot flashes and putting on a few pounds, I try to ignore all of that by inviting my menopausal friends over to party. I get some edibles or roll a few joints and whip up a batch of margaritas or something fun. We smoke, we drink, we laugh. It doesn't help with any of our symptoms or problems, but it does help us forget about them for a little while. Like last Tuesday night. I made some pot brownies and my spiked espresso milkshakes, and the girls and I played poker. Once we had our buzz on we were feeling kind of wild. My neighbor, who happens to be a very hot 60-something I've had my eye on for a while, and a couple of his buddies, were looking very attractive washing their motorcycles in his driveway. I put on some lip gloss, adjusted my cleavage, went over there with some of those brownies, and invited them over to party. It turned into an all-night bash. I won't go into detail, but, wow! What a night! In the morning, I made Drew, that's motorcycle neighbor's name, Drew, some Bloody Marys, and scrambled eggs.

(beat)

When I was younger, I was always worried about how I looked to everyone.

Behaving appropriately was everything to me and it drove my ex crazy, hence the ex-part.

I never let loose.

(beat)

When I turned 50, I wracked my brain trying to figure out who I was behaving so appropriately for. Turns out no one cared so I'm using it as an excuse to be unabashedly myself for the rest of my life.

DOPEY

Normally, I meditate to release any negative feelings, but lately not so much. Now, I like to tell people how it is. You should all try it. If anyone looks at you funny while you're having a hot flash and you're feeling particularly irritable that day, give them a piece of your mind. Just let it rip. Busy bodies love that. Forget taking deep breaths or reciting affirmations on being enough. Punch them in the face with your words.

(beat)

Hell yes, I'm angry. Thus the weekly visits to the dispensary to calm my nerves. In addition to this fabulous tire around my belly I suddenly woke up with one morning out of the blue, I'm losing my mind. NOT COOL. No one warned me about this bullshit.

Wikipedia generously let me know that I had "brain fog" which is a polite way of describing the mush my brain has become in menopause. Whenever I try to tell anyone anything, I forget what the hell I'm trying to say. It even happened at a job interview. It's hard enough getting a new job at my age without coming across like an airhead. I've told my daughter that the neighbors sold their house at least 15 times already, and I've been to the market at least a dozen times to get...um...the... because...I'm out of the...the uh...Go figure. I can't remember it now either.

> (beat)

I need to hit something. Or smoke a joint. Or smoke a joint and hit something.

DOC

Before I had my hysterectomy, I had a lot of nightmares. My therapist said I was grieving my fertility and what I thought was the loss of my femininity. Whatever the reason, the nightmares were so bad I didn't want to go to bed at night. I added reading something positive to what my husband refers to as my elaborate bedtime routine as if I could alter my subconscious mind or something. The night before my hysterectomy, I was lulled into a false sense of security. At first, everything felt ethereal and lovely, like a good dream. I was pregnant with both of my children at the same time like they were twins instead of being two years apart. My belly was huge, and it was blissful.

> (beat)

One minute I'm holding a little boombox to my belly so the kids can listen to the Beatles, and the next I'm on a gurney being wheeled into surgery, except I didn't know about any surgery.

And it isn't glaringly bright from those horrible fluorescent lights like most hospitals. It's all dark and ominous, kind of like the episode of Criminal Minds when the unsub sets up a "hospital" in his garage so he can remove the leg from one person and attach it to another, whom he subsequently removed a leg from all so he could give his wife a "new," working leg.

Anyway, there I am being wheeled into God knows where, and I'm like What. The. Actual. Fuck. I start screaming at the top of my lungs, "What kind of surgery am I having?" but they just wheel me down this never-ending hallway to the operating room. When we finally get there, it's dingy and unwelcoming and not at all sanitary…I can see dust and dirt and what I think is blood…Plus, there's no anesthesiologist. No one knocks me out. I'm wide awake. And I'm not in a hospital gown with my ass hanging out. I'm in that cute maternity romper with the daisies I practically lived in.

                                                    (beat)

Suddenly, someone slices me open and rips everything out… all of it in one fell swoop.

                                                    (beat)

Gone…no more babies…no way to make babies.

                                                    (beat)

I was just…empty.

Aurora & Ruly

Gina Rae Duran

Dramedy

Characters:

AURORA: Age 43, Queer, Gender Non-conforming/ Gender Fluid, doesn't actually believe in pronouns but uses she/he/they, Indigenous Xicanx, mother, can't stand colonial constructs, activist, twice divorced, makes poor romantic choices, buoyant, "strong," has PTSD, a little neurotic with some eccentricities, has five jobs and one of them is substitute teaching, loves her children, sacrifices everything for the ones she loves.

RULY: Age 23, Aurora's son, nerdy, looks like Clark Kent and Superman, loves comic books and films, husky energy, is a D&D Dungeon Master, a journalism major in community college, works on the college newspaper, and has a side job in a strip mall, has a moderate case of OCD.

Setting: Kitching / dining room. Minimalist stage.

Synopsis: Aurora makes a mistake…Alright, alright several mistakes. Ruly walks in to find his mother, Aurora, bandaging up her hand, as she falls deeper into her mess.

This play is fictional. Characters and events of Aurora and Ruly are loosely based on the very real moment that I accidentally cut the tip of my finger off while slicing pickles. All other mentioned characters and events are an amalgamation of other people, events, rumors and gossip about my life. In fiction, I have the opportunity to ask: "What if?"

SCENE THREE

A minimalist kitchen.

AURORA is in the kitchen slicing pickling cucumbers from her garden. SHE has the brine in a jar.

Without a safe guard for her Japanese mandolin (vegeta ble slicer), SHE slices pickles while talking on the phone.

AURORA

Okay, let's do it, Marcus... Go on a date... Yeah. Let's get dinner...It's not like we haven't had dinner together before... Yeah, only this time it'll be a... date...I do not have trouble saying the word date. Date... see, I just said it. Date. I am going on a date, with you. Date, Date, Date, Date,

(AURORA gasps in pain.)

Fuck!

(She looks down and sees she sliced open the tip of her middle finger.)

Fuck! Shit, Fuck, Shit, Fuck.... Uhhhhh, I sliced off the tip of my fucking middle finger... Because the tip of my middle finger

288

is dangling from my hand. I have to go.... I need to wrap it...
Yeah, I have them all over my house. I'm a military brat. Piss
poor planning and all that. I'll be fine, but it won't stop bleed-
ing and I have to cut off the circulation.

> AURORA puts down the phone, grabs paper
> towels, and wraps her finger.

> Climbs up the counter and gets out her first aid
> kit.

> Quickly wraps gauze and tape around her finger,
> cutting off the blood and raises her hand above
> her head.

> Picks up the phone.

AURORA

Oh, great tip. I didn't know it coagulated the blood. Thank you.
I'll take vitamin C, now.

> AURORA hangs up.

> RULY, enters the front door.

RULY

Hey, Ma. You'd never believe what happened at work today.

> AURORA walks towards RULY with her hand
> raised above her head.

RULY

Oh, Fuck! What happened to your hand?

AURORA

I sort of cut off the tip of my middle finger on the mandoline.

RULY

OH My God, Mom? What the hell?

AURORA laughs.

AURORA

Clearly, the universe was preventing me from going on a date.

RULY

Oh My God, Mom. You're worrying me…What did you do?

RULY inhales and exhales while blinking his eyes
three times.

AURORA

I'll tell you later I gotta call an advice nurse.

RULY paces.

RULY

Oh My God, Mom. I don't want you going to the ER.

AURORA

The ER? Fuck, I don't know. I can't afford this shit. I can't
afford the deductible. Maybe, I can go to family care if we rush.

(Long beat)

Or, maybe I should just super glue it together.

RULY laughs.

RULY

Seriously?

AURORA

 Yeah, I superglued my friend Tami's finger once, because she didn't have insurance.

RULY

What the fuck? Who raised me?!

AURORA

Yeah! Your dad told me they did it on the construction field, all the time.

(Beat)

Let me call the advice nurse first.

RULY

If you're seriously thinking of doing this I'm getting the alcohol rub and bandages and...

RULY points his pointer finger up into the air as

though he has a brilliant idea.

                              RULY

I'll be right back!

                          HE exits.

                            AURORA

 Great idea... Okay, you do that and I'll call.

                 AURORA makes a phone call.

                            AURORA

Hello, yes...Aurora Rivera, my medical number is 33457. Yeah,
I chopped of my finger on a mandoline…Well, not the whole
thing. The tip of my middle finger. Yes, the skin is sort of...
hanging... no, more like dripping... no hanging. It's hanging
dripping. It's bleeding everywhere. I can't get it to stop.

        AURORA lowers her hand to check the bandage.

                            AURORA

Actually, I think I finally got it to stop.

            RULY enters holding out his phone.

                             RULY

Ma! Do we have needles?

                            AURORA

Do you know how much the co-pay would be?

(to RULY)

I don't know? Yeah…in the bathroom…

RULY exits.

AURORA

Wait. What? What do you need needles for?

(into phone)

I'm sorry, my kid is…was asking me something? How much?

RULY rushes back in.

RULY

Ma? I found them. Where do you keep the fishing wire?

AURORA

So I have to go in to find out? What? Wait, what?…Just a second…

(to RULY)

Fishing wire? What do you need fish…ing…? I don't know Brody. Check my art studio.

RULY exits.

AURORA

(into phone)

I'm sorry. I'm back. Why can't you just tell me my co-pay over the phone. Can I just go into Family Medicine…err…Then

Urgent Care?

> RULY enters, a little breathless, as if he went for a jog.

RULY

Ma? Ma? Where would you keep it in the studio? I just see containers.

AURORA

I don't know, Ruly…On the shelf.

RULY

Which shelf? There are two.

AURORA

On the big one, next to the massage room. Wait, What…What do you need fishing wire…?

RULY

I got it!

> RULY exits.

AURORA

(into phone)
Why do I have to go to the ER? …Family Medicine is full?

Seriously? And you won't tell me how much stitches will cost?
I mean are we talking 500 dollars? A thousand dollars? What is
this Let's Make a Deal? I choose door number...

(Beat)

You know what. Fuck it. I'll do it myself.

AURORA hangs up. RULY enters.

AURORA

I figured it out.

RULY puts a pile of medical supplies and his
cell phone on the table.

AURORA

When did you get all of that?

RULY

When you were on the phone. Sit down.

RULY lines up all of the supplies.

AURORA

It's okay, I already bandaged it up. I just need to find the
superglue.

RULY

No, you don't. I'm going to give you stitches. That's what the dental floss is for.

AURORA

Instead of string?

RULY

Yeah, string collects bacteria and will infect the wound. Fishing wire is best, but all I could find is dental floss. Gosh, Ma. I thought everyone knew that.

AURORA

Whatever, man.

RULY snickers then turns on his phone.

RULY

Just kidding. I saw it on Grey's Anatomy.

AURORA starts laughing.

AURORA

 Is that a YouTube video? Did you look up a How To video, to stitch up my finger?

RULY

Sshhh! Yeah. I gotta see what to do with…This needle.

RULY disinfects the table. Then gets up and
starts opening kitchen drawers. AURORA stays in
the chair and watches.

RULY

Where is the lighter?

AURORA gets up to get the lighter from a small
table stand and hand it to RULY.

AURORA

This DIY project of yours reminds me of when Rambo goes
into a cave, pulls shrapnel from his wound and then lights it on
fire…Wait, are you planning to light my wound on fire?…If so,
just let me know in advance.

RULY chuckles as he puts on his gloves. Then
snaps the glove around his wrist.

RULY

Nah, Ma. Don't you know? This is more like Supernatural .
Now, get me some whiskey.

AURORA

What, you're operating drunk now?

RULY

It's for disinfecting.

AURORA

That would be vodka.

RULY

Then vodka.

> SHE grabs the bottle from the freezer and hands
> it to him.

AURORA

I'm Dean.

RULY

No, I'm Dean. You're Sam. This is a Sam move.

AURORA

What...The...Fuck? Hmm...Maybe, it was a Sam move. But I'm
still Dean.

> RULY gives a deep maniacal laugh. Grabs the
> needle nosed pliers and bends the needle.

AURORA

What the heck? Why are you bending the needle?

RULY

It needs to be curved so it can come back up through the skin.

AURORA

I'm starting to question this idea.

RULY

Shh!...Quiet, Sam.

> Both AURORA and RULY sweat profusely.
> AURORA wipes RULY's forehead with a towel
> for him, like he's a surgeon.

RULY

Okay, I got it. Sit down and put your hand on the table.

AURORA

Okay. You know the tips of the fingers have a lot of nerves
in them, so let me work up some courage. I have to take my
bandage off too.

> RULY gulps. Then lights the needle.

RULY

Okay. Here we go.

> RULY closes his eyes and exhales.

AURORA

Um, if we're doing this, you need to open your eyes.

> HE does. AURORA puts out her hand.

299

AURORA

Okay, I believe in you.

> RULY grabs the needle. AURORA winces.
> Then...

RULY

Fuck!...I'm Sorry...I can't do this...I'm sorry, Ma! I just can't.

AURORA

Oh, thank god...You chickened out. That means I'm still Dean...I'll super glue it.

> AURORA gets up, wipes her brow, grabs the
> superglue laying on the kitchen table.

RULY

Nah, I just don't accept Kaiser..Can I help you? You can tell me what to do.

AURORA

Okay, this is easier. Put glue all around, especially the edges... But let me disinfect it first.

> RULY hands AURORA the alcohol rub. Then
> AURORA pours alcohol rub on her wound.

RULY

This really sucks.

AURORA

What? That I chopped off my finger or the American Health
Care system.

RULY

Well, both. But especially the American Health Care system.

AURORA

Yep, we're living in a panopticon.

RULY

Good word, Ma.

AURORA

A prison. We're living under constant surveillance even though
no one's watching.

RULY

What is this, the DC's OMAC Project?

AURORA

Yeah, is this some AI bullshit?

RULY

Well, technically the AI stole people's natural abilities in that storyline.

AURORA

It could happen!...But how hard is it to tell a person their co-pay before their visit?

RULY

Seriously, we're poor ...as fuck.

AURORA

Poor? We're lucky we aren't homeless. How many more jobs do I need to have?

RULY

How are you supposed to be a massage therapist with a missing finger?

AURORA

Good point.

RULY

We're screwed.

AURORA

I need to Zoom with my therapist.

RULY

Such a Sam move...Speaking of Sam...

AURORA

Oh, my god. You're not going to let it go, are you?

RULY

So what happened?

AURORA

Marcus split up with his wife and started flirting. And I normal-
ly would ignore it, but...

RULY

Oh, my god. Mom!...You're Gay.

AURORA

I know that. I know I'm Gay. I don't know what I was think-
ing...I mean he was like...Oh, you're single? You aren't seeing
Marin anymore?...Dude, I wasn't seeing her in the first place...
she has Friends...ugh. I'm so dumb. She's straight. I was in love.

(beat)

But you know what, Ruly...I actually rarely say Gay anymore. I identify as Queer...And you know what else...I'm gender fluid... And you know that...And I've dated more men than women... And it's not like I don't find men attractive. I just find women more attractive. Sexuality and gender aren't that cut and dry, you know. You act all progressive and then you say things like that. And I know I'm not always all that open about my sexual and gender identity and I called myself a lesbian while I was married to your step-mom, but that was just because men kept asking me if they could join in.

RULY

Oh my god, Mom. I don't want to hear about...

AURORA

Don't interrupt. I need you to listen...Thank you.

(beat)

I got tired of explaining myself. I got tired of the questions. I deal with it enough as Xicanx ...And even though I don't go around calling myself Native American, because I didn't grow up on a reservation. People can tell. Men. Can tell. I get men approaching men and telling me how much they like Native women...Objectifying me. Sexualizing me. Exotifying. Me...I get enough. I'm tired of being over sexualized. Exotified. I'm also tired of being alone. And even though I don't find Marcus attractive like that, he's my friend. We've been friends for fourteen or so years. I don't even remember how long. And he calls me family. He knows I'm Queer. He showed up for me and made sure I was safe during my art exhibition, when I performed naked in front of hundreds of people. He was a friend to me during my divorce. And I am exhausted by this long term, on again-off again, non-relationship relationship with Marin. I feel used. I feel like an experiment. And Marcus' wife has had several affairs, just like ....Well, You know. But the point is that he understands. Plus, my grandmother just died and I guess all I can think about is how she was so heartbroken when my grandfather died that she never remarried or dated. She just decided to wait to see him again in death. He died when my mom was seven. Seven. That's a long time to be alone. And, I don't even know what happens to us when we die. She kept crying about how lonely she was...I don't want to die alone. You know...One of my friends even told me I was going to die alone after they met Marin. I stopped talking to them, but still...I don't want to die alone! I know it's ridiculous! But. I. Don't. Want. To . Die . Alone.

RULY sighs.

RULY

Sorry, Mom. I mean it. I really am.

AURORA

Thank you, I appreciate it.

RULY

But she was still your professor.

AURORA

Ugh! And she was your professor too.

RULY

That's not my fault.

AURORA

I told you not to take her class...I begged you.

RULY

She was the only Journalism professor. What was I supposed to do?

AURORA

Go to another school.

RULY

I'm not going to another school just because you liked my teacher.

AURORA

You knew she and I kissed when we were dancing in the rain! I told you.

RULY

I didn't want to commute. But she was your professor first. Boundaries, Mom.

AURORA

I just got tired and...and...It was a mistake.

RULY smiles.

RULY

Which part? Marin or Marcus?

AURORA

Both. All of it. But especially talking on the phone while slicing
pickles on a mandoline...Wait...Aren't you going to superglue
my finger?

RULY

Gosh. I don't know, Ma. You've only been here nine minutes. I
need at least 50 minutes.

RULY superglues AURORA'S finger.

RULY

Mmm...Now take two ibuprofen. That'll be a thousand dollars.
Plus your co-pay.

END SCENE

Every Day is a Protest

Rhema Boston

Characters:

Cree   ..... Female ..... 20s-30s, African-American, free spirit.

John   .....Male   ..... 20s-40s, Mixed race, hesitant.

Miriam .....Female..... 50s-70s, White, Jewish, a true ally.

Darius .....Male   ..... 20s-50s, African-American,

Amy   .....Female..... 30s-50s, White, "Karen".

Officer Cooper .....Male   ..... 30s-50s, White/Racially ambiguous, just doing his job.

Setting: An empty stage.

Notes: * In the dialogue, when words are in CAPS, all characters say that word.

FIVE SILHOUETTES stand side by side
CREE, African American, steps forward.

CREE

Cree Angelique insert generic black last name, like Williams, Johnson, or Brown. My mother named me Cree, hoping that one day I'd create something BEAUTIFUL. That, or she was just ghetto like the rest of the teenage moms who thought giving their child a unique name would help them in life... either way, I'm convinced she didn't know what the fuck she was talking about.

> SHE steps back. JOHN, light-skinned, could pass for white, steps forward.

JOHN

I grew up in a run-down neighborhood and didn't come from money or generational wealth like you might ASSUME. I straddle the fence between both worlds. On the inside I'm JUST LIKE YOU. On the outside, I'm ONE OF THEM. My life may not have been easy, but I'm sure yours is worse. Because I can switch what people see when necessary... YOU CAN'T.

> ALL Five, point to the audience.

> MIRIAM, older Jewish, walks forward.

MIRIAM

My eyes have seen a lot. Between me and the people who came before me, I've seen my fair share of HATE. Sure, I've known antisemites, misogynists and even Republicans, but the RACISTS. They're the worst. Some of the people I thought were the nicest had the most hate in their hearts. I've spent my whole life waiting for CHANGE. I guess I'm still waiting. I hope I

309

can see it in this lifetime. My eyes have seen a lot... and I've had cataract surgery, so I suppose they've seen a lot twice. There are many mysteries in the world, but what I do know is that RESPECT is the first step.

AMY, Caucasian, steps forward

AMY

Sure, racism exists, but honestly, what's happening right now has been blown way out of proportion. Should cops be a little more careful? Of course, but their job is to PROTECT AND SERVE. So if you look suspicious or are doing something wrong, then of course, they are going to take affirmative action. You want to defund police, but if your house gets broken into, who are you going to call? Ghostbusters? You say FUCK THE POLICE but they keep order. What do you want us to be, a bunch of uncivilized animals?

MIRIAM

Republican.

CREE

Hashtag, Stay Woke.

AMY stays where SHE is. DARIUS, African American, steps forward.

DARIUS

I'm confused on what to do. PAIN stirs quick. HATE stirs even quicker, that's what my dad always told me. Just like him, I end up drinking to try to ease my soul. And no, not Hennessy or Ciroc. Black people only drink Ciroc because Diddy makes them think it'll give them some higher level of "black excellence", it also conveniently rhymes with Barak. And Hennessy? That's just for people who purposely want to suffer. Me? I like red wine. I'm like a white woman who shops at Targét, complains about her only child who has a fulltime nanny, and is in a book club just for the finger sized hors d'oeuvres. Wine may not be the most potent thing to drink but it manages to numb my PAIN. I spend endless nights contemplating if I should be doing more, but does MY VOICE even matter? I live in a world that only sees me as a way to make money. Always has, and always will. From private corporations benefitting from mass incarceration to parading around, showing off our God-given talents, possibly leading to fatal injuries, all for others' entertainment. I'm not even good at basketball, or football, or any other sport that my height and build would make you automatically assume I'm gifted. I play the violin. I'm taking an extension course in Mandarin and when no one's looking, I blast Beethoven's Moonlight Sonata while pondering my existence in the world.

 (beat)

I feel like I should PROTEST. Like my ancestors who got beat, abused, and even KILLED FOR CRIMES THEY DIDN'T DO. But they never got discouraged and somehow still paved the way. I wonder if I don't stand my ground, with my fist up proud...

 ALL FIVE put THEIR fists in the air.

DARIUS

Am I a disgrace to them? Should I pick up my cross like Jesus, WHEN WE PRAY I HOPE HE HEARS US, put my fear aside and walk with them?

 (beat)

I just want a cabernet.

 A beat. AMY puts HER phone to HER
 ear.

AMY

Hello. Hello, can you hear me? THERE IS A BLACK MAN DISTURBING THE PEACE. PLEASE HURRY.

CREE

I see a beautiful black man, and you see a THUG. And White people, thug is not synonymous with black. You can't just toss it into sentences whenever you feel like it to try and paint us in a worser light. Thug also isn't synonymous with Nig-

AMY

Ah! Oh, my good.

CREE

I know that's what y'all really want to say.

    (beat)

You know what? Why don't you just erase all of the words that you use to denigrate us? It's funny because denigrate comes from the Latin word denigrare, which means "to blacken." This is just another example of how being black is looked at as a negative, and there's a whole list of words like that, but it's NOT MY RESPONSIBILITY TO EDUCATE YOU. Why? Because you see me everywhere but never actually see me. How can you have a conversation about race when YOU DON'T LISTEN? You look, and you judge, and you make assumptions merely by the color of my skin. I'VE DONE NOTHING. HANDS UP, DON'T SHOOT.

        ALL except AMY, put THEIR hands up.

CREE

To curse God for the cards I was dealt is pointless. But if I could look God in his eyes, I would tell him...IT DOESN'T MATTER, Right? Cause I know that looking someone in their eyes doesn't really mean much. Lies can be told with a smile and with tears. Hell, even the woman who gave life to me fed me lies. She told me "I'll create something beautiful". Right now, I just want to create moments that aren't filled with PAIN. Oh, and white people, Juneteenth isn't the fucking fourth of July; they were already free, but you kept us as slaves despite the law.

> (beat)

Who's a lawbreaker now?

                              AMY

Oh, thank God!

                    OFFICER COOPER, enters and walks
                    to CREE. SHE runs in between the Four,
                    THEY don't react. THEY can't see HER.

                              CREE

If I could paint, all my canvases would be RED OR BLACK. Sometimes red and black. Either smeared together in an unidentified CHAOS or delicately placed black circles on a red background to represent my emptiness. Or to represent my blackness and the red that continually gets shed by people who look just like me. But why are canvases always white? And why does white mean pure? And what is that saying about the opposite? Why do you hate us? And why am I expected to be content with just painting my black sorrows and red grief over your never-ending heavenly white clouds? If I could look God in his eyes, I would ask him WHAT DID I DO TO DESERVE THIS, and why can't I see any other colors?

                              JOHN

I'm trying to tiptoe on eggshells because I see BOTH SIDES.

DARIUS

I'm trying to be peaceful like Doctor King, but he DIED.

MIRIAM

The more things change, the more they stay the same.

DARIUS

Breonna Taylor, Ahmaud Arbery, George Floyd.

CREE

THERE'VE BEEN THOUSANDS. SAY THEIR NAME.

JOHN

I don't know where I stand. Am I black enough? Well, I sure as hell ain't white. My mind can take me anywhere, but my skin won't let me. Help.

AMY

Help. All I want is to protect my children and my family.

DARIUS

Help. All I want is to stay alive long enough to create a family.

CREE

Help. In a sea of only eyes what do you see? A Gangster? A beautiful black man who you reduce to a CRIMINAL? Whatever you see, the actions you decide to take afterward CAN NOT BE CONTROLLED, and I know that that means that in a game where there should be one God, there are many.

MIRIAM

I hear chants and crying, sirens and orders being yelled like they're prisoners. I HATE what's going on but how can I change it? I write letters. I make calls. I attend protests. But it's not enough. It's never enough. I will never truly understand what you feel. Talk to me. I want to be an Ally.

DARIUS

My parents taught me to be open-minded, but why? Was that
all just to keep me from being KILLED for speaking my mind?
I tried to pretend like it doesn't affect me. But it's even stranger
to be able to witness a side that doesn't get affected. Being an
ALLY when it's convenient does not make you a friend.

JOHN

Why am I so SILENT?

    (beat)

I mean, I post on FaceBook. Isn't that enough?

ALL

NO. SILENCE IS COMPLIANCE.

    OFFICER COOPER pins CREE to the
    ground.

CREE

The odds were stacked against me from the moment I was born.
I don't want to give up, but you're making it impossible.

    CREE fights back.

OFFICER COOPER

Stop resisting!

CREE

I HATE YOU! I hate you for hating me! The world was set up
to take more than it gives and pin us against each other. Is it too
much to want more?

    OFFICER COOPER cuffs CREE.

AMY

We all have the same 24 hours in a day, and if you don't make something of yourself, that's no one's fault but your own.

AMY takes out HER phone.

AMY

Hello? There is a black man threatening my life. I called earlier but they got the other black, not the black I was talking about, although I'm sure getting them all off the streets will help. They're taking up my air, and their presence makes it hard for me to breathe.

CREE

I'm suffocating from your ignorance.

MIRIAM

They suffocated them.

    (to Cree)

I wonder if they will take you to the same place they took my grandparents.

    (beat)

Hashalóm, aléyem-hashólem.

JOHN

My father is black, but you'd never be able to tell just by looking at me. I'm the person they bring in as a way to DIVERSIFY when they know they really don't want to be diverse. I was told to capitalize on this moment. I'm light enough, so my existence doesn't offend you. But I'm able to check off the box that gives you more money for being INCLUSIVE. I know what I am, and I own it. If they want to throw me a bone, who am I not to take it?

316

DARIUS

I grew up knowing I was different and did everything in my
power to make that a false reality. That's why I have a plan for
my life. Become an anesthesiologist. Four years of undergrad,
four years of medical school, and four years in a residency.
I've done eleven of my twelve-year bid, but if I go down there
to protest, I might be arrested, which will cause my future
employers to view me as VIOLENT. UNEDUCATED. THUG.
Imagine having a higher education than any random Joe off of
the street but still being talked down to when they call me a
grown man, BOY. Or when I'm questioned about why I'm in
locations where I don't belong. Like I'm a newly freed slave who
has to show his freedom papers to any person who demands
them, and even then, you still tell me that I look SUSPICIOUS
and am up to no good. Tell me then, where do I belong? It's like
I'm trying to pave a new path in a blizzard, but the snow just
keeps falling.

CREE

Am I being detained? What did I do? What law did I break?
Why are you arresting me!? What's your badge number?

OFFICER COOPER

Hey, Welfare Queen, shut up, will ya?

CREE

I have never been on welfare. My mother, although terrible at
giving names, always told me never to take anyone's pity money
because once you take it, you're no better than a slave, and the
person who controls the money will always be the master.

(beat)

And while I'm at it, black men calling us Queen and then
treating us like complete dog shit doesn't really help the situ-
ation, does it? We should be unified, now more than ever. I'm
disappointed in you and the system.

MIRIAM waves DARIUS OVER. HE
hides behind HER.

AMY

Oh, stop it; if cops really wanted black people dead, all they'd
have to do is stop patrolling your neighborhoods and wait.
Eventually, you'd kill each other off.

CREE

I know you think MY VOICE doesn't matter. But I will not be
quiet. Not for you. Not for anybody.

JOHN

Why am I so SILENT?

 (beat)

I mean, I voted for Obama and correct white people who say
the N-word in rap songs... isn't that enough?

MIRIAM

No.

SHE steps up to the OFFICER. Sings
Adon Olam.

MIRIAM

Adon olam, asher malach,

b'terem kol y'tzir nivra.

L'et na'asah v'cheftzo kol,

azai melech sh'mo nikra.

V'acharey kichlot hakol,

l'vado yimloch nora.

V'hu haya, v'hu hoveh,

v'hu yih'yeh b'tifara.

CREE

Why am I being arrested? Someone record this! Someone record. If you're not outraged, YOU'RE NOT PAYING ATTENTION.

OFFICER COOPER

Ma'am I have cause to believe a dangerous fugitive is taking refuge behind you. For your own protection make sure you clutch your purse tightly to ensure that he does not rob you. They are very sneaky.

(beat)

Black male. Hair not specified. Ages 14-34. Wearing cloth-ing, probably baggy. Height anywhere from 5'5-6'5. Come out with your hands up.

MIRIAM

V'hu echad, v'eyn sheni

l'hamshil lo, l'hachbira.

B'li reishit, b'li tachlit,

v'lo ha'oz v'hamisrah.

V'hu Eli, v'chai go'ali,

v'tzur chevli b'et tzarah.

V'hu nisi umanos li,

m'nat kosi b'yom ekra.

B'yado afkid ruchi

b'et ishan v'a'irah.

V'im ruchi g'viyati,

Adonai li v'lo ira.

AMY

Ma'am, for your own good, you need to step aside so this kind officer can do his job.

MIRIAM

I didn't see anything.

AMY

We're trying to protect you.

CREE

Protect her from what?

> CREE stands up, wrists cuffed.

AMY

Whoa, I'm not the bad guy here. I don't give a crap what color you are. I have a black friend. I'm the one who suggested that my book club read The Help.

> AMY and CREE stand face to face.

CREE

I guess being a racist makes your breath smell, huh?

AMY

If you don't want to have interactions with law enforcement, don't break the law. I feel sorry for you. Slinging around the word racist like it's going to fix your problems.

CREE

Never said it would. But shutting the fuck up and some gum

might fix yours.

AMY

And you wonder why people like you are never taken seriously or get jobs. You're an illiterate child who's channeling her inner daddy issues to be angry at the world... Grow up.

> OFFICER COOPER pulls out a weapon.

OFFICER COOPER

Black male. Come out with your HANDS UP!

> (beat)

And don't breathe, blink, or move in any way that I might misinterpret as a threat. Remember, I see violence on a daily basis. My father used to beat me. My badge gives me powers. When I was five, I wore a cape to escape. I pull over black men in nice cars. My wife is about to leave me. I have PTSD and haven't yet been evaluated for biases that have been implanted since my upbringing. I'm human. I make mistakes.

AMY

I think I saw a gun. He has a gun!

> OFFICER COOPER aims his weapon at MIRIAM.

CREE

Since when did brushes, shower heads, and smartphones look like weapons to you?

AMY

Officer, please!

OFFICER COOPER

Ma'am, I need you to step aside.

321

MIRIAM does not move.

MIRIAM

I saw no fugitive.

OFFICER COOPER tries to pull
MIRIAM. SHE holds fast.

MIRIAM

I will not move.

OFFICER COOPER

(into walkie)

I'm going to need backup.

CREE

No justice, NO PEACE. No racist. POLICE. Black lives
MATTER. Black LIVES MATTER. BLACK LIVES MATTER.

JOHN

Why am I always so silent? I mean, I--

CREE

--You what!? Post a photo to save face? Plaster on a hashtag to
ride for a cause you wouldn't walk for? Actions speak louder
than words. You're a hypocrite. If you know what's happening is
wrong, say something. And not just behind a screen, in every-
thing you do. You want to support the cause for a moment. But
for me, everyday day of my life is a protest. Not an event you
can check into on Facebook.

AMY

Are you serious? This isn't one of your "I think I'm making a difference" protests. What's next? Looting? Well, I tell you what, when the looting starts, the shooting starts. I know my rights. Officer, control her.

> CREE links arms with MIRIAM. THEY look at EACH OTHER, then at OFFICER COOPER.

OFFICER COOPER

Criminal sit down.

(to Miriam)

Ma'am I tried to be nice but now you are obstructing the law.

JOHN

Last time I checked, being black wasn't a crime.

> JOHN walks forward and links arms with MIRIAM on the other side.

AMY

Of course! Always making things about race. This is about the law. Officer!

OFFICER COOPER

Step aside.

JOHN

No. SILENCE IS COMPLIANCE.

AMY

If you won't do your job, I'll do it for you. Where is he!?

MIRIAM

He's hidden under the floorboards. Protected in secret passage-ways and locked away in the attic.

JOHN

Together, we can clear a path for everyone.

CREE

We are the change we've been waiting for.

> DARIUS comes from behind MIRIAM
> and locks arms with JOHN.

DARIUS

A life lived in fear isn't really living.

AMY

Shoot them. Tear gas them. Beat them. Do something.

> OFFICER COOPER looks conflicted.

MIRIAM

I, more than anyone know the importance of an ally. My voice matters.

JOHN

My voice matters?

CREE

Our voice matters.

DARIUS

… My voice matters.

ALL

YOUR VOICE MATTERS. YOUR VOICE MATTERS. YOUR VOICE MATTERS. YOUR VOICE MATTERS. YOUR VOICE MATTERS.

EVERYONE points to different people in the audience until… LIGHTS GO DOWN.

Burning Anyway

(The Suburbs After Moving From the City, 1985)

Jay Halsey

Stagnant waters pool around my feet. Only I can smell the decay.

Hot algae ferment the breezes. An environment clinching its jaws.

> The sun finds its way to eyes,
>
> magnifies the July sweat on my face.
>
> Sweat is proof of a heart beating life.

The oppression of sun is bored house mothers peering through thin

white curtains hanging in living room windows.

The oppression of sun is the weight of a quick verdict.

> The sun began as shadow before it was born.

I rummage alone through untamed thistle and new construction
litter in the undeveloped lot beside our house. The green retention
pond buzzes with hungry mosquitoes and gentle dragonflies. I
search for hidden stories.

> *The sun cooks my skin to deeper Brown,*
>
> *and the neighborhood kids always ask,*
>
> *What are you*
>
> *anyway?*

I am a just boy.

Mom is Brown, like the muddy Stillwater River that flows near our home. I am Brown like her. Sister is White that turns to red-clay Brown in summer, like the father who left us before I knew him. The father who Mom is married to now is pale as the Ohio summer is thick.

What are you

anyway?

is another way of saying,

We know what we are,

and you are not what we are.

I want to be Mr. T in "The A-Team,"

neck dripping gold jewelry

instead of dripping sweat.

I want to be Mr. T, with friends helping him fight evil forces. With friends whose parents don't call him names by the color of his skin.

I stare at myself in the bathroom mirror. Sister wets my black curls. She shapes and smooths them into a mohawk with her hair gel. Mom's fake gold chains reflect the dim sink lights. I turn the rope chains between my fingers; they dance and sparkle. Mr. T's defiant face stares back at me from my t-shirt:

I'm gonna get you, sucka!

The sun began as shadow before it was born.

The oppression of sun is eyes burning my movements through thin white curtains, waving like truce flags in summer breezes.

But truce is not an option.

> *What am I*
> *anyway?*

Author Biographies

1.   **Dan Acosta Jr, Ph.D.**, is a first-generation Mexican American, whose mother and grandparents emigrated from Mexico. He is a former professor, research scientist, and administrator. His career spanned 45 years in academia and the federal government. He writes about his experiences as a Mexican American trying to succeed in white America.

2.   From Imperial Valley, **Gracie Azua** is a Latina poet writing about her family, mental illness, and her culture. Her first collection of poetry, *You Will Know Our Name*, processes the grief of losing the most important women in her life. She received her Bachelor's in literature and Writing in 2022.

3.   **Karen Beatty** was reared in Eastern Kentucky and later served as a Peace Corps Thailand Volunteer. She settled in NYC, where she trained as a trauma-informed counselor. Karen's stories and essays have appeared in over 30 publications. Her first novel, "Dodging Prayers and Bullets," was released in September 2023.

4.   **Rhema Boston** is a writer, director, and playwright from Upstate New York, known for her blend of comedy and introspection. With a BFA and MFA in Creative Dramatic Writing, she champions overlooked voices through genre-bending storytelling that empowers characters to embrace authenticity and challenge societal norms.

5.   **Mary Camarillo** is the author of the award-winning novels "Those People Behind Us" and "The Lockhart Women." Her poems and short fiction have appeared in publications such as Citric Acid, California Writers' Club Literary Anthology,

Inlandia, 166 Palms, Sonora Review, and The Ear. Mary lives in Huntington Beach, California.

6.   **Kevin Carver's** storytelling is deeply inspired by an obsession with old vinyl records, too much coffee, and the stern timelessness of John Steinbeck and Denis Johnson. When he's not weaving tales or crafting immersive literary soundtracks, you can find him chasing the sunset with his family on the California coast.

7.   **Karla Cordero** is a 2021 California Arts Fellow. Her poetry collection, *How To Pull Apart The Earth*, is a San Diego Book Award winner and finalist for the International Latino Book Awards. Karla's work has appeared on NPR, Academy of American Poets, among other publications. Follow her on IG @ karlaflaka13

8.   **Carly Creley** is an educator and Certified Naturalist from Los Angeles, California. She uses art to share her experiences in the natural world with others. She holds Master's degrees in Environmental Science and in Education, alongside a bachelor's degree in Agribusiness Management that helps her seek unique solutions to environmental issues from multiple perspectives.

9.   **Thomas Davila** will be completing his Bachelor of Arts degree in Journalism in August 2025. He has been working in Journalism for almost 5 years. Thomas may have a physical disability, but he doesn't let that stop him from reaching for the stars, despite any setbacks he's faced in his life.

10.   **Isaiah Kye Diaz-Mays** is an Afro-Boricua writer, poet and scholar from Hoboken, New Jersey. His work has been published in Free the Verse and Poetry Breakfast, among others. He holds an MA from Dartmouth College and is a current MFA candidate at California College of the Arts in San Francisco.

11.   **Gina Rae Duran** is a Xixanx, Interdisciplinary artist, trauma informed educator, and lecturer. Was Editor of the Rio Grande Valley International Poetry Festival's Boundless 2022, author of, "…and so, the Wind was Born" (FlowerSong Press), The Collective's radio host, and founder of IE Hope Collective; an outreach for disadvantaged youth.

12.   **Audrey Harris Fernández** teaches at the University of California, Los Angeles, and has also taught in women's prisons. Her writing has been published in the Los Angeles Review of Books, Huizache, Sunstone, MELUS (Multi-Ethnic Literature in the United States) and elsewhere. She lives in Long Beach, CA with her husband and daughter.

13.   **Emily Fernandez** is the author of two poetry chapbooks: *Pliny and Other Problems* (Bamboo Dart Press, 2023) and *Procession of Martyrs* (Finishing Line Press, 2018). She is an Assistant Professor of English at Pasadena City College, where she also teaches creative writing & advocates for sustainability.

14.   **Sunee Lyn Foley** is a writer and playwright. She received her MFA from Antioch University Los Angeles, with an emphasis in Playwriting and young adult fiction. Her plays have toured high schools and universities, and her blogs have been published in Lunch Ticket. She lives in Torrance, California.

15.   **Rosemary Frisino Toohey** has had more than 400 productions of her plays across four continents. Twelve of her comedies are available through publishers, and a half-dozen of her dramas are in anthologies and online journals. She's a proud member of both The Dramatists Guild, and as a retired broadcaster, SAG/AFTRA.

16.   **Audrey Gaines** is an attempting writer based in Boston, Massachusetts. She hopes you enjoy.

17.   **Julio Puente Garcia's** debut short story collection, *Acrobacias Angelinas,* was recognized as "Best Latino Focus Fiction" at the International Latino Book Awards in 2021. His stories have appeared in The Common, Acentos Review, Literary Hub, and Latino Book Review. Julio holds a Ph.D. in Hispanic Literatures from UCLA.

18.   **Flora Gamez Grateron** is a retired educator. Her first book, *Through the Door, Cuentos de Casa* published in 2023, received a Silver Medal for First Best Book at the International Latino Book Awards. Her second book *Open Doors, Cuentos de Familia* was published July 2024. She lives in Tucson, Arizona.

19.   **Jay Halsey's** poetry and prose have been published in many online journals and print anthologies. Several poetry collections and novels feature his photography as cover art. In 2023, Agape Editions published the second edition of his photography and multi-genre writing collection, *Barely Half in an Awkward Line.*

20.   **Bonnie Hearn Hill** loves everything about writing even when she hates it. She is the author of essays, short stories, and 16 traditionally published novels, and she holds an MFA from Antioch University Los Angeles. Bonnie has co-hosted a Central California television network's book segment since 2002. https://www.bonniehhill.com/

21.   **Mark Hein** lives and writes in a forest canyon in Los Angeles. "Fleeing the Farm" is the opening chapter of his second novel, HOUSE OF SECRETS, HOUSE OF LIES (due out mid-2025). His first novel, FATHER DREAM, was longlisted for the 2022 Novel London Prize.

22.   **Maggie Nerz Iribarne** is a 55 year old woman, lives in Syracuse, NY, writes about witches, priests/nuns, the very very old, struggling teachers, neighborhood ghosts, and whatever else strikes her fancy. She keeps a portfolio of her published work at https://www.maggienerziribarne.com.

23.   **Anna Y. Loebe**, Ed. D., has worked in the child welfare arena supporting adoptive, fostercare, and kinship families since 2006. Between 1976 and 2005, she worked as an educator in various teaching, administrative, and research capacities. She writes essays, memoirs, and prose. She lives in Tucson, Arizona.

24.   **Juanita E. Mantz** ("JEM") is a writer, lawyer, performer and podcaster. JEM has 2 award winning books, "Tales of an Inland Empire Girl" and "Portrait of a Deputy Public Defender, or how I became a punk rock lawyer". Find her & her Life of JEM podcast and blog at https://juanitaemantz.com.

25.   **Maximilian Martini** writes, teaches, and sings in Chattanooga, Tennessee. He is an artist with River to River Community Records. His work has been published by Caveat Lector, Signal Mountain Review, and Walnut Street Publishing, among others.

26.   **Roberta H. Martinez'** work can be found in Altadena Poetry Anthology 2021; The Covid Monologues; Hometown Pasadena; Women Who Submit Anthologies, 2021, 2023; Slow Lightning, 21, 23, 25. Her plays include: EL ARROYO, XOCHIMILCO BAKERY No. 3, RULES ARE RULES, MIS JOTITOS, ESPIE, LA VENTURA. She's the Artistic Director of Amapola Players.

27.   **Sylvia Merino** is native to Tucson, Arizona with roots in Rayon, Sonora, Mexico. Sylvia's corporate career ended in 2021. Her dream to publish, became fruitful with her first two books published in 2024. Her stories include a touch of Spanish and imaginable colors carrying over to her love for acrylic painting.

28.   **Regina Garza Mitchell** is a proud Chicana/Latina writer and professor, proof that being a teenage mother does not ruin your life. She is the author of *Shadow of the Vulture* and has published about two dozen short stories. Originally from the Rio Grande Valley, she now lives in Michigan.

29.   **Tomás Montoya** is a multidisciplinary artist community worker. Tomás received his B.S. in Digital Film and Video Production from The Art Institute of Sacramento., Tomás is currently the Lead Teaching Artist for the Juvenile Justice Arts Education Program. The Program serves youth incarcerated and on probation.

30.   **Ute Orgassa** was born and raised in Germany. She now lives with her family in the Bay Area. Her short stories have been published by Shortwave Media, Haunted Word, Alternative Milk, Punk Noir, Alien Buddha, and Infested. Her play A Different Track was produced by Awkward Pigeons Theater.

31.   Having lived in conflict/post-conflict zones such as Iraq, the West Bank, and Ukraine, **Alex Poppe** writes about fierce and funny women rebuilding their lives in the wake of violence. She is the award-winning author of four works of literary fiction. *Breakfast Wine*is her first memoir-in-essay.

32.   **Thea Pueschel** is a multi-hyphenated writer, among other things creative and technical, that enjoys collecting pieces of paper that typically add letters behind surnames. The collection of letters remains rarely used.

33.   **Raquel Reyes-Lopez** is a first generation Latinx poet. Her poetry advocates mental health awareness, speaks of infertility struggles, highlights tones of death, and loss. Her debut poetry chapbook 'Born to Electrify' was published by Sadie Girl Press. Her work appears in Rattle #52, Wild Roof Journal #20, and other publications.

34.   Chicana Feminist and former Rodeo Queen, **Tisha Marie Reichle-Aguilera** is the author of *Breaking Pattern* (Inlandia Books) and *Stories All Our Own* (Bottlecap Press). Her short stories have been anthologized and nominated for awards. She is a Macondista and works for literary equity through Women Who Submit.

35.   **Jeff Rogers** grew up in Michigan college towns but moved to Los Angeles in 1983, then Crestline in the San Bernardino Mountains in 2022. His poetry collection *Right Wrong Night Song* is available from World Stage Press. He's published widely and performs his work frequently. LefthandedJeff.com | @lefthandedjeff

36.   **Facundo Rompehuevos** is the author of two books of poetry: *Irreconcilable Contradictions* (2017) and *Grabbing the Stars from the Sky* (2021), both published by Fourth Sword Publications. His debut novel, *Children Chasing Tigers*, published by Anxiety Press, will be out this winter. You can find him on Substack at facundorompehuevos.substack.com.

37.   **Terry Sanville** lives in San Luis Obispo, California with his artist-poet wife and two plump cats. Over 450 journals, magazines, and anthologies have published his stories and essays. Four of his stories were nominated for Pushcart Prizes and one for inclusion in the Best of the Net Anthology.

38.   **Jo Scott-Coe** has authored three nonfiction books: *Teacher at Point Blank*; *MASS: A Sniper, a Father, and a Priest*; and most recently, *Unheard Witness*. Her writing has appeared in many publications, including TIME, Salon, and Fourth Genre. Jo is a professor of English and creative writing at Riverside City College.

39.   **Barbara Ellen Sorensen** has had three books of poetry published: *Song from the Deep Middle Brain* (Main Street Rag, 2010), *Compositions of the Dead Playing Flutes* (Able Muse Press, 2013), and *Mary's River* (Kelsay Books, 2018). Her first book was a finalist in the 2011 Colorado Book Awards.

40.   **Karen Cline-Tardiff** has been writing as long as she could hold a pen. Her works have appeared in several anthologies and journals, both online and in print. She is founder and Editor-in-Chief of Gnashing Teeth Publishing. Find her at karenthepoet.com

41.   **Tezozomoc** is a Los Angeles Chicano Essayist, Poet and 2009 Oscar Nominated Activist, internationally published and has been published by Amoxcalco Books for "I am not your Chihuahua", and by Floricanto Press, "Gashes!: Poems and Pain from the halls of injustice", a collection of poetry, ISBN-13: 978-1951088040, 9/2019.

42.   **Angela Townsend** is a five-time Pushcart Prize nominee and seven-time Best of the Net nominee. Her work appears or is forthcoming in Arts & Letters, Chautauqua, Pleiades, SmokeLong, and West Trade Review, among others. She graduated from Princeton Seminary and Vassar College and writes for a cat sanctuary.

43.   **Sahara Williamson**, a Black queer poet, playwright, and mother of three, lives in the Bay Area. An MFA graduate from Antioch University, she is a Fiction Editor for Lunch Ticket. Her work includes literary profiles & articles. Poetry in Parenthesis Journal, Chestnut Review, and forthcoming in ZAUM & Kinsman Quarterly.

44.   **Christian Vazquez**, was previously published in the Big Muddy Journal 2021 issue, Four Palaces Publishing Fall 2022 Fiction Anthology and the LatineLit Spring 2024 issue, Christian Vazquez is a gay writer born in Brownsville, Texas. He is currently an English Professor at Houston Community College. His Instagram is christian77vazquez, and Twitter is @ christian77v

45.   **Donald R. Vogel** is a fundraiser by profession, writer by aspiration, who lives in Long Island, New York with his wife and son. He holds a master's degree in English from Stony Brook University and has published both fiction and nonfiction in several literary journals.

46.   **Angélica M. Yañez**, PhD in Ethnic Studies from UCSD, is a professor, poet, and Aztec Dancer. She leads a BIPOC-focused writing group and founded The Ancestral Teachings Institute for Indigenous wisdom. Her work has been featured in Latina: Struggles and Protest, The San Diego Poetry Annual, and by Planned Parenthood.

47.   **Nick Young** is a retired award-winning CBS News Correspondent. His writing has appeared in dozens of reviews, journals and anthologies. His first novel, "Deadline," was published in 2023. He lives outside Chicago.